PHILOSOPHY IN A NEW KEY

PHILOSOPHY IN A NEW KEY

A STUDY IN THE SYMBOLISM
OF REASON, RITE, AND ART

BY

SUSANNE K. LANGER

CAMBRIDGE, MASSACHUSETTS
HARVARD UNIVERSITY PRESS

To

ALFRED NORTH WHITEHEAD

my great Teacher and Friend

A PREFATORY NOTE TO THE THIRD EDITION

FIVE years ago, when the second edition of *Philosophy in a New Key* appeared, the book had already taken on, for its author, the character of a prolegomenon to a larger work. A decade had elapsed since its composition, and in that time the theory of music proposed in Chapter VIII had undergone a considerable expansion and had, indeed, grown into a philosophy not only of music, but of all the arts. But this change of character was, as yet, only for the author; the philosophy of art had not appeared in print. Since then it has met its public, and *Philosophy in a New Key* now is frankly a prelude to *Feeling and Form*.

Now; what is "now"? We cannot step twice into the same river. We cannot arrest a day, a melody, or a thought. Now, even as the third edition goes to press, the philosophy of art here engendered has in turn become a mere station in the progress of ideas. These ideas, tentative and imperfect as their expression in this first book had to be, now promise to transcend the realm of "aesthetics" (to use the unfortunate current word), and lead us to a new philosophy of living form, living nature, mind, and some of the very deep problems of human society that we usually designate as ethical problems. In the course of such a long development they are sure to undergo changes, like babies grown into men, whose fading snapshots in the family album are hard to reconcile with their football frowns or Rotarian smiles in the newspaper today. Some readers, therefore, who are dissatisfied with many things in this book, may find some misgivings allayed if they pursue the development of certain paradoxical or arbitrary-sounding assertions through their subsequent history; others, who like forensic argument, will triumphantly find that the earlier and later versions of many a concept are inconsistent, so the whole philosophy goes down refuted. But consistency should be demanded only within the compass of a book, including, of course, whatever former work is reaffirmed in it; between two distinct phases of a long thought, improvement is more important, even if it amounts to self-reversal.

So *Philosophy in a New Key* goes out once more, still the beginning of an unfinished story, but also still its indispen-.sable prologue. It contains the foundations of *Feeling and Form*, and whatever, with good fortune, may follow from that philosophical excursion into the arts; and above all, it still proclaims the work of a brilliant, though strangely assorted, intellectual generation — Whitehead, Russell, Wittgenstein, Freud, Cassirer, to name but a few — who launched the attack on the formidable problem of symbol and meaning, and established the keynote of philosophical thought in our day.

S. K. L.

November, 1956

PREFACE TO THE EDITION OF 1951

IN offering *Philosophy in a New Key* to the public once more, this time to a larger part of the English-speaking world, I have made no changes (except for small corrections) in the original text. After nine years one naturally sees the imperfections of a work and wishes it were better; but so long as one can still subscribe to its contents as a whole it is more important, perhaps, to carry the intellectual venture forward than to revise small details of its first formulation.

Modern theory of knowledge, leading naturally to a critique of science, represents the best philosophical work of our time. But "knowledge" is not synonymous with "human mentality." It is the intent of this book to establish a *theory of mind* which shall support that excellent treatment of science, and furthermore lead to an equally serious and detailed critique of art. Chapters VIII and IX — "On Significance in Music" and "The Genesis of Artistic Import" — purport to point the way to that second inquiry. They are, of course, no more than preliminary and limited studies, and do not establish the power of the premises here assumed to cope with the entire problem of the nature and structure of art; but they assay the new ground.

A book which is the beginning of a line of thought can be judged only in retrospect, when the relative importance of its several ideas emerges by virtue of the further developments of which they show themselves capable and any major defects in their foundations have had time to come to light. In the years which have elapsed since the first edition of this book appeared, I have put its general tenets to the test by working out the philosophy of art they promised, and so far I have found them amazingly fertile, leading from novelty to novelty in a realm of theory that has long been imponderable or purely academic. It is with this pragmatic assurance, therefore, that I reaffirm my little work by offering it to the public once more in unaltered form.

If, however, I were writing it now, there would be at least one difference in terminology, affecting especially Chapter III, "The Logic of Signs and Symbols"; that chapter heading would read "The Logic of *Signals* and Symbols." Charles Morris, in his *Signs, Language and Behavior*, employed a usage which I find superior to my own and have accordingly adopted since the publication of his book. Morris uses the word "signal" for what I called "sign." The term "signal" is stretched, of course, to cover not only explicitly recognized signals — red lights, bells, et cetera — but also those phenomena which we tacitly respect as signals to our sense, e.g. the sight of objects and windows whereby we are oriented in a room, the sensation evoked by a fork in a person's hand that guides him in raising it to his mouth; in short, to cover everything that I called "sign." But such a stretching of a semi-technical term is easily accepted and perfectly legitimate. The great advantage of Morris's usage is that it leaves us the word "sign" to denote any vehicle of meaning, signal or symbol, whereas in my own vocabulary there was no generic term, and the need of it was sometimes obvious.

Another, intellectually much more important, change I should like to make, if I could have twenty-four hours' "second chance" like Sartre's shades from Limbo, is to replace the unsatisfactory notion of music as an essentially ambiguous symbol by a much more precise, though somewhat difficult, concept of musical significance, involving a theory (not yet quite completed) of artistic abstraction in general. This I would consider a distinct advance in the theory of art as "expressive form"; but it has to wait upon the later elaboration of certain ideas that are still young and therefore half poetic in *Philosophy in a New Key*. The process of philosophical thought moves typically from a first, inadequate, but ardent apprehension of some novel idea, figuratively expressed, to more and more precise comprehension, until language catches up to logical insight, the figure is dispensed with, and literal expression takes its place. Really new concepts, having no names in current language, always make their earliest appearance in metaphorical statements; therefore the beginning of any theoretical structure is inevitably marked by fantastic inventions. There is an air of such metaphor, or "philosophical myth," in the treatment of musical "meaning," which I think I could improve on were I given another fling at it today.

Yet perhaps not; perhaps, in the course of rendering that mild extravaganza more literally and logically, one would necessarily raise new issues, which again would invite the imagination to project their answers in a tentative, figurative way; for all the vastly ramified questions of art — of creation, abstraction, and import — are still in the offing. So it may be wiser to let the book go out just as it was before, even with its unfinished thoughts and half-spoken answers, instead of tinkering with any part. A book is like a life: all that is in it is really of a piece. *Les jeux sont fait.*

S. K. L.

Columbus, Ohio
May 7, 1951

PREFACE TO THE FIRST EDITION

THE "new key" in Philosophy is not one which I have struck. Other people have struck it, quite clearly and repeatedly. This book purports merely to demonstrate the unrecognized fact that it *is* a new key, and to show how the main themes of our thought tend to be transposed into it. As every shift of tonality gives a new sense to previous passages, so the reorientation of philosophy which is taking place in our age bestows new aspects on the ideas and arguments of the past. Our thinking stems from that past, but does not continue it in the ways that were foreseen. Its cleavages cut across the old lines, and suddenly bring out new motifs that were not felt to be implicit in the premises of the schools at all; for *it changes the questions of philosophy.*

The universality of the great key-change in our thinking is shown by the fact that its tonic chord could ring true for a mind essentially preoccupied with logic, scientific language, and empirical fact, although that chord was actually first sounded by thinkers of a very different school. Logic and science had indeed prepared the harmony for it, unwittingly; for the study of mathematical "transformations" and "projections," the construction of alternative descriptive systems, etc., had raised the issue of *symbolic modes* and of the variable relationship of form and content. But the people who recognized the importance of expressive forms for all human understanding were those who saw that not only science, but myth, analogy, metaphorical thinking, and art are intellectual activities determined by "symbolic modes"; and those people were for the most part of the idealist school. The relation of art to epistemology was first revealed to them through reflection on the phenomenal character of experience, in the course of the great transcendentalist "adventure of ideas" launched by Immanuel Kant. And, even now, practically all serious and penetrating philosophy of art is related somehow to the idealistic tradition. Most studies of artistic significance, of art as a symbolic form and a vehicle of conception, have been made in the spirit of post-Kantian metaphysics.

Yet I do not believe an idealistic interpretation of Reality is necessary to the recognition of art as a symbolic form. Professor Urban speaks of "the assumption that the more richly and energetically the human spirit builds its languages and symbolisms, the nearer it comes . . . to its ultimate being and reality," as "the idealistic minimum necessary for any adequate theory of symbolism." If there be such a "Reality" as the idealists assume, then access to it, as to any other intellectual goal, must be through some adequate symbolism; but I cannot see that *any* access to the source or "principle" of man's being is presupposed in the logical and psychological study of symbolism itself. We need not assume the presence of a transcendental "human spirit," if we recognize, for instance, the function of *symbolic transformation* as a natural activity, a high form of nervous response, characteristic of man among the animals. The study of symbol and meaning is a starting-point of philosophy, not a derivative from Cartesian, Humean, or Kantian premises; and the recognition of its fecundity and depth may be reached from various positions, though it is a historical fact that the idealists reached it first, and have given us the most illuminating literature on non-discursive symbolisms — myth, ritual, and art. Their studies, however, are so intimately linked with their metaphysical speculations that the new key they have struck in philosophy impresses one, at first, as a mere modulation within their old strain. Its real vitality is most evident when one realizes that even studies like the present essay, springing from logical rather than from ethical or metaphysical interests, may be actuated by the same generative idea, the essentially *transformational* nature of human understanding.

The scholars to whom I owe, directly or indirectly, the material of my thoughts represent many schools and even many fields of scholarship; and the final expression of those thoughts does not always give credit to their influence. The writings of the sage to whom this book is dedicated receive but scant explicit mention; the same thing holds for the works of Ernst Cassirer, that pioneer in the philosophy of symbolism, and of Heinrich Schenker, Louis Arnaud Reid, Kurt Goldstein, and many others. Sometimes a mere article or essay, like Max Kraussold's "Musik und Mythus in ihrem Verhältnis" (*Die Musik*, 1925), Étienne Rabaud's "Les hommes au point de vue biologique" (*Journal de Psychologie*, 1931), Sir Henry Head's "Disorders of Symbolic Thinking and Expression" (*British Journal of Psychology*, 1920), or Hermann Nohl's *Stil und Weltanschauung*, can give one's thinking a new slant or suddenly organize one's scattered knowledge into a significant idea, yet be completely swallowed up in the theories it has influenced so that no specific reference can be made to it at any particular point of their exposition. Inevitably, the philosophical ideas of every thinker stem from all he has read as well as all he has heard and seen, and if consequently little of his material is really original, that only lends his doctrines the continuity of an old intellectual heritage. Respectable ancestors, after all, are never to be despised.

Though I cannot acknowledge all my literary debts, I do wish to express my thanks to several friends who have given me the benefit of their judgment or of their aid: to Miss Helen Sewell for the comments of an artist on the whole theory of non-discursive symbolism, and especially on chapters VIII and IX; to Mr. Carl Schorske for his literary criticism of those same long chapters; to my sister, Mrs. Dunbar, for some valuable suggestions; to Mrs. Dan Fenn for reading the page proofs, and to Miss Theodora Long and my son Leonard for their help with the index. Above all I want to thank Mrs. Penfield Roberts, who has read the entire manuscript, even after every extensive revision, and given me not only intellectual help, but the constant moral support of enthusiasm and friendship; confirming for me the truth of what one lover of the arts, J. M. Thorburn, has said — that "all the genuine, deep delight of life is in showing people the mud-pies you have made; and life is at its best when we confidingly recommend our mud-pies to each other's sympathetic consideration."

S. K. L.

Cambridge, 1941

CONTENTS

I. THE NEW KEY 3

Every epoch characterized by its questions — "generative ideas": their rise and decline — examples from Greek philosophy — rise and exhaustion of Christian philosophy — rise and exhaustion of modern philosophy — philosophical interests stifled by technological — only mathematics remains both "abstract" and respectable — mathematics a science of symbols and meanings — sense-data and interpretation in science — data as symbols and laws as their meanings — power of symbols a new theme — "dynamic" psychology — symbolic logic — extravagance of young "generative ideas" — limits of the "field" of an idea — promise of the "new key."

II. SYMBOLIC TRANSFORMATION 26

Influence of semantic problems on genetic psychology — presuppositions of genetic theory: identity of animal and human needs, and derivation of symbol-responses from sign-responses — the mind as a transmitter — sources of error — error grows with complication — impractical effects of symbol-using — absurdity of a theory that reduces intelligence to folly — such theory contradicted by the persistence of impractical ritual — by the seriousness of art — by the phenomenon of dream — inventory of human needs reconsidered — special functions presuppose special needs — need of symbolization — the human mind as a transformer — impractical behavior symbolistic — this view explains many anthropological puzzles — several uses of symbolism call for separate investigations.

III. THE LOGIC OF SIGNS AND SYMBOLS 53

Existing analyses of meaning-relation mainly acceptable — historical survey — "quality" of meaning elusive — meaning a *function* of terms — patterns as contexts — subject, symbol, and object — "meanings of 'meaning'" relative to choice of terms in a pattern — signs and symbols — wide scope of sign-relations — mistake — logical simplicity of signs — symbols and conceptions — names — as signs and as symbols — distinction illustrated by case of Helen Keller — signification, denotation, and connotation — relatedness of denotation and connotation — proper names excepted — symbols and discourse — literal meanings and propositions — syntactical structures — the "logical picture" as a symbol — progressive abstraction — conceptions and concepts — abstraction the basis of rationality — logical virtues of language — truth and falsity.

IV. DISCURSIVE FORMS AND PRESENTATIONAL FORMS   79

"Logical projection" — discursive form a "projection" — Carnap's conclusion: syntax of language the limit of conceivability — non-literal
symbolism "emotive" — Russell and Wittgenstein on metaphysics —
philosophy a development of meanings — symbolic function wider than
language — limitation to language leaves too much of mentality non-
sensical — rationality begins with articulation — sense-experience an
articulation — conceptual character of "things" — "*Gestalt*" the forerunner of symbolic uses — apprehension of non-discursive forms — such
forms not "linguistic" even in a derived sense — logical characteristics
of language — of presentational symbolisms — primitive understanding
— forms of feeling — progressive articulation of presentational forms —
key to major developments of culture.

V. LANGUAGE 103

All men have completely articulate language — no beasts have any
language — animal communication — mutism of apes — lack of babbling-
impulse in the young — enigma of linguistic origins — sometimes sought
in "speech-instinct" — deaf children and "wild" children do not speak —
problem rejected by philologists — Sapir's reason: it requires general
theory of symbolism — its roots always sought in communication —
should be sought in early symbol-functions — primitive symbolic behavior
of apes — lack of "lalling-instinct" precludes speech — symbols and free
forms — utilitarian view a mistake — Furness' ape — the Wild Boy of
Aveyron — human "lalling" a transient instinct — conditions for learning
language — Donovan's theory of origin — connotation probably before
denotation — use — always propositional — Bühler and Wegener on development — emendation — generality through metaphor — Wegener on
"faded metaphors" — evolution of conceptual thinking — universality of
language explained.

VI. LIFE–SYMBOLS: THE ROOTS OF SACRAMENT . . 144

Sense-images and concepts — metaphorical uses — primitive abstraction
— fantasies — desire and dream — primitive imagination — confusion of
symbol and meaning in dream — in savage thought — power of "sacra"
— intellectual excitement in contemplation — emotional expression and
gesture — ritual — mimetic rites — mimicry in play — Dewey's theory rejected — ritual as assent to sacred concepts — magic not essentially practical — familiar acts acquire strictest forms — sacrament — derivation of
divinities from "sacra" — animal forms — totemism — Jane Harrison on
the making of gods.

VII. LIFE–SYMBOLS: THE ROOTS OF MYTH 171

Ritual and myth have different origins — dream and story — primitive
story — characters and acts symbolical — growth of fairytale — fairytale

and myth — difference of functions — realistic elements in fairytale — generalization of forms — problem of "nature myths" — the "culture hero" — link between fairytale and myth — nature symbols in his story — evolution of a lunar deity — personification of moon is lunarization of Woman — mythical elaboration — influence of poetic formulation — the *Kalevala* as transitional form — epic phase the consummation of myth.

VIII. ON SIGNIFICANCE IN MUSIC 204

Art and artifact — "Significant Form" — meaning as central problem of modern aesthetics — problem of artistic significance — psychoanalytic theory not helpful — form the source of artistic merit — music the best example — theories of music as pleasure — as emotional stimulus — as communication of feeling — fallacy of self-expression theory — music not symptom but symbol — its "significance" a logical problem of art — language of music — program music — language of feeling — logical structure of music and of feeling — analogy of language misleading — Huber on semantic elements in music — presentational symbol not translatable — Urban's theory of art rejected — difficulties of analysis — emotional attitudes of critics — autonomy defended — music as "algebra of feelings" — fallacies — music an unconsummated symbol — assignment of meanings a crutch to musical thinking — musical meanings real but "implicit" — form and content experienced as one.

IX. THE GENESIS OF ARTISTIC IMPORT 246

Origins of music not artistic — sources of folk music — genetic fallacy — materials furnished by casual sounds — benefit of models in plastic arts — danger of models — confusion of standards — articulation the aim of art — artistic vision — late development of music — due to lack of models — rhythms and words its only guides — airs — emancipation from models — artistic import — Pater's dictum — no comparison of arts implied — content of various arts — unity sought in "aesthetic emotion" — nature of that emotion — not the content of art — artist and audience — "artistic truth" as adequacy of symbol — distinguished from literal truth — artistic insight — standards of art not absolute — new forms not lucid — old forms become exhausted — literal interpretation and artistic vision — mysticism the limit of meaning.

X. THE FABRIC OF MEANING 266

Practical vision — appreciation of fact — propositional form of fact — truth and falsity — interest in fact the destruction of myth — "discoveries" secondary — tendency toward realism develops with maturity — systematization of facts an intellectual challenge — fact as standard of reality — history its typical expression — more factual than science — causation — and verification — combination of symbols and signs — power of realistic thought — change in man's world — nature-symbols outgrown — modern life — signs and symbols the warp and woof of thought — sign-functions

CONTENTS

— symbol-functions — complexity of meanings — "charged" symbols — complexity of mental life — hardships of moral life — need of orientation — lack of potent life-symbols — modern reality too new to furnish new "sacra" — freedom of action depends on fixed values — values depend on symbols — ritual acts — meaninglessness in modern life — reorientation a rational need — modern barbarism the effect of new emergent mythologies.

PHILOSOPHY IN A NEW KEY

CHAPTER I

The New Key

EVERY age in the history of philosophy has its own preoccupation. Its problems are peculiar to it, not for obvious practical reasons — political or social — but for deeper reasons of intellectual growth. If we look back on the slow formation and accumulation of doctrines which mark that history, we may see certain *groupings* of ideas within it, not by subject-matter, but by a subtler common factor which may be called their "technique." It is the mode of handling problems, rather than what they are about, that assigns them to an age. Their subject-matter may be fortuitous, and depend on conquests, discoveries, plagues, or governments; their treatment derives from a steadier source.

The "technique," or treatment, of a problem begins with its first expression as a question. The way a question is asked limits and disposes the ways in which any answer to it — right or wrong — may be given. If we are asked: "Who made the world?" we may answer: "God made it," "Chance made it," "Love and hate made it," or what you will. We may be right or we may be wrong. But if we reply: "Nobody made it," we will be accused of trying to be cryptic, smart, or "unsympathetic." For in this last instance, we have only seemingly given an answer; in reality we have *rejected the question*. The questioner feels called upon to repeat his problem. "Then how did the world become as it is?" If now we answer: "It has not 'become' at all," he will be really disturbed. This "answer" clearly repudiates the very framework of his thinking, the orientation of his mind, the basic assumptions he has always entertained as common-sense notions about things in general. Everything has become what it is; everything has a cause; every change must be to some end; the world is a thing, and must have been made by some agency, out of some original stuff, for some reason. These are natural ways of thinking. Such implicit "ways" are not avowed by the average man, but simply followed. He is not conscious of assuming any basic principles. They are what a German would call his "Weltanschauung," his attitude of mind, rather than specific articles of faith. They constitute his outlook; they are deeper than facts he may note or propositions he may moot.

But, though they are not stated, they find expression in the *forms of his questions*. A question is really an ambiguous proposition; the answer is its determination.[1] There can be only a certain number of alternatives that will complete its sense. In this way the intellectual treatment of any datum, any experience, any subject, is determined by the nature of our questions, and only carried out in the answers.

In philosophy this disposition of problems is the most important thing that a school, a movement, or an age contributes. This is the "genius" of a great philosophy; in its light, systems arise and rule and die. Therefore a philosophy is characterized more by the *formulation* of its problems than by its solution of them. Its answers establish an edifice of facts; but its questions make the frame in which its picture of facts is plotted. They make more than the frame; they give the angle of perspective, the palette, the style in which the picture is drawn — everything except the subject. In our questions lie our *principles of analysis*, and our answers may express whatever those principles are able to yield.

There is a passage in Whitehead's *Science and the Modern World*, setting forth this predetermination of thought, which is at once its scaffolding and its limit. "When you are criticizing the philosophy of an epoch," Professor Whitehead says, "do not chiefly direct your attention to those intellectual positions which its exponents feel it necessary explicitly to defend. There will be some fundamental assumptions which adherents of all the variant systems within the epoch uncon-

[1] Cf. Felix Cohen, "What is a Question?" *The Monist*, XXXIX (1929), 3: 350–364.

sciously presuppose. Such assumptions appear so obvious that people do not know what they are assuming because no other way of putting things has ever occurred to them. With these assumptions a certain limited number of types of philosophic systems are possible, and this group of systems constitutes the philosophy of the epoch." [2]

Some years ago, Professor C. D. Burns published an excellent little article called "The Sense of the Horizon," in which he made a somewhat wider application of the same principle; for here he pointed out that every civilization has its limits of knowledge — of perceptions, reactions, feelings, and ideas. To quote his own words, "The experience of any moment has its horizon. Today's experience, which is not tomorrow's, has in it some hints and implications which are tomorrow on the horizon of today. Each man's experience may be added to by the experience of other men, who are living in his day or have lived before; and so a common world of experience, larger than that of his own observation, can be lived in by each man. But however wide it may be, that common world also has its horizon; and on that horizon new experience is always appearing. . . ." [3]

"Philosophers in every age have attempted to give an account of as much experience as they could. Some have indeed pretended that what they could not explain did not exist; but all the great philosophers have allowed for more than they could explain, and have, therefore, signed beforehand, if not dated, the death-warrant of their philosophies." [4]

". . . The history of Western philosophy begins in a period in which the sense of the horizon lifts men's eyes from the myths and rituals, the current beliefs and customs of the Greek tradition in Asia Minor. . . . In a settled civilization, the *regularity* of natural phenomena and their connection over large areas of experience became significant. The myths were too disconnected; but behind them lay the conception

---

[2] From Chapter III: The Century of Genius. By permission of The Macmillan Company, publishers.

[3] *Philosophy*, VIII (1933), 31: 301–317. This preliminary essay was followed by his book, *The Horizon of Experience* (1934). See p. 301.

[4] "The Sense of the Horizon," pp. 303–304.

of Fate. This perhaps provided Thales and the other early philosophers with the first hint of the new formulation, which was an attempt to allow for a larger scale of certainty in the current attitude toward the world. From this point of view the early philosophers are conceived to have been not so much disturbed by the contradictions in the tradition as attracted by certain factors on the horizon of experience, of which their tradition gave no adequate account. They began the new formulation in order to include the new factors, and they boldly said that 'all' was water or 'all' was in flux." [5]

The formulation of experience which is contained within the intellectual horizon of an age and a society is determined, I believe, not so much by events and desires, as by the *basic concepts* at people's disposal for analyzing and describing their adventures to their own understanding. Of course, such concepts arise as they are needed, to deal with political or domestic experience; but the same experiences could be seen in many different lights, so the light in which they do appear depends on the genius of a people as well as on the demands of the external occasion. Different minds will take the same events in very different ways. A tribe of Congo negroes will react quite differently to (say) its first introduction to the story of Christ's passion, than did the equally untutored descendants of Norsemen, or the American Indians. Every society meets a new idea with its own concepts, its own tacit, fundamental way of seeing things; that is to say, *with its own questions*, its peculiar curiosity.

The horizon to which Professor Burns makes reference is the limit of clear and sensible questions that we can ask. When the Ionian philosophers, whom he cites as the innovators of Greek thought, asked what "all" was made of, or how "all" matter behaved, they were assuming a general notion, namely that of a parent substance, a final, universal *matter* to which all sorts of accidents could happen. This notion dictated the terms of their inquiries: what things were, and how they changed. Problems of right and wrong, of wealth and poverty, slavery and freedom, were beyond

[5] *Ibid.*, pp. 306–307.

their scientific horizon. On these matters they undoubtedly adopted the wordless, unconscious attitudes dictated by social usage. The concepts that preoccupied them had no application in those realms, and therefore did not give rise to new, interesting, leading questions about social or moral affairs.

Professor Burns regards all Greek thought as one vast formulation of experience. "In spite of continual struggles with violent reversals in conventional habits and in the use of words," he says, "work upon the formulation of Greek experience culminated in the magnificent doctrines of Plato and Aristotle. Both had their source in Socrates. He had turned from the mere assertions of the earlier philosophers to the question of the validity of any assertion at all. Not what the world was but how one could know what it was, and therefore what one could know about one's self seemed to him to be the fundamental question. . . . The formulation begun by Thales was completed by Aristotle." [6]

I think the historical continuity and compactness of Hellenic civilization influences this judgment. Certainly between Thales and the Academy there is at least one further shift of the horizon, namely with the advent of the Sophists. The questions Socrates asked were as new to Greek thought in his day as those of Thales and Anaximenes had been to their earlier age. Socrates did not continue and complete Ionian thought; he cared very little about the speculative physics that was the very breath of life to the nature-philosophers, and his lifework did not further that ancient enterprise by even a step. He had not new answers, but new questions, and therewith he brought a new conceptual framework, an entirely different perspective, into Greek philosophy. His problems had arisen in the law-courts and the Sophists' courses of oratory; they were, in the main, and in their significant features, irrelevant to the academic tradition. The validity of knowledge was only one of his new puzzles; the *value* of knowing, the *purpose* of science, of political life, practical arts, and finally of the course of nature, all became problematical to him. For he was operating with a new idea.

[6] *Ibid.*, p. 307.

Not prime matter and its disguises, its virtual products, its laws of change and its ultimate identity, constituted the terms of his discourse, but the notion of *value*. That everything had a value was too obvious to require statement. It was so obvious that the Ionians had not even given it one thought, and Socrates did not bother to state it; but his questions centered on what values things had — whether they were good or evil, in themselves or in their relations to other things, for all men or for few, or for the gods alone. In the light of that newly-enlisted old concept, *value*, a whole world of new questions opened up. The philosophical horizon widened in all directions at once, as horizons do with every upward step.

The limits of thought are not so much set from outside, by the fulness or poverty of experiences that meet the mind, as from within, by the power of conception, the wealth of formulative notions with which the mind meets experiences. Most new discoveries are suddenly-seen things that were always there. A new idea is a light that illuminates presences which simply had no form for us before the light fell on them. We turn the light here, there, and everywhere, and the limits of thought recede before it. A new science, a new art, or a young and vigorous system of philosophy, is generated by such a basic innovation. Such ideas as identity of matter and change of form, or as value, validity, virtue, or as outer world and inner consciousness, are not theories; they are the terms in which theories are conceived; they give rise to specific questions, and are articulated only in the form of these questions. Therefore one may call them *generative ideas* in the history of thought.

A tremendous philosophical vista opened when Thales, or perhaps one of his predecessors not known to us, asked: "What is the world made of?" For centuries men turned their eyes upon the changes of matter, the problem of growth and decay, the laws of transformation in nature. When the possibilities of that primitive science were exhausted, speculations deadlocked, and the many alternative answers were stored in every learned mind to its confusion, Socrates propounded his simple and disconcerting questions — not,

"Which answer is true?" but: "What is Truth?" "What is Knowledge, and why do we want to acquire it?" His questions were disconcerting because they contained the new principle of explanation, the notion of value. Not to describe the motion and matter of a thing, but to see its purpose, is to understand it. From this conception a host of new inquiries were born. What is the highest good of man? Of the universe? What are the proper principles of art, education, government, medicine? To what purpose do planets and heavens revolve, animals procreate, empires rise? Wherefore does man have hands and eyes and the gift of language?

To the physicists, eyes and hands were no more interesting than sticks and stones. They were all just varieties of Prime Matter. The Socratic conception of *purpose* went beyond the old physical notions in that *it gave importance to the differences* between men's hands and other "mixtures of elements." Socrates was ready to accept tradition on the subject of elements, but asked in his turn: "*Why* are we made of fire and water, earth and air? Why have we passions, and a dream of Truth? Why do we live? Why do we die?" — Plato's ideal commonwealth and Aristotle's science rose in reply. But no one stopped to explain what "ultimate good" or "purpose" *meant*; these were the generative ideas of all the new, vital, philosophical problems, the measures of explanation, and belonged to common sense.

The end of a philosophical epoch comes with the exhaustion of its motive concepts. When all answerable questions that can be formulated in its terms have been exploited, we are left with only those problems that are sometimes called "metaphysical" in a slurring sense — insoluble problems whose very statement harbors a paradox. The peculiarity of such pseudo-questions is that they are capable of two or more equally good answers, which defeat each other. An answer once propounded wins a certain number of adherents who subscribe to it despite the fact that other people have shown conclusively how wrong or inadequate it is; since its rival solutions suffer from the same defect, a choice among them really rests on temperamental grounds. They are not intellectual discoveries, like good answers to appropriate questions, but *doctrines*. At this point philosophy becomes academic; its watchword henceforth is Refutation, its life is argument rather than private thinking, fair-mindedness is deemed more important than single-mindedness, and the whole center of gravity shifts from actual philosophical issues to peripheral subjects — methodology, mental progress, the philosopher's place in society, and apologetics.

The eclectic period in Greco-Roman philosophy was just such a tag-end of an inspired epoch. People took sides on old questions instead of carrying suggested ideas on to their further implications. They sought a *reasoned belief*, not new things to think about. Doctrines seemed to lie around all ready-made, waiting to be adopted or rejected, or perhaps dissected and recombined in novel aggregates. The consolations of philosophy were more in the spirit of that time than the disturbing whispers of a Socratic dæmon.

Yet the human mind is always active. When philosophy lies fallow, other fields bring abundance of fruit. The end of Hellenism was the beginning of Christianity, a period of deep emotional life, military and political enterprise, rapid civilization of barbarous hordes, possession of new lands. Wild northern Europe was opened to the Mediterranean world. Of course the old cultural interests flagged, and old concepts paled, in the face of such activity, novelty, and bewildering challenge. A footloose, capricious modernity took the place of deep-rooted philosophical thought. All the strength of good minds was consumed by the practical and moral problems of the day, and metaphysics seemed a venerable but bootless refinement of rather sheltered, educated people, a peculiar and lonely amusement of old-fashioned scholars. It took several centuries before the great novelties became an established order, the emotional fires burned themselves out, the modern notions matured to something like permanent principles; then natural curiosity turned once more toward these principles of life, and sought their essence, their inward ramifications, and the grounds of their security. *Interpretations* of doctrines and commandments became more and more urgent. But interpretation of general propositions is nothing more nor less than philosophy; and so another vital age of Reason began.

The wonderful flights of imagination and feeling inspired by the rise and triumph of Christianity, the questions to which its profound revolutionary attitude gave rise, provided for nearly a thousand years of philosophical growth, beginning with the early Church Fathers and culminating in the great Scholastics. But, at last, its generative ideas — sin and salvation, nature and grace, unity, infinity, and kingdom — had done their work. Vast systems of thought had been formulated, and all relevant problems had been mooted. Then came the unanswerable puzzles, the paradoxes that always mark the limit of what a generative idea, an intellectual vision, will do. The exhausted Christian mind rested its case, and philosophy became a reiteration and ever-weakening justification of faith.

Again "pure thought" appeared as a jejune and academic business. History teachers like to tell us that learned men in the Middle Ages would solemnly discuss how many angels could dance on the point of a needle. Of course that question, and others like it, had perfectly respectable deeper meanings — in this case the answer hinged on the material or immaterial nature of angels (if they were incorporeal, then an infinite number of them could occupy a dimensionless point). Yet such problems, ignorantly or maliciously misunderstood, undoubtedly furnished jokes in the banquet hall when they were still seriously propounded in the classroom. The fact that the average person who heard them did not try to understand them but regarded them as cryptic inventions of an academic class — "too deep for us," as our Man in the Street would say — shows that the issues of metaphysical speculation were no longer vital to the general literate public. Scholastic thought was gradually suffocating under the pressure of new interests, new emotions — the crowding modern ideas and artistic inspiration we call the Renaissance.

After several centuries of sterile tradition, logic-chopping, and partisanship in philosophy, the wealth of nameless, hereti-

cal, often inconsistent notions born of the Renaissance crystal-
lized into general and ultimate problems. A new outlook on
life challenged the human mind to make sense out of its
bewildering world; and the Cartesian age of "natural and
mental philosophy" succeeded to the realm.

This new epoch had a mighty and revolutionary generative
idea: the dichotomy of all reality into *inner experience and
outer world*, subject and object, private reality and public
truth. The very language of what is now traditional epistemology betrays this basic notion; when we speak of the
"given," of "sense-data," "the phenomenon," or "other
selves," we take for granted the immediacy of an internal
experience and the continuity of the external world. Our
fundamental questions are framed in these terms: What is
actually given to the mind? What guarantees the truth of
sense-data? What lies behind the observable order of phenomena? What is the relation of the mind to the brain?
How can we know other selves? — All these are familiar problems of today. Their answers have been elaborated into
whole systems of thought: empiricism, idealism, realism, phe-
nomenology, *Existenz-Philosophie*, and logical positivism.
The most complete and characteristic of all these doctrines
are the earliest ones: empiricism and idealism. They are the
full, unguarded, vigorous formulations of the new generative
notion, *Experience*; their proponents were the enthusiasts
inspired by the Cartesian method, and their doctrines are the
obvious implications derived by that principle, from such a
starting-point. Each school in its turn took the intellectual
world by storm. Not only the universities, but all literary
circles, felt the liberation from time-worn, oppressive concepts, from baffling limits of inquiry, and hailed the new
world-picture with a hope of truer orientation in life, art, and
action.

After a while the confusions and shadows inherent in the
new vision became apparent, and subsequent doctrines sought
in various ways to escape between the horns of the dilemma
created by the subject-object dichotomy, which Professor
Whitehead has called "the bifurcation of nature." Since then,

our theories have become more and more refined, circumspect, and clever; no one can be quite frankly an idealist, or go the whole way with empiricism; the early forms of realism are now known as the "naive" varieties, and have been superseded by "critical" or "new" realisms. Many philosophers vehemently deny any systematic *Weltanschauung*, and repudiate metaphysics in principle.

The springs of philosophical thought have run dry once more. For fifty years at least, we have witnessed all the characteristic symptoms that mark the end of an epoch — the incorporation of thought in more and more variegated "isms," the clamor of their respective adherents to be heard and judged side by side, the defense of philosophy as a respectable and important pursuit, the increase of congresses and symposia, and a flood of text-criticism, surveys, popularizations, and collaborative studies. The educated layman does not pounce upon a new philosophy book as people pounced upon *Leviathan* or the great *Critiques* or even *The World as Will and Idea*. He does not expect enough intellectual news from a college professor. What he expects is, rather, to be argued into accepting idealism or realism, pragmatism or irrationalism, as his own belief. We have arrived once more at that counsel of despair, to find a reasoned faith.

But the average person who has any faith does not really care whether it is reasoned or not. He uses reason only to satisfy his curiosity — and philosophy, at present, does not even arouse, let alone satisfy, his curiosity. It only confuses him with impractical puzzles. The reason is not that he is dull, or really too busy (as he says he is) to enjoy philosophy. It is simply that the generative ideas of the seventeenth century — "the century of genius," Professor Whitehead calls it — have served their term. The difficulties inherent in their constitutive concepts balk us now; their paradoxes clog our thinking. If we would have new knowledge, we must get us a whole world of new questions.

Meanwhile, the dying philosophical epoch is eclipsed by a tremendously active age of science and technology. The roots of our scientific thinking reach far back, through the whole period of subjective philosophy, further back than any explicit empiricism, to the brilliant, extravert genius of the Renaissance. Modern science is often said to have sprung from empiricism; but Hobbes and Locke have given us no physics, and Bacon, who expressed the scientists' creed to perfection, was neither an active philosopher nor a scientist; he was essentially a man of letters and a critic of current thought. The only philosophy that rose directly out of a contemplation of science is positivism, and it is probably the least interesting of all doctrines, an appeal to common-sense against the difficulties of establishing metaphysical or logical "first principles."

Genuine empiricism is above all a reflection on the validity of sense-knowledge, a speculation on the ways our concepts and beliefs are built up out of the fleeting and disconnected reports our eyes and ears actually make to the mind. Positivism, the scientists' metaphysic, entertains no such doubts, and raises no epistemological problems; its belief in the veracity of sense is implicit and dogmatic. Therefore it is really out of the running with post-Cartesian philosophy. It repudiates the basic problems of epistemology, and creates nothing but elbow-room for laboratory work. The very fact that it rejects *problems*, not answers, shows that the growing physical sciences were geared to an entirely different outlook on reality. They had their own so-called "working notions"; and the strongest of these was the concept of *fact.*

This central concept effected the *rapprochement* between science and empiricism, despite the latter's subjective tendencies. No matter what problems may lurk in vision and hearing, there is something final about the guarantees of sense. Sheer observation is hard to contradict, for sense-data have an inalienable semblance of "fact." And such a court of last appeal, where verdicts are quick and ultimate, was exactly what scientists needed if their vast and complicated work was to go forward. Epistemology might produce intriguing puzzles, but it could never furnish facts for conviction to rest upon. A naive faith in sense-evidence, on the other hand, provided just such terminals to thought. Facts are something we can all observe, identify, and hold in common; in the last resort, seeing is believing. And science, as against philosophy even in that eager and active philosophical age, professed to look exclusively to the visible world for its un-questioned postulates.

The results were astounding enough to lend the new atti-tude full force. Despite the objections of philosophical thinkers, despite the outcry of moralists and theologians against the "crass materialism" and "sensationalism" of the scientists, physical science grew like Jack's beanstalk, and overshadowed everything else that human thought produced to rival it. A passion for observation displaced the scholarly love of learned dispute, and quickly developed the experi-mental technique that kept humanity supplied thrice over with facts. Practical applications of the new mechanical knowledge soon popularized and established it beyond the universities. Here the traditional interests of philosophy could not follow it any more; for they had become definitely relegated to that haven of unpopular lore, the schoolroom. No one really cared much about consistency or definition of terms, about precise conceptions, or formal deduction. The senses, long despised and attributed to the interesting but improper domain of the devil, were recognized as man's most valuable servants, and were rescued from their classical dis-grace to wait on him in his new venture. They were so effi-cient that they not only supplied the human mind with an incredible amount of food for thought, but seemed presently to have most of its cognitive business in hand. Knowledge from sensory experience was deemed the only knowledge that carried any affidavit of truth; for truth became identified, for all vigorous modern minds, with empirical fact.

And so, a scientific culture succeeded to the exhausted philosophical vision. An undisputed and uncritical empiri-cism — not skeptical, but positivistic — became its official metaphysical creed, experiment its avowed method, a vast hoard of "data" its capital, and correct prediction of future occurrences its proof. The programmatic account of this great adventure, beautifully put forth in Bacon's *Novum*

Organum, was followed only a few centuries later by the complete, triumphant summary of all that was scientifically respectable, in J. S. Mill's Canons of Induction — a sort of methodological manifesto.

As the physical world-picture grew and technology advanced, those disciplines which rested squarely on "rational" instead of "empirical" principles were threatened with complete extinction, and were soon denied even the honorable name of science. Logic and metaphysics, aesthetics and ethics, seemed to have seen their day. One by one the various branches of philosophy — natural, mental, social, or religious — set up as autonomous sciences; the natural ones with miraculous success, the humanistic ones with more hope and fanfare than actual achievement. The physical sciences found their stride without much hesitation; psychology and sociology tried hard and seriously to "catch the tune and keep the step," but with mathematical laws they were never really handy. Psychologists have probably spent almost as much time and type avowing their empiricism, their factual premises, their experimental techniques, as recording experiments and making general inductions. They still tell us that their lack of laws and calculable results is due to the fact that psychology is but young. When physics was as old as psychology is now, it was a definite, systematic body of highly general facts, and the possibilities of its future expansion were clearly visible in every line of its natural progress. It could say of itself, like Topsy, "I wasn't made, I growed." But our scientific psychology is *made* in the laboratory, and especially in the methodological forum. A good deal has, indeed, been made; but the synthetic organism still does not grow like a wild plant; its technical triumphs are apt to be discoveries in physiology or chemistry instead of psychological "facts."

Theology, which could not possibly submit to scientific methods, has simply been crowded out of the intellectual arena and gone into retreat in the cloistered libraries of its seminaries. As for logic, once the very model and norm of science, its only salvation seemed to lie in repudiating its most precious stock-in-trade, the "clear and distinct ideas," and professing to argue only from empirical facts to equally factual implications. The logician, once an investor in the greatest enterprise of human thought, found himself reduced to a sort of railroad linesman, charged with the task of keeping the tracks and switches of scientific reasoning clear for sensory reports to make their proper connections. Logic, it seemed, could never have a life of its own; for it had no foundation of facts, except the psychological fact that we do think thus and so, that such-and-such forms of argument lead to correct or incorrect predictions of further experience, and so forth. Logic became a mere reflection on tried and useful methods of fact-finding, and an official warrant for that technically fallacious process of generalizing known as "induction."

Yes, the heyday of science has stifled and killed our rather worn-out philosophical interests, born three and a half centuries ago from that great generative idea, the bifurcation of nature into an inner and an outer world. To the generations of Comte, Mill, and Spencer, it certainly seemed as though all human knowledge could be cast in the new mold; certainly as though nothing in any other mold could hope to jell. And indeed, nothing much *has* jelled in any other mold; but neither have the non-physical disciplines been able to adopt and thrive on the scientific methods that did such wonders for physics and its obvious derivatives. The truth is that science has not really fructified and activated all human thought. If humanity has really passed the philosophical stage of learning, as Comte hopefully declared, and is evolving no more fantastic ideas, then we have certainly left many interesting brain-children stillborn along the way.

But the mind of man is always fertile, ever creating and discarding, like the earth. There is always new life under old decay. Last year's dead leaves hide not merely the seeds, but the full-fledged green plants of this year's spring, ready to bloom almost as soon as they are uncovered. It is the same with the seasons of civilization: under cover of a weary Greco-Roman eclecticism, a baffled cynicism, Christianity grew to its conquering force of conception and its clear interpretation of life; obscured by creed, canon, and curriculum, by learned disputation and demonstration, was born the great ideal of *personal experience*, the "rediscovery of the inner life," as Rudolph Eucken termed it, that was to inspire philosophy from Descartes's day to the end of German idealism. And beneath our rival "isms," our methodologies, conferences, and symposia, of course there is something brewing, too.

No one observed, amid the first passion of empirical fact-finding, that the ancient science of mathematics still went its undisturbed way of pure reason. It fell in so nicely with the needs of scientific thought, it fitted the observed world of fact so neatly, that those who learned and used it never stopped to accuse those who had invented and evolved it of being mere reasoners, and lacking tangible data. Yet the few conscientious empiricists who thought that *factual* bases must be established for mathematics made a notoriously poor job of it. Few mathematicians have really held that numbers were discovered by observation, or even that geometrical relationships are known to us by inductive reasoning from many observed instances. Physicists may think of certain facts in place of constants and variables, but the same constants and variables will serve somewhere else to calculate other facts, and the mathematicians themselves give no set of data their preference. They deal only with items whose sensory qualities are quite irrelevant: their "data" are arbitrary sounds or marks called *symbols*.

Behind these symbols lie the boldest, purest, coolest abstractions mankind has ever made. No schoolman speculating on essences and attributes ever approached anything like the abstractness of algebra. Yet those same scientists who prided themselves on their concrete factual knowledge, who claimed to reject every proof except empirical evidence, never hesitated to accept the demonstrations and calculations, the bodiless, sometimes avowedly "fictitious" entities of the mathematicians. Zero and infinity, square roots of negative numbers, incommensurable lengths and fourth dimensions, all found unquestioned welcome in the laboratory, when the average thoughtful layman, who could still take an invisible soul-substance on faith, doubted their logical respectability.

What is the secret power of mathematics, to win hardheaded empiricists, against their most ardent beliefs, to its purely rational speculations and intangible "facts"? Mathematicians are rarely practical people, or good observers of events. They are apt to be cloistered souls, like philosophers and theologians. Why are their abstractions taken not only seriously, but as indispensable, fundamental facts, by men who observe the stars or experiment with chemical compounds?

The secret lies in the fact that a mathematician does not profess to say anything about the existence, reality, or efficacy of *things* at all. His concern is the possibility of *symbolizing things*, and of symbolizing the relations into which they might enter with each other. His "entities" are not "data," but *concepts*. That is why such elements as "imaginary numbers" and "infinite decimals" are tolerated by scientists to whom invisible agents, powers, and "principles" are anathema. Mathematical constructions are only symbols; they have meanings in terms of relationships, not of substance; something in reality answers to them, but they are not supposed to be items in that reality. To the true mathematician, numbers do not "inhere in" denumerable things, nor do circular objects "contain" degrees. Numbers and degrees and all their ilk only *mean* the real properties of real objects. It is entirely at the discretion of the scientist to say, "Let x mean this, let y mean that." All that mathematics determines is that *then* x and y must be related thus and thus. If experience belies the conclusion, then the formula does not express the relation of *this* x and *that* y; then x and y may not mean this thing and that. But no mathematician in his professional capacity will ever tell us that *this is x*, and has therefore such and such properties.

The faith of scientists in the power and truth of mathematics is so implicit that their work has gradually become less and less observation, and more and more calculation. The promiscuous collection and tabulation of data have given way to a process of assigning possible meanings, merely supposed real entities, to mathematical terms, working out the logical results, and then staging certain crucial experiments to check the hypothesis against the actual, empirical results. But the facts which are accepted by virtue of these tests are not actually *observed* at all. With the advance of mathematical technique in physics, the tangible results of experiment have become less and less spectacular; on the other hand, their *significance* has grown in inverse proportion. The men in the laboratory have departed so far from the old forms of experimentation — typified by Galileo's weights and Franklin's kite — that they cannot be said to observe the actual objects of their curiosity at all; instead, they are watching index needles, revolving drums, and sensitive plates. No psychology of "association" of sense-experiences can relate these data to the objects they signify, for in most cases the objects have never been experienced. Observation has become almost entirely indirect; and *readings* take the place of genuine witness. The sense-data on which the propositions of modern science rest are, for the most part, little photographic spots and blurs, or inky curved lines on paper. These data are empirical enough, but of course they are not themselves the phenomena in question; the actual phenomena stand behind them as their supposed causes. Instead of watching the process that interests us, that is to be verified — say, a course of celestial events, or the behavior of such objects as molecules and ether-waves — we really see only the fluctuations of a tiny arrow, the trailing path of a stylus, or the appearance of a speck of light, and *calculate to the "facts" of our science*. What is directly observable is only a sign of the "physical fact"; it requires interpretation to yield scientific propositions. Not simply seeing is believing, but *seeing and calculating, seeing and translating*.

This is bad, of course, for a thoroughgoing empiricism. Sense-data certainly do not make up the whole, or even the major part, of a scientist's material. The events that are given for his inspection could be "faked" in a dozen ways — that is, the same visible events could be made to occur, but with a different significance. We may at any time be wrong

about their significance, even where no one is duping us; we
may be nature's fools. Yet if we did not attribute an elaborate,
purely reasoned, and hypothetical history of causes to the
little shivers and wiggles of our apparatus, we really could
not record them as momentous results of experiment. The
problem of observation is all but eclipsed by the problem of
meaning. And the triumph of empiricism in science is
jeopardized by the surprising truth that *our sense-data are
primarily symbols.*

Here, suddenly, it becomes apparent that the age of science
has begotten a new philosophical issue, inestimably more
profound than its original empiricism: for in all quietness,
along purely rational lines, mathematics has developed just
as brilliantly and vitally as any experimental technique, and,
step by step, has kept abreast of discovery and observation;
and all at once, the edifice of human knowledge stands before
us, not as a vast collection of sense reports, but as a structure
of *facts that are symbols* and *laws that are their meanings.*
A new philosophical theme has been set forth to a coming
age: an epistemological theme, the comprehension of science.
The power of symbolism is its cue, as the finality of sense-data
was the cue of a former epoch.

In epistemology — really all that is left of a worn-out philosophical heritage — a new generative idea has dawned. Its
power is hardly recognized yet, but if we look at the actual
trend of thought — always the surest index to a general prospect — the growing preoccupation with that new theme is
quite apparent. One needs only to look at the titles of some
philosophical books that have appeared within the last fifteen
or twenty years: *The Meaning of Meaning;* [7] *Symbolism and
Truth;* [8] *Die Philosophie der symbolischen Formen;* [9] *Language, Truth and Logic;* [10] *Symbol und Existenz der Wissenschaft;* [11] *The Logical Syntax of Language;* [12] *Philosophy and*

[7] C. K. Ogden and I. A. Richards (1923).
[8] Ralph Munroe Eaton (1925).
[9] Ernst Cassirer, 3 vols. (1923, 1924, 1929).   [10] A. J. Ayer (1936).
[11] H. Noack, *Symbol und Existenz der Wissenschaft: Untersuchungen zur
Grundlegung einer philosophischen Wissenschaftslehre* (1936).
[12] Rudolf Carnap (1935; German ed. 1934).

Logical Syntax; [13] *Meaning and Change of Meaning;* [14] *Symbolism: its Meaning and Effects;* [15] *Foundations of the Theory of Signs;* [16] *Seele als Äusserung;* [17] *La pensée concrète: essai sur le symbolisme intellectuel;* [18] *Zeichen, die Fundamente des Wissens;* [19] and recently, *Language and Reality.*[20] The list is not nearly exhaustive. There are many books whose titles do not betray a preoccupation with semantic, for instance Wittgenstein's *Tractatus Logico-Philosophicus,*[21] or Grudin's *A Primer of Aesthetics.*[22] And were we to take an inventory of articles, even on the symbolism of science alone, we would soon have a formidable bibliography.

But it is not only in philosophy proper that the new keynote has been struck. There are at least two limited and technical fields, which have suddenly been developed beyond all prediction, by the discovery of the all-importance of symbol-using or symbol-reading. They are widely separate fields, and their problems and procedures do not seem to belong together in any way at all: one is modern psychology, the other modern logic.

In the former we are disturbed — thrilled or irritated, according to our temperaments — by the advent of psychoanalysis. In the latter we witness the rise of a new technique known as symbolic logic. The coincidence of these two pursuits seems entirely fortuitous; one stems from medicine and the other from mathematics, and there is nothing whatever on which they would care to compare notes or hold debate. Yet I believe they both embody the same generative idea, which is to preoccupy and inspire our philosophical age: for each in its own fashion has discovered the power of symbolization.

---

[13] Rudolf Carnap (1935; German ed. 1934).
[14] Gustav Stern (1931).
[15] A. N. Whitehead (1927).
[16] Charles W. Morris (1938).
[17] Paul Helwig (1936).
[18] A. Spaier (1927).
[19] R. Gätschenberger (1932).
[20] Wilbur M. Urban, *Language and Reality; the Philosophy of Language and the Principles of Symbolism* (1939).
[21] Ludwig Wittgenstein (1922).   [22] Louis Grudin (1930).

They have different conceptions of symbolism and its functions. Symbolic logic is not "symbolic" in the sense of
Freudian psychology, and *The Analysis of Dreams* makes no
contribution to logical syntax. The emphasis on symbolism
derives from entirely different interests, in their respective
contexts. As yet, the cautious critic may well regard the one
as a fantastic experiment of "mental philosophy," and the
other as a mere fashion in logic and epistemology.

When we speak of fashions in thought, we are treating
philosophy lightly. There is disparagement in the phrases,
"a fashionable problem," "a fashionable term." Yet it is the
most natural and appropriate thing in the world for a new
problem or a new terminology to have a vogue that crowds
out everything else for a little while. A word that everyone
snaps up, or a question that has everybody excited, probably
carries a generative idea — the germ of a complete reorientation in metaphysics, or at least the "Open Sesame" of some
new positive science. The sudden vogue of such a key-idea
is due to the fact that all sensitive and active minds turn at
once to exploiting it; we try it in every connection, for every
purpose, experiment with possible stretches of its strict meaning, with generalizations and derivatives. When we become
familiar with the new idea our expectations do not outrun
its actual uses quite so far, and then its unbalanced popu-
larity is over. We settle down to the problems that it has
really generated, and these become the characteristic issues
of our time.

The rise of technology is the best possible proof that the
basic concepts of physical science, which have ruled our
thinking for nearly two centuries, are essentially sound. They
have begotten knowledge, practice, and systematic understanding; no wonder they have given us a very confident and definite *Weltanschauung*. They have delivered all physical nature
into our hands. But strangely enough, the so-called "mental
sciences" have gained very little from the great adventure.
One attempt after another has failed to apply the concept of
causality to logic and aesthetics, or even sociology and psychology. Causes and effects could be found, of course, and

could be correlated, tabulated, and studied; but even in psychology, where the study of stimulus and reaction has been carried to elaborate lengths, no true science has resulted. No prospects of really great achievement have opened before us in the laboratory. If we follow the methods of natural science our psychology tends to run into physiology, histology, and genetics; we move further and further away from those problems which we ought to be approaching. That signifies that the generative idea which gave rise to physics and chemistry and all their progeny — technology, medicine, biology — does not contain any vivifying concept for the humanistic sciences. The physicist's scheme, so faithfully emulated by generations of psychologists, epistemologists, and aestheticians, is probably blocking their progress, defeating possible insights by its prejudicial force. The scheme is not false — it is perfectly reasonable — but it is bootless for the study of mental phenomena. It does not engender leading questions and excite a constructive imagination, as it does in physical researches. Instead of a method, it inspires a militant methodology.

Now, in those very regions of human interest where the age of empiricism has caused no revolution, the preoccupation with symbols has come into fashion. It has not sprung directly from any canon of science. It runs at least two distinct and apparently incompatible courses. Yet each course is a river of life in its own field, each fructifies its own harvest; and instead of finding mere contradiction in the wide difference of forms and uses to which this new generative idea is put, I see in it a promise of power and versatility, and a commanding philosophical problem. One conception of symbolism leads to logic, and meets the new problems in theory of knowledge; and so it inspires an evaluation of science and a quest for certainty. The other takes us in the opposite direction — to psychiatry, the study of emotions, religion, fantasy, and everything but knowledge. Yet in both we have a central theme: the *human response,* as a constructive, not a passive thing. Epistemologists and psychologists agree that symbolization is the key to that constructive process, though they may be ready to kill each other over the issue of what

a symbol is and how it functions. One studies the structure
of science, the other of dreams; each has his own assumptions
— that is all they are — regarding the nature of symbolism
itself. Assumptions, generative ideas, are what we fight for.
Our conclusions we are usually content to demonstrate by
peaceable means. Yet the assumptions are philosophically our
most interesting stock-in-trade.

  In the fundamental notion of symbolization — mystical,
practical, or mathematical, it makes no difference — we have
the keynote of all humanistic problems. In it lies a new conception of "mentality," that may illumine questions of life
and consciousness, instead of obscuring them as traditional
"scientific methods" have done. If it is indeed a generative
idea, it will beget tangible methods of its own, to free the
deadlocked paradoxes of mind and body, reason and impulse,
autonomy and law, and will overcome the checkmated arguments of an earlier age by discarding their very idiom and
shaping their equivalents in more significant phrase. The
philosophical study of symbols is not a technique borrowed
from other disciplines, not even from mathematics; it has
arisen in the fields that the great advance of learning has left
fallow. Perhaps it holds the seed of a new intellectual harvest, to be reaped in the next season of the human understanding.

CHAPTER II

Symbolic Transformation

The vitality and energies of the imag-
ination do not operate at will; they are
fountains, not machinery.

D. G. JAMES, Skepticism and Poetry.

ACHANGED approach to the theory of knowledge naturally
has its effect upon psychology, too. As long as sense
was supposed to be the chief factor in knowledge,
psychologists took a prime interest in the organs that were
the windows of the mind, and in the details of their functioning; other things were accorded a sketchier and sometimes
vaguer treatment. If scientists demanded, and philosophers
dutifully admitted, that all true belief must be based on
sense-evidence, then the activity of the mind had to be conceived purely as a matter of recording and combining; then
intelligence had to be a product of impression, memory, and
association. But now, an epistemological insight has uncovered a more potent, howbeit more difficult, factor in scientific procedure — the use of symbols to attain, as well as to
organize, belief. Of course, this alters our conception of
intelligence at a stroke. Not higher sensitivity, not longer
memory or even quicker association sets man so far above
other animals that he can regard them as denizens of a lower
world: no, it is the power of using symbols — the power of
speech — that makes him lord of the earth. So our interest
in the mind has shifted more and more from the acquisition
of experience, the domain of sense, to the *uses* of sense-data,
the realm of conception and expression.

The importance of symbol-using, once admitted, soon becomes paramount in the study of intelligence. It has lent a

new orientation especially to genetic psychology, which traces the growth of the mind; for this growth is paralleled, in large measure, by the observable uses of language, from the first words in infancy to the complete self-expression of maturity, and perhaps the relapse into meaningless verbiage that accompanies senile decline. Such researches have even been extended from the development of individuals to the evolution of mental traits in nations and races. There is an increasing *rapprochement* between philology and psychology — between the science of language and the science of what we do with language. The recent literature of psychogenetics bears ample witness to the central position which symbol-using, or language in its most general sense, holds in our conception of human mentality. Frank Lorimer's *The Growth of Reason* bears the sub-title: "A Study of the Role of Verbal Activity in the Growth and Structure of the Human Mind." Grace De Laguna's *Speech: its Function and Development* treats the acquisition of language as not only indicative of the growth of concepts, but as the principal agent in this evolution. Much the same view is held by Professor A. D. Ritchie, who remarks, in *The Natural History of the Mind*: "As far as thought is concerned, and at all levels of thought, it [mental life] is a symbolic process. It is mental not because the symbols are immaterial, for they are often material, perhaps always material, but because they are symbols. . . . The essential act of thought is symbolization." [1] There is, I think, more depth in this statement than its author realized; had he been aware of it, the proposition would have occurred earlier in the book, and given the whole work a somewhat novel turn. As it is, he goes on to an excellent account of sign-using and sign-making, which stand forth clearly as the essential means of intellection.

Quotations could be multiplied almost indefinitely, from an imposing list of sources — from John Dewey and Bertrand Russell, from Brunschwicg and Piaget and Head, Köhler and Koffka, Carnap, Delacroix, Ribot, Cassirer, Whitehead — from philosophers, psychologists, neurologists, and

[1] Pages 278–279.

anthropologists — to substantiate the claim that symbolism is the recognized key to that mental life which is characteristically human and above the level of sheer animality. Symbol and meaning make man's world, far more than sensation; Miss Helen Keller, bereft of sight and hearing, or even a person like the late Laura Bridgman, with the single sense of touch, is capable of living in a wider and richer world than a dog or an ape with all his senses alert.

Genetic psychology grew out of the study of animals, children, and savages, both from a physiological and from a behavioristic angle. Its fundamental standpoint is that the responses of an organism to the environment are adaptive, and are dictated by that organism's *needs*. Such needs may be variously conceived; one school reduces them all to one basic requirement, such as keeping the metabolic balance, persisting in an ideal status; [2] others distinguish as elementary more specific aims — e.g., nutrition, parturition, defense — or even such differentiated cravings as physical comfort, companionship, self-assertion, security, play.[3] The tenor of these primary concepts is suggested largely by the investigator's starting point. A biologist tends to postulate only the obvious needs of a clam or even an infusorian; an animal-psychologist generalizes somewhat less, for he makes distinctions that are relevant, say, to a white rat, but hardly to a clam. An observer of childhood conceives the cardinal interests on a still higher level. But through the whole hierarchy of genetic studies there runs a feeling of continuity, a tendency to identify the "real" or "ultimate" motive conditions of human action with the needs of primitive life, to trace all wants and aims of mankind to some initial protoplasmic response. This dominant principle is the most important thing that the evolutionist school has bestowed upon psychology — the assumption, sometimes avowed, more often tacit, that "*Nihil est in homine quod non prius in amoeba erat.*"

When students of mental evolution discovered how great a

[2] Cf. Eugenio Rignano, *The Psychology of Reasoning* (1927).

[3] Cf. William James, *The Principles of Psychology* (1899; first published in 1890), II, 348.

role in science is played by symbols, they were not slow to exploit that valuable insight. The acquisition of so decisive a tool must certainly be regarded as one of the great landmarks in human progress, probably the starting point of all genuinely intellectual growth. Since symbol-using appears at a late stage, it is presumably a highly integrated form of simpler animal activities. It must spring from biological needs, and justify itself as a practical asset. Man's conquest of the world undoubtedly rests on the supreme development of his brain, which allows him to synthesize, delay, and modify his reactions by the interpolation of *symbols* in the gaps and confusions of direct experience, and by means of "verbal signs" to add the experiences of other people to his own.

There is a profound difference between using symbols and merely using signs. The use of signs is the very first manifestation of mind. It arises as early in biological history as the famous "conditioned reflex," by which a concomitant of a stimulus takes over the stimulus-function. The concomitant becomes a *sign* of the condition to which the reaction is really appropriate. This is the real beginning of mentality, for here is the birthplace of *error*, and therewith of truth. If truth and error are to be attributed only to belief, then we must recognize in the earliest misuse of signs, in the inappropriate conditioned reflex, not error, but some prototype of error. We might call it *mistake*. Every piano player, every typist, knows that the hand can make mistakes where consciousness entertains no error. However, whether we speak of truth and error, or of their respective prototypes, whether we regard the creature liable to them as conscious or preconscious, or dispense with such terms altogether, the use of signs is certainly a *mental* function. It is the beginning of intelligence. As soon as sensations function as signs of conditions in the surrounding world, the animal receiving them is moved to exploit or avoid those conditions. The sound of a gong or a whistle, itself entirely unrelated to the process of eating, causes a dog to expect food, if in past experience this sound has always preceded dinner; it is a sign, not a part, of his food. Or, the smell of a cigarette, in itself not necessarily displeasing, tells a wild animal that there is danger, and drives it into hiding. The growth of this sign-language runs parallel with the physical development of sense organs and synaptic nerve-structure. It consists in the transmission of *sense messages* to muscles and glands — to the organs of eating, mating, flight and defense — and obviously functions in the interest of the elementary biological requirements: self-preservation, growth, procreation, the preservation of the species.

Even animal mentality, therefore, is built up on a primitive semantic; it is the power of learning, by trial and error, that certain phenomena in the world are signs of certain others, existing or about to exist; adaptation to an environment is its purpose, and hence the measure of its success. The environment may be very narrow, as it is for the mole, whose world is a back yard, or it may be as wide as an eagle's range and as complicated as a monkey's jungle preserve. That depends on the variety of *signals* a creature can receive, the variety of combinations of them to which he can react, and the fixity or adjustability of his responses. Obviously, if he have very fixed reactions, he cannot adapt himself to a varied or transient environment; if he cannot easily combine and integrate several activities, then the occurrence of more than one stimulus at a time will throw him into confusion; if he be poor in sensory organs — deaf, or blind, hard-shelled, or otherwise limited — he cannot receive many signals to begin with.

Man's superiority in the race for self-preservation was first ascribed to his wider range of signals, his greater power of integrating reflexes, his quicker learning by trial and error; but a little reflection brought a much more fundamental trait to light, namely his peculiar use of "signs." Man, unlike all other animals, uses "signs" not only to *indicate* things, but also to *represent* them. To a clever dog, the name of a person is a signal that the person is present; you say the name, he pricks up his ears and looks for its object. If you say "dinner," he becomes restive, expecting food. You cannot make any communication to him that is not taken as a signal of something immediately forthcoming. His mind is a simple and direct *transmitter* of messages from the world to his motor centers. With man it is different. We use certain "signs" among ourselves that do not point to anything in our actual surroundings. Most of our words are not signs in the sense of signals. They are used to talk *about* things, not to direct our eyes and ears and noses toward them. Instead of announcers of things, they are reminders. They have been called "substitute signs," for in our present experience they take the place of things that we have perceived in the past, or even things that we can merely imagine by combining memories, things that *might* be in past or future experience. Of course such "signs" do not usually serve as vicarious stimuli to actions that would be appropriate to their meanings; where the objects are quite normally not present, that would result in a complete chaos of behavior. They serve, rather, to let us develop a characteristic attitude toward objects *in absentia*, which is called "thinking of" or "referring to" what is not here. "Signs" used in this capacity are not *symptoms* of things, but *symbols*.

The development of language is the history of the gradual accumulation and elaboration of verbal symbols. By means of this phenomenon, man's whole behavior-pattern has undergone an immense change from the simple biological scheme, and his mentality has expanded to such a degree that it is no longer comparable to the minds of animals. Instead of a direct transmitter of coded signals, we have a system that has sometimes been likened to a telephone-exchange,[4] wherein messages may be relayed, stored up if a line is busy, answered by proxy, perhaps sent over a line that did not exist when they were first given, *noted down and kept* if the desired number gives no answer. Words are the plugs in this super-switchboard; they connect impressions and let them function together; sometimes they cause lines to become crossed in funny or disastrous ways.

This view of mentality, of its growth through trial and error, its apparently complicated but essentially simple aims

[4] The simile of the telephone-exchange has been used by Leonard Troland in *The Mystery of Mind* (1926), p. 100 ff.

— namely, to advance the persistence, growth, and procreation of the organism, and to produce, and provide for, its progeny — brings the troublesome concept of Mind into line with other basic ideas of biology. Man is doing in his elaborate way just what the mouse in his simplicity is doing, and what the unconscious or semiconscious jellyfish is performing after its own chemical fashion. The ideal of *"Nihil est in homine . . ."* is supported by living example. The speech line between man and beast is minimized by the recognition that speech is primarily an instrument of social control, just like the cries of animals, but has acquired a representative function, allowing a much greater degree of cooperation among individuals, and the focussing of personal attention on absent objects. The passage from the sign-function of a word to its symbolic function is gradual, a result of social organization, an instrument that proves indispensable once it is discovered, and develops through successful use.

If the theoretic position here attributed to students of genetic psychology requires any affidavit, we can find it in the words of a psychologist, in Frank Lorimer's *The Growth of Reason*:

"The apes described by Köhler," he says, "certainly have quite elaborate 'ape-ways' into which a newcomer is gradually acculturated, including among other patterns ways of using available instruments for reaching and climbing, a sort of rhythmic play or dance, and types of murmurs, wails and rejoicings. . . .

"It is not surprising that still more intelligent animals should have developed much more definite and elaborate 'animal ways,' including techniques of tool-uses and specific mechanisms of vocal social control, which gradually developed into the 'folk-ways' of the modern anthropologist. . . .

"Vocal acts are originally involved in the intellectual correlation of behaviour just as other physiological processes are. During the whole course of meaningless vocal chatter, vocal processes gradually accumulate intensity and dominance in behaviour. . . . Specific vocables become dominant *foci* of fixed reactions to various situations and the instruments of specific social adjustments. . . . The gradual differentiation and expansion of the social functions of vocal activity, among a race of animals characterized by increasingly complex nervous systems, is the fundamental principle of the historic trend of *vocal* activity to *verbal* activity, and the emergence of language." [5]

An interpretation of observed facts that adjusts them to a general scientific outlook, a theory that bridges what used to appear as a *saltus naturae*, a logical explanation displacing a shamefaced resort to miracle, has so much to recommend it that one hates to challenge it on any count. But the best ideas are also the ones most worth reflecting on. At first glance it seems as though the genetic conception of language, which regards the power of symbol-using as the latest and highest device of practical intelligence, an added instrument for gaining animal ends, must be the key to all essential features of human mentality. It makes rationality plausible, and shows at once the relationship of man and brute, and the gulf between them as a fairly simple phenomenon.

The difficulty of the theory arises when we consider how people with synaptic switchboards between their sense organs and their muscles should use their verbal symbols to make the telephone-exchange work most efficiently. Obviously the only proper use of the words which "plug in" the many complicated wires is the denotation of *facts*. Such facts may be concrete and personal, or they may be highly general and universal; but they should be chosen for the sake of orientation in the world for better living, for more advantageous practice. It is easy to see how *errors* might arise, just as they occur in overt action; the white rat in a maze makes mistakes, and so does the trout who bites at a feather-and-silk fly. In so complicated an organ as the human cortex, a confusion of messages or of responses would be even more likely than in the reflex arcs of rodents or fish. But of course the mistakes should be subject to quick correction by the world's punishments; behavior should, on the whole, be rational and

[5] Pages 76–77.

realistic. Any other response must be chalked up as failure, as a miscarriage of biological purposes.

There are, indeed, philosophical and scientific thinkers who have accepted the biogenetic theory of mind on its great merits, and drawn just the conclusions indicated above. They have looked at the way men really use their power of symbolic thinking, the responses they actually make, and have been forced to admit that the cortical telephone-exchange does business in most extraordinary ways. The results of their candid observations are such books as W. B. Pitkin's *Short Introduction to the History of Human Stupidity*, Charles Richet's *L'homme Stupide* (which deals not with men generally regarded as stupid, but with the impractical customs and beliefs of aliens, and the folly of religious convictions), and Stuart Chase's *The Tyranny of Words*. To contemplate the unbelievable folly of which symbol-using animals are capable is very disgusting or very amusing, according to our mood; but philosophically it is, above all, confounding. How can an instrument develop in the interests of better practice, and survive, if it harbors so many dangers for the creature possessed of it? How can language increase a man's efficiency if it puts him at a biological disadvantage beside his cat?

Mr. Chase, watching his cat Hobie Baker, reflects:

"Hobie can never learn to talk. He can learn to respond to my talk, as he responds to other signs. . . . He can utter cries indicating pain, pleasure, excitement. He can announce that he wants to go out of doors. . . . But he cannot master words and language. This in some respects is fortunate for Hobie, for he will not suffer from hallucinations provoked by bad language. He will remain a realist all his life. . . . He is certainly able to think after a fashion, interpreting signs in the light of past experience, deliberately deciding his course of action, the survival value of which is high.

"Instead of words, Hobie sometimes uses a crude gesture language. We know that he has a nervous system corresponding to that of man, with messages coming in to the receptors in skin, ear and eye and going over the wires to the cortex, where memories are duly filed for reference. There are fewer switchboards in his cortex than in mine, which may be one of the reasons why he cannot learn to talk. . . .

"Meaning comes to Hobie as it comes to me, through past experience. . . .

"Generally speaking, animals tend to learn cumulatively through experience. The old elephant is the wisest of the herd. This selective process does not always operate in the case of human beings. The old are sometimes wise, but more often they are stuffed above the average with superstitions, misconceptions, and irrational dogmas. One may hazard the guess that erroneous identifications in human beings are pickled and preserved in words, and so not subject to the constant check of the environment, as in the case of cats and elephants. . . .

"I find Hobie a useful exhibit along this difficult trail of semantics. What 'meaning' connotes to him is often so clear and simple that I have no trouble in following it. I come from a like evolutionary matrix. 'Meaning' to me has like roots, and a like mechanism of apprehension. I have a six-cylinder brain and he has a one-lunger, but they operate on like principles.

". . . Most children do not long maintain Hobie Baker's realistic appraisal of the environment. Verbal identifications and confused abstractions begin at a tender age. . . . Language is no more than crudely acquired before children begin to suffer from it, and to misinterpret the world by reason of it." [6]

A cat with a "stalking-instinct," or other special equipment, who could never learn to use that asset properly, but was forever stalking chairs or elephants, would scarcely rise in animal estate by virtue of his talent. Men who can use symbols to facilitate their practical responses, but use them constantly to confuse and inhibit, warp and misadapt their actions, *and gain no other end by their symbolic devices*, have no prospect of inheriting the earth. Such an "instinct" would have no chance to develop by any process of successful

[6] Stuart Chase, *The Tyranny of Words* (1938), pp. 46–56.

exercise. The error-quotient is too great. The commonly recognized biological needs — food and shelter, security, sexual satisfaction, and the safety of young ones — are probably better assuaged by the realistic activities, the meows and gestures, of Hobie Baker than by the verbal imagination and reflection of his master. The cat's world is not falsified by the beliefs and poetic figments that language creates, nor his behavior unbalanced by the bootless rites and sacrifices that characterize religion, art, and other vagaries of a word-mongering mind. In fact, his vital purposes are so well served without the intervention of these vast mental constructions, these flourishes and embellishments of the cerebral switchboard, that it is hard to see why such an overcomplication of the central exchange was ever permitted, in man's "higher centers," to block the routes from sensory to motor organs and garble all the messages.

The dilemma for philosophy is bad enough to make one reconsider the genetic hypothesis that underlies it. If our basic needs were really just those of lower creatures much refined, we should have evolved a more realistic language than in fact we have. If the mind were essentially a recorder and transmitter, typified by the simile of the telephone-exchange, we should act very differently from the way we actually do. Certainly no "learning-process" has caused man to believe in magic; yet "word-magic" is a common practice among primitive peoples, and so is vicarious treatment — burning in effigy, etc. — where the proxy is plainly a mere symbol of the desired victim. Another strange, universal phenomenon is ritual. It is obviously symbolic, except where it is aimed at concrete results, and then it may be regarded as a communal form of magic. Now, all magical and ritual practices are hopelessly inappropriate to the preservation and increase of life. My cat would turn up his nose and his tail at them. To regard them as mistaken attempts to control nature, as a result of wrong synapses, or "crossed wires," in the brain, seems to me to leave the most rational of animals too deep in the slough of error. If a savage in his ignorance of physics tries to make a mountain open its caverns by dancing round it, we must admit with shame that no rat in a psychologist's maze would try such patently ineffectual methods of opening a door. Nor should such experiments be carried on, in the face of failure, for thousands of years; even morons should learn more quickly than that.

Another item in human behavior is our serious attitude toward art. Genetic psychology usually regards art as a form of play, a luxury product of the mind. This is not only a scientific theory, it is a common-sense view; we *play an instrument*, we *act a play*. Yet like many common-sense doctrines, it is probably false. Great artists are rarely recruited from the leisure class, and it is only in careless speech that we denote music or tragedy as our "hobby"; we do not really class them with tennis or bridge. We condemn as barbarous people who destroy works of art, even under the stress of war — blame them for ruining the Parthenon, when only a recent, sentimental generation has learned to blame them for ruining the homes that surrounded the sanctuary of Beauty! Why should the world wail over the loss of a play product, and look with its old callousness on the destruction of so much that dire labor has produced? It seems a poor economy of nature that men will suffer and starve for the sake of play, when play is supposed to be the abundance of their strength after their needs are satisfied. Yet artists as a class are so ready to sacrifice wealth and comfort and even health to their trade, that a lean and hollow look has become an indispensable feature in the popular conception of genius.

There is a third factor in human life that challenges the utilitarian doctrine of symbolism. That is the constant, ineffectual process of *dreaming* during sleep. The activity of the mind seems to go on all the time, like that of the heart and lungs and viscera; but during sleep it serves no practical purpose. That dream-material is symbolic is a fairly established fact. And symbols are supposed to have evolved from the advantageous use of *signs*. They are representative signs, that help to retain things for later reference, for comparing, planning, and generally for purposive thinking. Yet the symbolism of dreams performs no such acquired function.

At best it presents us with the things we do *not* want to think about, the things which stand in the way of practical living. Why should the mind produce symbols that do not direct the dreamer's activities, that only mix up the present with unsuitable past experiences?

There are several theories of dream, notably, of course, the Freudian interpretation. But those which — like Freud's — regard it as more than excess mental energy or visceral disturbance do not fit the scientific picture of the mind's growth and function at all. A mind whose semantic powers are evolved from the functioning of the motor arc should *only think*; any vagaries of association are "mistakes." If our viscera made as many mistakes in sleep as the brain, we should all die of indigestion after our first nursing. It may be replied that the mistakes of dream are harmless, since they have no motor terminals, though they enter into waking life as memories, and we have to learn to discount them. But why does the central switchboard not rest when there is no need of making connections? Why should the plugs be popped in and out, and set the whole system wildly ringing, only to end with a universal "Excuse it, please"?

The love of magic, the high development of ritual, the seriousness of art, and the characteristic activity of dreams, are rather large factors to leave out of account in constructing a theory of mind. Obviously the mind is doing something else, or at least something more, than just connecting experiential items. It is not functioning simply in the interest of those biological needs which genetic psychology recognizes. Yet it is a natural organ, and presumably does nothing that is not relevant to the total behavior, the response to nature that constitutes human life. The moral of this long critique is, therefore, *to reconsider the inventory of human needs*, which scientists have established on a basis of animal psychology, and somewhat hastily set up as the measure of a man. An unrecorded motive might well account for many an unexplained action. I propose, therefore, to try a new general principle: to conceive the mind, still as an organ in the service of primary needs, but of *characteristically human needs*; instead of assuming that the human mind tries to do the same things as a cat's mind, but by the use of a special talent which miscarries four times out of five, I shall assume that the human mind is *trying to do something else*; and that the cat does not act humanly *because he does not need to*. This difference in fundamental needs, I believe, determines the difference of function which sets man so far apart from all his zoölogical brethren; and the recognition of it is the key to those paradoxes in the philosophy of mind which our too consistently zoölogical model of human intelligence has engendered.

It is generally conceded that men have certain "higher" aims and desires than animals; but what these are, and in what sense they are "higher," may still be mooted without any universal agreement. There are essentially two schools of opinion: one which considers man the highest animal, and his supreme desires as products of his supreme mind; and another which regards him as the lowest spirit, and his unique longings as a manifestation of his otherworldly admixture. To the naturalists, the difference between physical and mental interests, between organismic will and moral will, between hungry meows and harvest prayers, or between faith in the mother cat and faith in a heavenly father, is a difference of complexity, abstractness, articulateness, in short: a difference of degree. To the religious interpreters it seems a radical distinction, a difference, in each case, of kind and cause. The moral sentiments especially are deemed a sign of the ultimate godhead in man; likewise the power of prayer, which is regarded as a gift, not a native and natural power like laughter, tears, language, and song. The Ancient Mariner, when suddenly he could pray, had not merely found his speech; he had received grace, he was given back the divine status from which he had fallen. According to the religious conception, man is at most half-brother to the beast. No matter how many of his traits may be identified as simian features, there is that in him yet which springs from a different source and is forever unzoölogical. This view is the antithesis of the naturalistic; it breaks the structure of genetic psychology in principle. For, the study of psychogenesis has grown up on exactly the opposite creed — that man is a true-blooded, full-franchised denizen of the animal kingdom, without any alien ancestors, *and therefore has no features or functions which animals do not share in some degree.*

That man is an animal I certainly believe; and also, that he has no supernatural essence, "soul" or "entelechy" or "mind-stuff," enclosed in his skin. He is an organism, his substance is chemical, and what he does, suffers, or knows, is just what this sort of chemical structure may do, suffer, or know. When the structure goes to pieces, it never does, suffers, or knows anything again. If we ask how physical objects, chemically analyzable, can be conscious, how ideas can occur to them, we are talking ambiguously; for the conception of "physical object" is a conception of chemical substance *not* biologically organized. What causes this tremendous organization of substances, is one of the things the tremendous organisms do not know; but with their organization, suffering and impulse and awareness arise. It is really no harder to imagine that a chemically active body wills, knows, thinks, and feels, than that an invisible, intangible something does so, "animates" the body without physical agency, and "inhabits" it without being in any *place.*

Now this is a mere declaration of faith, preliminary to a confession of heresy. The heresy is this: that I believe there is a primary need in man, which other creatures probably do not have, and which actuates all his apparently unzoölogical aims, his wistful fancies, his consciousness of value, his utterly impractical enthusiasms, and his awareness of a "Beyond" filled with holiness. Despite the fact that this need gives rise to almost everything that we commonly assign to the "higher" life, it is not itself a "higher" form of some "lower" need; it is quite essential, imperious, and general, and may be called "high" only in the sense that it belongs exclusively (I think) to a very complex and perhaps recent genus. It may be satisfied in crude, primitive ways or in conscious and refined ways, so it has its own hierarchy of "higher" and "lower," elementary and derivative forms.

SYMBULIZATION

This basic need, which certainly is obvious only in man, is the *need of symbolization*. The symbol-making function is one of man's primary activities, like eating, looking, or moving about. It is the fundamental process of his mind, and goes on all the time. Sometimes we are aware of it, sometimes we merely find its results, and realize that certain experiences have passed through our brains and have been digested there.

Hark back, now, to a passage already quoted above, from Ritchie's *The Natural History of the Mind*: "As far as thought is concerned, and at all levels of thought, it is a symbolic process. . . . The essential act of thought is symbolization." [7] The significance of this statement strikes us more forcibly now. For if the material of thought is symbolism, then the thinking organism must be forever furnishing symbolic versions of its experiences, in order to let thinking proceed. As a matter of fact, it is not the essential act of thought that is symbolization, but an act *essential to thought*, and prior to it. Symbolization is the essential act of mind; and mind takes in more than what is commonly called thought. Only certain products of the symbol-making brain can be used according to the canons of discursive reasoning. In every mind there is an enormous store of other symbolic material, which is put to different uses or perhaps even to no use at all — a mere result of spontaneous brain activity, a reserve fund of conceptions, a surplus of mental wealth.

The brain works as naturally as the kidneys and the blood-vessels. It is not dormant just because there is no conscious purpose to be served at the moment. If it were, indeed, a vast and intricate telephone-exchange, then it should be quiescent when the rest of the organism sleeps, or at most transmit experiences of digestion, of wanted oxygen or itching toes, of after-images on the retina or little throbbings in pressed arteries. Instead of that, it goes right on manufacturing ideas — streams and deluges of ideas, that the sleeper is not using to *think* with about anything. But the brain is following its own law; it is actively translating experiences

[7] See p. 27.

into symbols, in fulfilment of a basic need to do so. It carries on a constant process of ideation.

Ideas are undoubtedly made out of impressions — out of sense messages from the special organs of perception, and vague visceral reports of feeling. The law by which they are made, however, is not a law of direct combination. Any attempt to use such principles as association by contiguity or similarity soon runs into sheer unintelligible complication and artifice. Ideation proceeds by a more potent principle, which seems to be best described as a principle of symbolization. The material furnished by the senses is constantly wrought into *symbols*, which are our elementary ideas. Some of these ideas can be combined and manipulated in the manner we call "reasoning." Others do not lend themselves to this use, but are naturally telescoped into dreams, or vapor off in conscious fantasy; and a vast number of them build the most typical and fundamental edifice of the human mind — religion.

Symbolization is pre-rationative, but not pre-rational. It is the starting point of all intellection in the human sense, and is more general than thinking, fancying, or taking action. For the brain is not merely a great transmitter, a super-switchboard; it is better likened to a great transformer. The current of experience that passes through it undergoes a change of character, not through the agency of the sense by which the perception entered, but by virtue of a primary use which is made of it immediately: it is sucked into the stream of symbols which constitutes a human mind.

Our overt acts are governed by representations whose counterparts can nowhere be pointed out, whose objects are "percepts" only in a Pickwickian sense. The representations on which we act are symbols of various kinds. This fact is recognized in a vague and general way by most epistemologists; but what has not received their due recognition is the enormous importance of the *kinds*. So long as we regard sensations as *signs* of the things which are supposed to give rise to them, and perhaps endow such signs with further reference to past sensations that were similar signs, we have not even scratched the surface of the symbol-mongering human mind. It is only when we penetrate into the varieties of symbolific activity — as Cassirer, for instance, has done — that we begin to see why human beings do not act as super-intelligent cats, dogs, or apes would act. Because our brain is only a fairly good transmitter, but a tremendously powerful transformer, we do things that Mr. Chase's cat would reject as too impractical, if he were able to conceive them. So they would be, for him; so are they for the psychologist who deems himself a cat of the nth degree.

The fact that the human brain is constantly carrying on a process of symbolic transformation of the experiential data that come to it causes it to be a veritable fountain of more or less spontaneous ideas. As all registered experience tends to terminate in action, it is only natural that a typically human function should require a typically human form of overt activity; and that is just what we find in *the sheer expression of ideas.* This is the activity of which beasts appear to have no need. And it accounts for just those traits in man which he does not hold in common with the other animals — ritual, art, laughter, weeping, speech, superstition, and scientific genius.

Only a part — howbeit a very important part — of our behavior is practical. Only some of our expressions are *signs,* indicative or mnemonic, and belong to the heightened animal wisdom called common sense; and only a small and relatively unimportant part are immediate *signs of feeling.* The remainder serve simply to express ideas that the organism yearns to express, i.e. to act upon, without practical purpose, without any view to satisfying other needs than the need of completing in overt action the brain's symbolic process.

How else shall we account for man's love of talk? From the first dawning recognition that words can *express* something, talk is a dominant interest, an irresistible desire. As soon as this avenue of action opens, a whole stream of symbolic process is set free in the jumbled outpouring of words — often repeated, disconnected, random words — that we observe in the "chattering" stage of early childhood. Psychologists generally, and perhaps correctly, regard such babble as *verbal play*, and explain it through its obvious utilitarian function of developing the lines of *communication* that will be needed later in life. But an explanation by final causes does not really account for the occurrence of an act. What gives a child the present stimulus to talk? Surely not the prospect of acquiring a useful tool toward his future social relations! The impulse must be motivated by a present need, not a prospective one. Mr. Chase, who sees no use in words except their practical effect on other people, admits the puzzling fact that "children practice them with as much gusto as Hobie stalks a mouse." [8] But we can hardly believe that they do so for the sake of practice. There must be immediate satisfaction in this strange exercise, as there is in running and kicking. The effect of words on other people is only a secondary consideration. Mrs. De Laguna has pointed this out in her book on the general nature of speech: "The little child," she says there, "spends many hours and much energy in vocal *play*. It is far more agreeable to carry on this play with others . . . but the little child indulges in language-play even when he is alone. . . . Internal speech, fragmentary or continuous, becomes the habitual accompaniment of his active behaviour and the occupation of his idle hours." [9] Speech is, in fact, the readiest active termination of that basic process in the human brain which may be called *symbolic transformation of experiences*. The fact that it makes elaborate communication with others possible becomes important at a somewhat later stage. Piaget has observed that children of kindergarten age pay little attention to the response of others; they talk just as blithely to a companion who does not understand them as to one who gives correct answers.[10] Of course they have long learned to use language practically; but the typically infantile, or "egocentric," function persists side by side with the progres-

[8] *Op. cit.*, p. 54.

[9] Grace De Laguna, *Speech: its Function and Development* (1927), p. 307.

[10] Jean Piaget, *Le langage et la pensée chez l'enfant* (1923). See esp. chaps. i and ii.

sively social development of communication. The sheer *symbolific* use of sounds is the more primitive, the easier use, which can be made before conventional forms are really mastered, just as soon as any *meaning*-experience has occurred to the vociferous little human animal. The practical use, though early, is more difficult, for it is not the direct fulfilment of a craving; it is an adaptation of language for the satisfaction of *other* needs.

Words are certainly our most important instruments of expression, our most characteristic, universal, and enviable tools in the conduct of life. Speech is the mark of humanity. It is the normal terminus of thought. We are apt to be so impressed with its symbolistic mission that we regard it as the only important expressive act, and assume that all other activity must be practical in an animalian way, or else irrational — playful, or atavistic (residual) past recognition, or mistaken, i.e., unsuccessful. But in fact, speech is the natural outcome of only one *kind* of symbolic process. There are transformations of experience in the human mind that have quite different overt endings. They end in acts that are neither practical nor communicative, though they may be *Ritual* both effective and communal; I mean the actions we call *ritual.*

Human life is shot through and through with ritual, as it is also with animalian practices. It is an intricate fabric of reason and rite, of knowledge and religion, prose and poetry, fact and dream. Just as the results of that primitive process of mental digestion, verbal symbolism, may be used for the satisfaction of other needs than symbolization, so all other instinctive acts may serve the expressive function. Eating, traveling, asking or answering questions, construction, destruction, prostitution — any or all such activities may enter into *rites*; yet rites in themselves are not practical, but expressive. Ritual, like art, is essentially the active termination of a symbolic transformation of experience. It is born in the cortex, not in the "old brain"; but it is born of an *elementary need* of that organ, once the organ has grown to human estate.

If the "impractical" use of language has mystified philosophers and psychologists who measured it by standards it is not really designed to meet, the apparent perversity of ritual from the same point of view has simply overcome them. They have had to invent excuses for its existence, to save the psychogenetic theory of mind. They have sought its explanation in social purposes, in ulterior motivations of the most unlikely sort, in "mistakes" of sense and reason that verge on complete imbecility; they have wondered at the incorrigibility of religious follies, at the docility of the poor dupes who let themselves be misled, and at the disproportionate cost of the supposed social advantages; but they have not been led to the assumption of a peculiarly human *need* which is fed, as every need must be, at the expense of other interests.

The ethnologists who were the first white men to interest themselves in the ritual of primitive races for any other purpose than to suppress or correct it were mystified by the high seriousness of actions that looked purely clownish and farcical to the European beholder; just as the Christian missionaries had long reported the difficulty of making the gospels plausible to men who were able to believe stories far more mysterious and fantastic in their own idiom. Andrew Lang, for instance, discussing the belief in magic, makes the following observation:

"The theory requires for its existence an almost boundless credulity. This credulity appears to Europeans to prevail in full force among savages. . . . But it is a curious fact that while savages are, as a rule, so credulous, they often 'laugh consumedly' at the religious doctrines taught them by missionaries. Savages and civilized men have different standards of credulity. Dr. Moffat remarks, 'To speak of the Creation, the Fall, and the Resurrection, seemed more fabulous, extravagant, and ludicrous to them than their own vain stories of lions and hyaenas.' . . . It is, apparently, in regard to imported and novel opinions about religion and science alone that savages imitate the conduct of the adder which, according to St. Augustine, is voluntarily deaf. . . ." [11]

Frobenius, also a pioneer in the study of primitive society,

[11] *Myth, Ritual, and Religion,* 2 vols. (1887), I, 91.

describes an initiation ceremony in New South Wales, in the course of which the older men performed a dog-dance, on all fours, for the benefit of the young acolytes who watched these rites, preliminary to the painful honor of having a tooth knocked out. Frobenius refers to the ritual as a "comedy," a "farce," and is amazed at the solemnity with which the boys sat through the "ridiculous canine display." "They acted as if they never caught sight of the comical procession of men." [12] A little later he describes a funeral among the Bougala, in the Southern Congo; again, each step in the performance seems to him a circus act, until at last "there now followed, if possible, a still more clownish farce. The deceased had now himself to declare what was the cause of his death." [13] The professor is at a loss to understand how even the least intelligent of men can reach such depths of folly. Perhaps the savages who "laughed consumedly" at a tonsured father's sacraments with Holy Water, his God-eating and his scriptural explanations, were having a similar difficulty!

Later scholars gradually realized that the irrationality of customs and rites was so great that they could not possibly be "mistakes" of practice, or rest on "erroneous" theories of nature. Obviously they serve some natural purpose to which their practical justification or lack of justification is entirely irrelevant. Mrs. De Laguna seeks this purpose in the social solidarity which a prescribed ritual imparts: "Those elaborate and monstrous systems of belief," she says, "cannot possibly be accounted for by any simple theory that beliefs are determined by their successful 'working' in practice. . . . The truth is . . . that some more or less organized system of beliefs and sentiments is an absolute necessity for the carrying on of social life. So long as group solidarity is secured by some such system, the particular beliefs which enter into it may to an indefinite degree lead to behavior ill-adapted to the objective order of nature." [14] But why should this social purpose not be served by a sensible dogma which the members

[12] Leo Frobenius, *The Childhood of Man* (1909; first published in 1901 under the title, *Aus den Flegeljahren der Menschheit*), p. 41 ff.
[13] *Ibid.*, p. 148.   [14] *Speech*, pp. 345–346.

of the society could reasonably be called on to believe, instead of "elaborate and monstrous" creeds issuing in all sorts of cruel rites, mutilations, and even human sacrifices, such as Baal or the Aztec gods demanded? Why did the Cults of Reason set up in post-Revolutionary France and in early Soviet Russia not serve the purpose of social solidarity every bit as well as the "Christian hocus-pocus" they displaced, and much better than the dog-dances and interrogation of the dead that disturbed Frobenius by their incredibility? Why should a priesthood primarily interested in accomplishing a social end demand that its laity should believe in immoral and unreasonable gods? Plato, who treated religion in just this sociological spirit, found himself confronted with this question. The established religion of Greece was not only irrational, but the social unity that might be achieved by participating in one form of worship and following one divine example was off-set by the fact that this worship was often degrading and the example bad. How could any wise ruler or rulers prescribe such ritual, or indorse such a mythology?

The answer is, of course, that ritual is not prescribed for a practical purpose, not even that of social solidarity. Such solidarity may be one of its effects, and sophisticated warlords may realize this fact and capitalize on it by emphasizing national religion or holding compulsory prayers before battle; but neither myth nor ritual arose originally for this purpose. Even the pioneers in anthropology, to whom the practices of savage society must have been more surprising than to us who are initiated through their reports, realized that the "farces" and "antics" of primitive men were profoundly serious, and that their wizards could not be accused of bad faith. "Magic has not its origin in fraud, and seems seldom practiced as an utter imposture," observed Tylor, seventy years ago. "It is, in fact, a sincere but fallacious system of philosophy, evolved by the human intellect by processes still in great measure intelligible to our minds, and it had thus an original standing-ground in the world." [15] Its roots lie much

[15] E. B. Tylor, *Primitive Culture*, 2 vols. (6th ed., 1920; first published in 1871), I, 134.

deeper than any conscious purpose, any trickery, policy, or practical design; they lie in that substratum of the mind, the realm of fundamental ideas, and bear their strange if not poisonous fruits, by virtue of the human need for *expressing* such ideas. Whatever purpose magical practice may serve, its direct motivation is the desire to symbolize great conceptions. It is the overt action in which a rich and savage imagination automatically ends. Its origin is probably not practical at all, but ritualistic; its central aim is to symbolize a Presence, to aid in the formulation of a religious universe. "Except ye see signs and wonders, ye will not believe." Magic is never employed in a commonplace mood, like ordinary causal agency; this fact belies the widely accepted belief that the "method of magic" rests on a mistaken view of causality. After all, a savage who beats a tom-tom to drive off his brother's malaria would never make such a practical mistake as to shoot his arrow blunt end forward or bait his fishline with flowers. It is not ignorance of causal relations, but the supervention of an interest stronger than his practical interest, that holds him to magical rites. This stronger interest concerns the *expressive* value of such mystic acts.

Magic, then, is not a method, but a language; it is part and parcel of that greater phenomenon, *ritual*, which is the language of religion. Ritual is a symbolic transformation of experiences that no other medium can adequately express. Because it springs from a primary human need, it is a spontaneous activity — that is to say, it arises without intention, without adaptation to a conscious purpose; its growth is undesigned, its pattern purely natural, however intricate it may be. It was never "imposed" on people; they acted thus quite of themselves, exactly as bees swarmed and birds built nests, squirrels hoarded food, and cats washed their faces. No one made up ritual, any more than anyone made up Hebrew or Sanskrit or Latin. The forms of expressive acts — speech and gesture, song and sacrifice — are the symbolic transformations which minds of certain species, at certain stages of their development and communion, naturally produce.

Franz Boas remarked, even in one of his early works, that

ritual resembled language in the unconscious development of its forms; and furthermore he saw, though less clearly, that it had certain symbolistic functions. After a discussion of the role played by language in the actual division and arrangement of sense experience, he says: "The behavior of primitive man makes it perfectly clear that all these linguistic classes have never risen to consciousness, and that consequently their origin must be sought, not in rational, but in entirely unconscious, processes of the mind. . . . It seems very plausible . . . that the fundamental religious notions . . . are in their origin just as little conscious as the fundamental ideas of language." [16] And a few pages later he touches, howbeit only tentatively and vaguely, upon the expressive nature of those practices which seem "impractical" to us:

"Primitive man views each action not only as adapted to its main object, each thought related to its main end, as we should perceive them, but . . . he associates them with other ideas, often of a religious or at least a symbolic nature. Thus he gives them a higher significance than they seem to us to deserve. Every taboo is an example of such associations of apparently trifling actions with ideas that are so sacred that a deviation from the customary mode of performance creates the strongest emotions of abhorrence. The interpretation of ornaments as charms, the symbolism of decorative art, are other examples of association of ideas that, on the whole, are foreign to our mode of thought." [17]

A year after Boas' book, there appeared the articles by Sigmund Freud which are now collected under the title of *Totem and Taboo*.[18] It was Freud who recognized that ritual acts are not genuine instrumental acts, but are motivated primarily *a tergo*, and carry with them, consequently, a feeling not of purpose, but of compulsion. They *must* be performed, not to any visible end, but from a sheer inward need; and he is familiar enough with such compulsive acts in other settings to suspect at once that in the religious sphere,

[16] *The Mind of Primitive Man* (1911), pp. 198–199.
[17] *Ibid.*, p. 209.
[18] Published in 1918.

too, they are best interpreted as *expressive* behavior. Empirically senseless, they are none the less important and justified when we regard them as symbolic presentations rather than practical measures. They are spontaneous transformations of experience, and the form they take is normal for the primitive mind. In civilized society, the same phenomena are apt to be pathological; there is a good reason for this, but that must be postponed to a later chapter.

The great contribution of Freud to the philosophy of mind has been the realization that human behavior is not only a food-getting strategy, but is also a language; that every *move* is at the same time a *gesture*. Symbolization is both an end and an instrument. So far, epistemology has treated it only in the latter capacity; and philosophers have ample reason to wonder why this purely utilitarian trait of man's mind so frequently plays him false, why nature permitted it to grow beyond the limits of usefulness, to assume a tyrant role and lure him into patently impractical ventures. The fact is, I believe, that it did not originate purely in the service of other activities. It is a primary interest, and may require a sacrifice of other ends, just as the imperative demand for food or sex-life may necessitate sacrifices under difficult conditions. This fundamentally — not adventitiously — symbolific function of the mind was suggested to Freud by his psychiatric studies, but in later works he has given it a very general development, notably in the book already cited, *Totem and Taboo*.[19] Certainly he has carried his theories far enough to make a philosophical study of "impractical" actions — rites, formalities, dramatizations, and above all, the unapplied arts — relevant and promising in the light of them. Yet few epistemologists have seriously taken advantage of the new ideas that fairly cry to be explored.

The reason is, probably, that traditional theory of mind is epistemology — theory of *knowledge*; and Freud's psychology is not directly applicable to the problems which compose this field. Symbolism, as it enters into the structure of knowledge, is better typified by mathematical "expressions" than

[19] See also, *Group Psychology and the Analysis of the Ego* (1922).

by swastikas or genuflexions. Language, not ritual, is its main representative.

In order to relate these two distinct conceptions of symbolism, and exhibit the respective parts they play in that general human response we call a *life*, it is necessary to examine more accurately that which makes *symbols* out of anything — out of marks on paper, the little squeaks and grunts we interpret as "words," or bended knees — the quality of *meaning*, in its several aspects and forms. Meaning rests upon a condition which is, in the last analysis, logical; therefore the next chapter will have to concern itself mainly with logical structure, and cannot help being somewhat technical. But without such a grounding the whole argument would remain intangible, unfounded, and would probably appear more fantastic than cogent; so a short account of what constitutes meaning, what characterizes symbols, and also the different kinds of symbolism and their logical distinctions, will have to precede any further elaborations of the ideas so far suggested.

CHAPTER III

The Logic of Signs and Symbols

S O MUCH work has already been done on the logic of meaning that it is not necessary to present long arguments in support of the theory here employed; let it suffice to outline the facts, or if you will, the assumptions, on which my further considerations are to rest.

Meaning has both a logical and a psychological aspect. Psychologically, any item that is to have meaning must be *employed* as a sign or a symbol; that is to say, it must be a sign or a symbol *to* someone. Logically, it must be *capable* of conveying a meaning, it must be the sort of item that can be thus employed. In some meaning-relations this logical requirement is trivial, and tacitly accepted; in others it is of the utmost importance, and may even lead us a merry chase through the labyrinths of nonsense. These two aspects, the logical and the psychological, are thoroughly confounded by the ambiguous verb "to mean"; for sometimes it is proper to say "*it* means," and sometimes "*I* mean." Obviously, a word — say, "London" — does not "mean" a city in just the same sense that a person employing the word "means" the place.

Both aspects, the logical and the psychological, are always present, and their interplay produces the great variety of meaning-relations over which philosophers have puzzled and fought for the last fifty years. The analysis of "meaning" has had a peculiarly difficult history; the word is used in many different ways, and a good deal of controversy has been wasted on the subject of *the* correct way, *the* meaning of "meaning." Whenever people find several species of a genius, they look for the prime form, the archetype that is supposed to be differently disguised in each special case; so, for a long time, philosophers hoped to find the true quality of meaning by collecting all its various manifestations and looking for a common ingredient. They talked more and more generally about "symbol-situations," believing that by generalization they might attain to the essential quality which all such situations had in common. But generalizing from vague and muddled special theories can never give us a clear general theory. The sort of generalization that merely substitutes "symbol-situation" for "denotation-or-connotation-or-signification-or-association-etc." is scientifically useless; for the whole purpose of general concepts is to make the distinctions between special classes clear, to relate all subspecies to each other in definite ways; but if such general concepts are simply composite photographs of all known types of meaning, they can only blur, not clarify, the relations that obtain among specialized senses of the word.

Charles Peirce, who was probably the first person to concern himself seriously with semantics, began by making an inventory of all "symbol-situations," in the hope that when all possible meanings of "meaning" were herded together, they would show empirical differentia whereby one could divide the sheep from the goats. But the obstreperous flock, instead of falling neatly into a few classes, each according to its kind, divided and subdivided into the most terrifying order of icons, qualisigns, legisigns, semes, phemes, and delomes, and there is but cold comfort in his assurance that his original 59,049 types can really be boiled down to a mere sixty-six.[1]

A few further attempts were made to grasp the essential quality of meaning by empirical methods, but the more varieties could be found, the less did they promise to reveal a common essence. Husserl, distinguishing each type of meaning as a special notion, ended with as many theories as there are "meanings." [2] But we have still the sheep and the

---

[1] From two letters to Lady Welby, 1904 and 1908 respectively, first cited by Ogden and Richards in *The Meaning of Meaning* (App. D, pp. 435–444), and now published in *The Collected Papers of Charles S. Peirce* (1932), II, 330.

[2] Edmund Husserl, *Logische Untersuchungen*, 2 vols. (1913 and 1921), vol. II, part I, *passim*.

goats and all their several relatives, and are still left wondering why one family name, Meaning, should apply where no family likeness can be detected.

There is in fact no quality of meaning; its essence lies in the realm of logic, where one does not deal with qualities, but only with relations. It is not fair to say: "Meaning is a relation," for that suggests too simple a business. Most people think of a relation as a two-termed affair — "A-in-relation-to-B"; but meaning involves several terms, and different types of meaning consist of different types and degrees of relationship. It is better, perhaps, to say: "Meaning is not a quality, but a *function* of a term." A function is a *pattern* viewed with reference to one special term round which it centers; this pattern emerges when we look at the given term *in its total relation to the other terms about it.* The total may be quite complicated. For instance, a musical chord may be treated as a function of one note, known as the "written bass," by writing this one note and indicating its relation to all the other notes that are to

go above it. In old organ music, the chord 𝄢 would be

written: 𝄢 , which means: "The A-chord with the

6
4
3

sixth, the fourth and the third notes above A." The chord is treated as *a pattern surrounding and including* A. It is expressed as a function of A.

The meaning of a term is, likewise, a function; it rests on a pattern, in which the term itself holds the key-position. Even in the simplest kinds of meaning there must be at least two other things related to the term that "means" — an object that is "meant," and a subject who uses the term; just as in a chord there must be at least two notes besides the "written bass" to determine what the chord is (one of these may be merely "understood" by musicians, but without it the combination would not be a determinate chord). The same may be said for a term with a meaning; the existence of a subject is often tacitly accepted, but if there is not at least one thing meant and one mind for which it is meant, then there is not a complete meaning — only a partial pattern which might be completed in different ways.

Any term in a pattern may be taken as a key-term to which the others are related. For instance, the chord ♮ may be regarded as a function of its lowest note, and expressed by the description ♮ ; or it may be treated with reference to the note on which it is built harmonically, which happens to be D. A musician analyzing the harmony would call this chord "the second inversion of the seventh-chord on the dominant, in the key of G." The "dominant" of that key is D, not A. He would treat the whole pattern as *a function of D*; that sounds more complicated than the other treatment, which fixed the notes from the A upward, but of course it is not really so, because it comes to just the same pattern.

Similarly, we may view a meaning-pattern from the point of view of any term in it, and our descriptions of the same pattern will differ accordingly. We may say that a certain symbol "means" an object to a person, or that the person "means" the object by the symbol. The first description treats meaning in the logical sense, the second in the psychological sense. The former takes the symbol as the key, and the latter the subject.[3] So, the two most controversial kinds of meaning — the logical and the psychological — are distinguished and at the same time related to each other, by the general principle of viewing meaning *as a function, not a property*, of terms.

In the further analyses that follow, "meaning" will be taken in the objective sense, unless some other is specified; that is to say, I shall speak of terms (such as words) as "meaning" something, not of people as "meaning" this or that. Later we

[3] Where the object is taken as the key, the resulting description begins with the "knowledge-content" postulated in some epistemologies.

shall have to distinguish various subjective functions; but at present let us consider the *relations of terms to their objects.* What *relates* the terms to their objects is, of course, a subject; that is always to be understood.

There are, first of all, two distinct functions of terms, which have both a perfectly good right to the name "meaning": for a significant sound, gesture, thing, event (e.g. a flash, an image), may be either a *sign* or a *symbol.*

A sign indicates the existence — past, present, or future — of a thing, event, or condition. Wet streets are a sign that it has rained. A patter on the roof is a sign that it is raining. A fall of the barometer or a ring round the moon is a sign that it is going to rain. In an unirrigated place, abundant verdure is a sign that it often rains there. A smell of smoke signifies the presence of fire. A scar is a sign of a past accident. Dawn is a herald of sunrise. Sleekness is a sign of frequent and plentiful food.

All the examples here adduced are *natural signs.* A natural sign is a part of a greater event, or of a complex condition, and to an experienced observer it signifies the rest of that situation of which it is a notable feature. It is a *symptom* of a state of affairs.[4]

The logical relation between a sign and its object is a very simple one: they are associated, somehow, to form a *pair;* that is to say, they stand in a one-to-one correlation. To each sign there corresponds one definite item which is its object, the thing (or event, or condition) signified. All the rest of that important function, signification, involves the third term, the subject, which *uses* the pair of items; and the relation of the subject to the other two terms is much more interesting than their own bare logical coupling. The subject is related, essen-

---

[4] There is a fine distinction between sign and symptom, in that the object signified by a symptom is the *entire condition* of which the symptom is a proper part; e.g., red spots are a symptom of measles, and "measles" is the entire condition begetting and including the red spots. A sign, on the other hand, may be one part of a total condition, which we associate with another separate part. Thus a ring round the moon is part of a weather condition, but what it signifies is rain — another proper part — and not the entire state of "low-pressure" weather.

tially, to the other two terms *as a pair*. What characterizes them is the fact that they are paired. Thus, a white bump on a person's arm, as a mere sense-datum, would probably not be interesting enough even to have a name, but such a datum *in its relation to the past* is noted and called a "scar." Note, however, that although the subject's relation is to the *pair* of other terms, he has also a relation to each one of them individually, which makes one of them the sign and the other the object. What is the difference between a sign and its object, by virtue of which they are not interchangeable? Two terms merely associated as a pair, like two socks, two balances of a scale, two ends of a stick, etc., could be interchanged without any harm.

The difference is, that the subject for which they constitute a pair must *find one more interesting than the other, and the latter more easily available than the former*. If we are interested in tomorrow's weather, the events now present, if coupled with tomorrow's weather-phenomena, are signs for us. A ring round the moon, or "mares' tails" in the sky, are not important in themselves; but as visible, present items coupled with something important but not yet present, they have "meaning." If it were not for the subject, or *interpretant*, sign and object would be interchangeable. Thunder may just as well be a sign that there has been lightning, as lightning may signify that there will be thunder. In themselves they are merely correlated. It is only where one is perceptible and the other (harder or impossible to perceive) is interesting, that we actually have a case of *signification belonging to a term*.[5]

Now, just as in nature certain events are correlated, so that the less important may be taken as signs of the more important, so we may also *produce* arbitrary events purposely correlated with important ones that are to be their meanings. A whistle means that the train is about to start. A gunshot means that the sun is just setting. A crêpe on the door means someone has just died. These are artificial signs, for they are not part of a condition of which they naturally signify the remainder or something in the remainder. Their logical relation to their

---

[5] Cf. Whitehead, *Symbolism*, pp. 9–13.

objects, however, is the same as that of natural signs — a one-to-one correspondence of sign and object, by virtue of which the interpretant, who is interested in the latter and perceives the former, may apprehend the existence of the term that interests him.

The interpretation of signs is the basis of animal intelligence. Animals presumably do not distinguish between natural signs and artificial or fortuitous signs; but they use both kinds to guide their practical activities. We do the same thing all day long. We answer bells, watch the clock, obey warning signals, follow arrows, take off the kettle when it whistles, come at the baby's cry, close the windows when we hear thunder. The logical basis of all these interpretations, the mere correlation of trivial events with important ones, is really very simple and common; so much so that there is no limit to what a sign may mean. This is even more obviously true of artificial signs than of natural ones. A shot may mean the beginning of a race, the rise of the sun, the sighting of danger, the commencement of a parade. As for bells, the world is mad with their messages. Somebody at the front door, the back door, the side door, the telephone — toast is ready — typewriter line is ended — school begins, work begins, church begins, church is over — street car starts — cashbox registers — knife grinder passes — time for dinner, time to get up — fire in town!

Because a sign may mean so many things, we are very apt to misinterpret it, especially when it is artificial. Bell signals, of course, may be either wrongly associated with their objects, or the sound of one bell may actually be confused with that of another. But natural signs, too, may be misunderstood. Wet streets are not a reliable sign of recent rain if the sprinkler wagon has passed by. The misinterpretation of signs is the simplest form of *mistake*. It is the most important form, for purposes of practical life, and the easiest to detect; for its normal manifestation is the experience called *disappointment*.

Where we find the simplest form of error, we may expect to find also, as its correlate, the simplest form of knowledge. This is, indeed, the interpretation of signs. It is the most elemen-

tary and most tangible sort of intellection; the kind of knowledge that we share with animals, that we acquire entirely by
experience, that has obvious biological uses, and equally obvious criteria of truth and falsehood. Its mechanism may be
conceived as an elaboration of the conditioned-reflex arc, with
the brain doing switchboard duty, and getting the right or the
wrong number for the sense organ that called up the muscula-
ture and expects an answer in terms of altered sensations. It
has all those virtues of simplicity, componability, and intelli-
gibility that recommend a concept for scientific purposes. So
it is not surprising that students of genetic psychology have
seized upon sign interpretation as the archetype of all knowledge, that they regard *signs* as the original bearers of meaning,
and treat all other terms with semantic properties as subspecies — "substitute signs," which act as proxy for their
objects and evoke conduct appropriate to the latter instead of
to themselves.

But "substitute signs," though they may be classed with
symbols, are of a very specialized sort, and play only a meagre
and restricted part in the whole process of mental life. I shall
return to them later, in discussing the relationship between
symbols and signs, for they do stand with a foot in either
domain. First, however, the characteristics of symbols in general, and their essential difference from signs, must go on
record.

A term which is used symbolically and not signally does
not evoke action appropriate to the presence of its object. If
I say: "Napoleon," you do not bow to the conqueror of Europe
as though I had introduced him, but merely think of him. If
I mention a Mr. Smith of our common acquaintance, you may
be led to tell me something about him "behind his back,"
which is just what you would *not* do in his presence. Thus
the symbol for Mr. Smith — his name — may very well initiate
an act appropriate peculiarly to his absence. Raised eyebrows
and a look at the door, interpreted as a *sign* that he is coming,
would stop you in the midst of your narrative; *that* action
would be directed toward Mr. Smith in person.

Symbols are not proxy for their objects, but are *vehicles for the conception of objects.* To conceive a thing or a situation is not the same thing as to "react toward it" overtly, or to be aware of its presence. In talking *about* things we have conceptions of them, not the things themselves; and *it is the conceptions, not the things, that symbols directly "mean."* Behavior toward conceptions is what words normally evoke; this is the typical process of thinking.

Of course a word may be used as a sign, but that is not its primary role. Its signific character has to be indicated by some special modification — by a tone of voice, a gesture (such as pointing or staring), or the location of a placard bearing the word. In itself it is a symbol, associated with a conception,[6] not directly with a public object or event. The fundamental difference between signs and symbols is this difference of association, and consequently of their *use* by the third party to the meaning function, the subject; signs *announce* their objects to him, whereas symbols *lead him to conceive* their objects. The fact that the same item — say, the little mouthy noise we call a "word" — may serve in either capacity, does not obliterate the cardinal distinction between the two functions it may assume.

The simplest kind of symbolistic meaning is probably that which belongs to proper names. A personal name evokes a conception of something given as a unit in the subject's experience, something concrete and therefore easy to recall in imagination. Because the name belongs to a notion so obviously and unequivocally derived from an individual object, it is often supposed to "mean" that object as a sign would "mean" it. This belief is reinforced by the fact that a name borne by a living person always is at once a symbol by which we think of the person, and a call-name by which we signal him. Through a confusion of these two functions, the proper name

---

[6] Note that I have called the terms of our thinking conceptions, not concepts. Concepts are abstract forms embodied in conceptions; their bare presentation may be approximated by so-called "abstract thought," but in ordinary mental life they no more figure as naked factors than skeletons are seen walking the street. Concepts, like decent living skeletons, are always embodied — sometimes rather too much. I shall return to the topic of pure concepts later on, in discussing communication.

is often deemed the bridge from animal semantic, or sign-using, to human language, which is symbol-using. Dogs, we are told, understand names — not only their own, but their masters'. So they do, indeed; but they understand them *only in the capacity of call-names.* If you say "James" to a dog whose master bears that name, the dog will interpret the sound as a sign, and *look for* James. Say it to a person who knows someone called thus, and he will ask: "What about James?" That simple question is forever beyond the dog; signification is the only meaning a name can have for him — a meaning which the master's name shares with the master's smell, with his footfall, and his characteristic ring of the door-bell. In a human being, however, the name evokes the *conception* of a certain man so called, and prepares the mind for further conceptions in which the notion of that man figures; therefore the human being naturally asks: "What about James?"

There is a famous passage in the autobiography of Helen Keller, in which this remarkable woman describes the dawn of Language upon her mind. Of course she had used signs before, formed associations, learned to expect things and identify people or places; but there was a great day when all sign-meaning was eclipsed and dwarfed by the discovery that a certain datum in her limited sense-world had a *denotation*, that a particular act of her fingers constituted a *word.* This event had required a long preparation; the child had learned many finger acts, but they were as yet a meaningless play. Then, one day, her teacher took her out to walk — and there the great advent of Language occurred.

"She brought me my hat," the memoir reads, "and I knew I was going out into the warm sunshine. This thought, if a wordless sensation may be called a thought, made me hop and skip with pleasure.

"We walked down the path to the well-house, attracted by the fragrance of the honeysuckle with which it was covered. Some one was drawing water and my teacher placed my hand under the spout. As the cool stream gushed over my hand she spelled into the other the word *water,* first slowly, then rapidly.

I stood still, my whole attention fixed upon the motion of her fingers. Suddenly I felt a misty consciousness as of something forgotten — a thrill of returning thought; and somehow the mystery of language was revealed to me. I knew then that w-a-t-e-r meant the wonderful cool something that was flowing over my hand. That living word awakened my soul, gave it light, hope, joy, set it free! There were barriers still, it is true, but barriers that in time could be swept away.

"I left the well-house eager to learn. Everything had a name, and each name gave birth to a new thought. As we returned to the house every object which I touched seemed to quiver with life. That was because I saw everything with the strange, new sight that had come to me." [7]

This passage is the best affidavit we could hope to find for the genuine difference between sign and symbol. The sign is something to act upon, or a means to command action; the symbol is an instrument of thought. Note how Miss Keller qualifies the mental process just preceding her discovery of words — "This thought, *if a wordless sensation may be called a thought.*" Real thinking is possible only in the light of genuine language, no matter how limited, how primitive; in her case, it became possible with the discovery that "w-a-t-e-r" was not necessarily a sign that water was wanted or expected, but was the *name* of this substance, by which it could be mentioned, conceived, remembered.

Since a name, the simplest type of symbol, is directly associated with a conception, and is employed by a subject to realize the conception, one is easily led to treat a name as a "conceptual sign," an artificial sign which announces the presence of a certain idea. In a sense this is quite justified; yet it strikes a strained and unnatural note, which is usually a fair warning that the attempted interpretation misses the most important feature in its material. In the present case, it misses *the relation of conceptions to the concrete world*, which is so close and so important that it enters into the very structure of "names." A name, above all, *denotes* something. "James" may represent a conception, but it *names* a certain person. In

[7] Helen Keller, *The Story of My Life* (1936; 1st ed. 1902), pp. 23–24.

the case of proper nouns this relation of the symbol to what it denotes is so striking that denotation has been confused with the direct relation of sign and object, signification. As a matter of fact, "James" does not, without further ado, signify a person; it denotes him — it is associated with a conception which "fits" the actual person. The relation between a symbol and an object, usually expressed by "S denotes O," is not a simple two-termed relation which S has to O; it is a complex affair: S is coupled, for a certain subject, with a conception that fits O, i.e. with a notion which O satisfies.

In an ordinary sign-function, there are three essential terms: subject, sign, and object. In denotation, which is the commonest kind of symbol-function, there have to be four: subject, symbol, conception, and object. The radical difference between sign-meaning and symbol-meaning can therefore be logically exhibited, for it rests on a difference of pattern, it is strictly a different function.[8]

Denotation is, then, the complex relationship which a name has to an object which bears it; but what shall the more direct relation of the name, or symbol, to its associated concept be called? It shall be called by its traditional name, connotation. The connotation of a word is the conception it conveys. Because the connotation remains with the symbol when the object of its denotation is neither present nor looked for, we are able to think about the object without reacting to it overtly at all.

Here, then, are the three most familiar meanings of the one word, "meaning": signification, denotation, and connotation. All three are equally and perfectly legitimate, but in no possible way interchangeable.

In every analysis of sign-using or symbol-using, we must be able to account not only for the genesis of knowledge, but also of that most human characteristic, error. How sign-

[8] If a symbol could be said normally to "signify" anything, its object would be the occurrence of an act of conception. But such a function of a symbol is casual, and crosses with its use as a symbol. In the latter function it is not the act of conception, but what is conceived, that enters into the meaning-pattern. We shall avoid much confusion and quibbling by recognizing that signification does not figure in symbolization at all.

interpretation can miscarry, has already been shown; but failures of denotation, or confusions of connotation, are unfortunately just as common, and have a claim to our attention, too.

There is a psychological act involved in every case of denotation, which might be called the *application* of a term to an object. The word "water," for instance, denotes a certain substance because people conventionally *apply* it to that substance. Such application has fixed its connotation. We may ask, quite reasonably, whether a certain colorless liquid is or is not water, but hardly whether water "really" means that substance which is found in ponds, falls from the clouds, has the chemical constitution H_2O, etc. The connotation of the word, though derived from an age-long application, is more definite now than some cases of the word's applicability. When we have *misapplied* a term, i.e. applied it to an object that does not satisfy its connotation, we do not say that the term "denoted" that object; one feature in the tetradic meaning-relation is missing, so there is no real denotation — only a psychological act of application, and that was a mistake. The word "water" was never guilty of *denoting* the drink that undid little Willy, in the pathetic laboratory rhyme:

> We had a little Willy,
> Now Willy is no more,
> For what he thought was H_2O
> Was H_2SO_4.

Willy had mistaken one object for another; he *misapplied* a term of which he knew the connotation well enough. But since connotations are normally fixed upon a word, originally, by its application to certain *things*, whose properties are but vaguely known, we may also be mistaken about the connotation, when we use the term as a vehicle of thought. We may know that the symbol "James" applies to our next-door neighbor, and quite mistakenly suppose it connotes a man with all sorts of virtues or frailties. This time we are not mistaking James for someone else, but we are *mistaken about James*.

It is a peculiarity of proper names that they have a *different connotation for every denotation.* Because their connotation is not fixed, they can be arbitrarily applied. In itself, a proper name has no connotation at all; sometimes it acquires a very general sort of conceptual meaning — it connotes a gender, or race, or confession (e.g. "Christian," "Wesley," "Israel") — but there is no actual *mistake* involved in calling a boy "Marion," a girl "Frank," a German "Pierre," or a Jew "Luther." In civilized society the connotation of a proper name is not regarded as a meaning applying to the bearer of the name; when the name is used to denote a certain person it takes on the connotation required by that function. In primitive societies this is less apt to be the case; names are often changed because their accepted connotations do not fit the bearer. The same man may in turn be *named* "Lightfoot," "Hawkeye," "Whizzing Death," etc. In an Indian society, the class of men named "Hawkeye" would very probably be a subclass of the class "sharp-eyed men." But in our own communities ladies named "Blanche" do not have to be albinos or even platinum blondes. A word that functions as a proper noun is excused from the usual rules of application.

So much, then, for the venerable "logic of terms." It appears a little more complicated than in the medieval books, since we must add to the long-recognized functions, connotation and denotation, a third one, signification, which is fundamentally different from the other two; and since, moreover, in discussing the semantic functions of terms we have made the rare discovery that they really are *functions*, not powers or mysterious properties or what-not, and have treated them accordingly. The traditional "logic of terms" is really a metaphysic of meaning; the new philosophy of meaning is first of all a logic of terms — of signs and symbols — an analysis of the relational patterns in which "meaning" may be sought.

But a semantic of separate symbols is only a rudimentary foundation for a more interesting aspect of meaning. Everything is mere propaedeutic until we come to *discourse.* It is in discursive thinking that truth and falsehood are born. Before terms are built into propositions, they assert nothing, preclude nothing; in fact, although they may *name* things, and convey ideas of such things, they *say* nothing. I have discussed them at such great length simply because most logicians have given them such cavalier treatment that even so obvious a distinction as that between sign-functions and symbol-functions passed unnoticed; so that careless philosophers have been guilty of letting ambitious genetic psychologists argue them from the conditioned reflex to the wisdom of G. Bernard Shaw, all in one skyrocketing generalization.

The logic of discourse has been much more adequately handled — so well, in fact, that practically nothing I have to say about it is new; yet it must at least be brought to mind here, because an understanding of discursive symbolism, the vehicle of propositional thinking, is essential to any theory of human mentality; for without it there could be no *literal meaning*, and therefore no scientific knowledge.

Anyone who has ever learned a foreign language knows that the study of its vocabulary alone will not make him master of the new tongue. Even if he were to memorize a whole dictionary, he would not be able to make the simplest statement correctly; for he could not form a sentence without certain *principles of grammar*. He must know that some words are nouns and some are verbs; he must recognize some as active or passive forms of verbs, and know the person and number they express; he must know where the verb stands in the sentence in order to make the sense he has in mind. Mere separate names of things (even of actions, which are "named" by infinitives) do not constitute a sentence. A string of words which we might derive by running our eye down the left-hand column in the dictionary — for instance, "especially espouse espringal espry esquire" — does not *say* anything. Each word has meaning, yet the series of words has none.

Grammatical structure, then, is a further source of significance. We cannot call it a symbol, since it is not even a term; but it has a symbolific mission. It ties together several symbols, each with at least a fragmentary connotation of its own, to make one complex term, whose meaning is a special constellation of all the connotations involved. What the special constellation is, depends on the syntactical relations within the complex symbol, or *proposition.*

Propositional structure has commanded more interest among logicians of the present generation than any other aspect of symbolism. Ever since Bertrand Russell [9] pointed out that the Aristotelian metaphysic of substance and attribute is a counterpart of the Aristotelian logic of subject and predicate — that the common-sense view of things and properties, agent and patient, object and action, etc., is a faithful counterpart of that common-sense logic embodied in our parts of *speech* — the ties between expressibility and conceivability, forms of language and forms of experience, propositions and facts, have been drawn closer and closer. It has become apparent that a proposition fits a fact not only because it contains names for the things and actions involved in the fact, but also because it combines them in a pattern analogous, somehow, to the pattern in which the named objects are "in fact" combined. *A proposition is a picture of a structure — the structure of a state of affairs.* The unity of a proposition is the same sort of unity that belongs to a picture, which presents one scene, no matter how many items may be distinguishable within it.

What property must a picture have in order to *represent* its object? Must it really share the visual appearance of the object? Certainly not to any high degree. It may, for instance, be black on white, or red on grey, or any color on any other color; it may be shiny whereas the object is dull; it may be much larger or much smaller than the object; it is certainly flat, and although the tricks of perspective sometimes give a perfect illusion of three-dimensionality, a picture without perspective — e.g. an architect's "elevation drawing" — is still unmistakably a picture, representing an object.

The reason for this latitude is that *the picture is essentially a symbol, not a duplicate, of what it represents.* It has certain salient features by virtue of which it can function as a symbol for its object. For instance, the childish outline drawing (fig. 1) on page 69 is immediately recognized as a rabbit,

[9] *A Critical Exposition of the Philosophy of Leibniz* (1900). See p. 12.

yet it really looks so unlike one that even a person nearly blind could not for a moment be made to think that he saw a rabbit sitting on the open page of his book. All it shares with the "reality" is a certain *proportion of parts* — the position and relative length of "ears," the dot where an "eye" belongs, the "head" and "body" in relation to each other, etc. Beside it is exactly the same figure with different ears and tail (fig. 2); any child will accept it as a cat. Yet cats don't look like long-tailed, short-eared rabbits, in reality. Neither are they flat and white, with a papery texture and a black

FIG. 1   FIG. 2

outline running round them. But all these traits of the pictured cat are irrelevant, because it is merely a symbol, not a pseudo-cat.[10]

Of course, the more detail is depicted by the image, the more unequivocal becomes the reference to a particular object. A good portrait is "true" to only one person. Yet even good portraits are not duplications. There are styles in portraiture as there are in any other art. We may paint in heightened, warm, melting colors, or in cool pastels; we may range from the clean line drawings of Holbein to the shimmering hues of French impressionism; and all the time the

[10] Tolstoi relates a little incident of his childhood which hinges on the sudden ingression of irrelevant factors into consciousness, to the detriment of artistic appreciation; I quote it here because it is quite the most charming record I have found of a semantic muddle:

"We settled ourselves about the round table at our drawing. I had only blue paint; nevertheless, I undertook to depict the hunt. After representing, in very lively style, a blue boy mounted on a blue horse, and some blue dogs, I was not quite sure whether I could paint a blue hare, and ran to Papa in his study to take advice on the matter. Papa was reading; and in answer to my question, 'Are there any blue hares?' he said, without raising his head, 'Yes, my dear, there are.' I went back to the round table and painted a blue hare. . . ." L. N. Tolstoi, *Childhood, Boyhood and Youth.*

object need not change. Our presentation of it is the variable factor.

The picture is a symbol, and the so-called "medium" is a type of symbolism. Yet there is something, of course, that relates the picture to its original, and makes it represent, say, a Dutch interior and not the crucifixion. What it may represent is dictated purely by its logic — by the arrangement of its elements. The disposition of pale and dark, dull and bright paints, or thin and thick lines and variously shaped white spaces, yield the determination of those *forms* that mean certain objects. They can mean all those and only those objects in which we recognize similar forms. All other aspects of the picture — for instance, what artists call the "distribution of values," the "technique," and the "tone" of the whole work — serve other ends than mere representation. The only characteristic that a picture must have in order to be a picture of a certain thing is an arrangement of elements analogous to the arrangement of salient visual elements in the object. A representation of a rabbit must have long ears; a man must feature arms and legs.

In the case of a so-called "realistic" picture, the analogy goes into great detail, so great that many people believe a statue or a painting to be a *copy* of its object. But consider how we meet such vagaries of style as modern commercial art produces: ladies with bright green faces and aluminum hair, men whose heads are perfect circles, horses constructed entirely of cylinders. We still recognize the objects they depict, as long as we find an element to stand for the head and one for the eye in the head, a white mark to connote a starched bosom, a line placed where it may represent an arm. With amazing rapidity our vision picks up these features and lets the whole fantasy convey a human form.

One step removed from the "styled" picture is the diagram. Here any attempt at *imitating* the parts of an object has been given up. The parts are merely indicated by conventional symbols, such as dots, circles, crosses, or what-not. The only thing that is "pictured" is the relation of the parts to each other. *A diagram is a "picture" only of a form.*

Consider a photograph, a painting, a pencil sketch, an architect's elevation drawing, and a builder's diagram, all showing the front view of one and the same house. With a little attention, you will recognize the house in each representation. Why?

Because each one of the very different images expresses the same relation of parts, which you have fastened on in formulating your conception of the house. Some versions show more such relations than others; they are more detailed. But those which do not show certain details at least show no others in place of these, and so it may be understood that the details are there left out. The things shown in the simplest picture, the diagram, are all contained in the more elaborate renderings. Moreover, they are contained in your conception of the house; so the pictures all answer, in their several ways, to your conception, although the latter may contain further items that are not pictured at all. Likewise, another person's conception of that same house will agree in its essential pattern with the pictures *and with your conception*, however many private aspects it may have.

It is by virtue of such a fundamental *pattern*, which all correct conceptions of the house have in common, that we can talk together about the "same" house despite our private differences of sense-experience, feeling, and purely personal associations. *That which all adequate conceptions of an object must have in common, is the concept of the object.* The same concept is embodied in a multitude of conceptions. It is a *form* that appears in all versions of thought or imagery that can connote the object in question, a form clothed in different integuments of sensation for every different mind. Probably no two people see anything just alike. Their sense organs differ, their attention and imagery and feelings differ so that they cannot be supposed to have identical impressions. But if their respective conceptions of a thing (or event, or person, etc.) embody the same *concept*, they will understand each other.

A concept is all that a symbol really conveys. But just as quickly as the concept is symbolized to us, our own imagination dresses it up in a private, personal *conception*, which we can distinguish from the communicable public concept only by a process of abstraction. Whenever we deal with a concept we must have some particular presentation of it, *through* which we grasp it. What we actually have "in mind" is always *universalium in re*. When we express this *universalium* we use another symbol to exhibit it, and still another *res* will embody it for the mind that sees through our symbol and apprehends the concept in its own way.

The power of understanding symbols, i.e. of regarding everything about a sense-datum as irrelevant except a certain *form* that it embodies, is the most characteristic mental trait of mankind. It issues in an unconscious, spontaneous process of *abstraction*, which goes on all the time in the human mind: a process of recognizing the concept in any configuration given to experience, and forming a conception accordingly. That is the real sense of Aristotle's definition of man as "the rational animal." *Abstractive seeing* is the foundation of our rationality, and is its definite guarantee long before the dawn of any conscious generalization or syllogism.[11] It is the function which no other animal shares. Beasts do not read symbols; that is why they do not see pictures. We are sometimes told that dogs do not react even to the best portraits because they live more by smell than by sight; but the behavior of a dog who spies a motionless real cat through the window glass belies this explanation. Dogs scorn our paintings because they see colored canvases, not pictures. A representation of a cat does not make them conceive one.

Since any single sense-datum can, logically, be a symbol for any single item, any arbitrary mark or counter may connote the conception, or publicly speaking: the concept, of any single thing, and thus denote the thing itself. A motion of fingers, apprehended as one unit performance, became the name of a substance to little deaf-and-blind Helen Keller. A word, likewise taken as a sound-unit, becomes a symbol to us, for some item in the world. And now the power of seeing

[11] Cf. Th. Ribot, *Essai sur l'imagination créatrice* (1921; 1st ed. 1900), p. 14.

configurations as symbols comes into play: we make patterns of denotative symbols, and they promptly symbolize the very different, but *analogous*, configurations of denoted things. A temporal order of words stands for a relational order of things. When pure word-order becomes insufficient, word-endings and prefixes "mean" relationships; from these are born prepositions and other purely relational symbols.[12] Just as mnemonic dots and crosses, as soon as they denote objects, can also enter into diagrams or simple pictures, so do sounds, as soon as they are words, enter into word-pictures, or *sentences*. A sentence is a symbol for a state of affairs, and pictures its character.

Now, in an ordinary picture, the terms of the represented complex are symbolized by so many visual items, i.e. areas of color, and their relations are indicated by relations of these items. So painting, being static, can present only a momentary state; it may suggest, but can never actually report, a *history*. We may produce a series of pictures, but nothing in the pictures can actually guarantee the conjunction of their several scenes in one serial order of events. Five baby-pictures of the little Dionne sisters in various acts may be taken either as a series representing successive acts of one child, or as separate views of five little girls in characteristic activities. There is no sure way of choosing between these two interpretations without captions or other indications.

But most of our interests center upon events, rather than upon things in static spatial relations. Causal connections, activities, time, and change are what we want most of all to conceive and communicate. And to this end pictures are poorly suited. We resort, therefore, to the more powerful, supple, and adaptable symbolism of language.

How are relations expressed in language? For the most part, they are not symbolized by other relations, as in pictures, but are *named*, just like substantives. We name two items, and place the name of a relation between; this means

[12] See Philip Wegener, *Untersuchungen über die Grundfragen des Sprachlebens* (1885), esp. pp. 88–89; also Karl Bühler, *Sprachtheorie* (1934), chs. iii and iv.

that the relation holds the two items together. "Brutus killed Caesar" indicates that "killing" holds between Brutus and Caesar. Where the relation is not symmetrical, the word-order and the grammatical forms (case, mood, tense, etc.) of the words symbolize its direction. "Brutus killed Caesar" means something different from "Caesar killed Brutus," and "Killed Caesar Brutus" is not a sentence at all. The word-order partly determines the sense of the structure.

The trick of naming relations instead of illustrating them gives language a tremendous scope; one word can thus take care of a situation that would require a whole sheet of drawings to depict it. Consider the sentence, "Your chance of winning is one among a thousand of losing." Imagine a pictorial expression of this comparatively simple proposition! First, a symbol for "you, winning"; another for "you, losing," pictured a thousand times! Of course a thousand anythings would be far beyond clear apprehension on a basis of mere visual *Gestalt*. We can distinguish three, four, five, and perhaps somewhat higher numbers as visible patterns, for instance:

But a thousand becomes merely "a great number." Its exact fixation requires an order of concepts in which it holds a definite place, as each number concept does in our number system. But to denote such a host of concepts and keep their relations to each other straight, we need a symbolism that can express both terms and relationships more economically than pictures, gestures, or mnesic signs.

It was remarked before that symbol and object, having a common logical form, would be interchangeable save for some psychological factors, namely: that the object is interesting, but hard to fixate, whereas the symbol is easy of apprehension though in itself perhaps quite unimportant. Now the little vocal noises out of which we make our words are extremely easy to produce in all sorts of subtle variations, and easy to perceive and distinguish. As Bertrand Russell has put it, "It is of course largely a matter of convenience that we do not use words of other kinds (than vocal). There is the deaf-and-dumb language; a Frenchman's shrug of the shoulders is a word; in fact, any kind of externally perceptible bodily movement may become a word, if social usage so ordains. But the convention which has given the supremacy to speaking is one which has a good ground, since there is no other way of producing a number of perceptively different bodily movements so quickly or with so little muscular effort. Public speaking would be very tedious if statesmen had to use the deaf-and-dumb language, and very exhausting if all words involved as much muscular effort as a shrug of the shoulders."[13] Not only does speech cost little effort, but above all it requires no instrument save the vocal apparatus and the auditory organs which, normally, we all carry about as part of our very selves; so words are *naturally available* symbols, as well as very economical ones.

Another recommendation for words is that they have no value except as symbols (or signs); in themselves they are completely trivial. This is a greater advantage than philosophers of language generally realize. A symbol which interests us *also* as an object is distracting. It does not convey its meaning without obstruction. For instance, if the word "plenty" were replaced by a succulent, ripe, real peach, few people could attend entirely to the mere concept of *quite enough* when confronted with such a symbol. The more barren and indifferent the symbol, the greater is its semantic power. Peaches are too good to act as words; we are too much interested in peaches themselves. But little noises are ideal conveyors of concepts, for they give us nothing but their meaning. That is the source of the "transparency" of language, on which several scholars have remarked. Vocables in themselves are so worthless that we cease to be aware of their physical presence at all, and become conscious only of their connotations, denotations, or other meanings. Our conceptual activity seems to flow *through* them, rather than merely to accompany them, as it accompanies other experi-

[13] *Philosophy* (1927), p. 44.

ences that we endow with significance. They fail to impress us as "experiences" in their own right, unless we have difficulty in using them as words, as we do with a foreign language or a technical jargon until we have mastered it.

But the greatest virtue of verbal symbols is, probably, their tremendous readiness to enter into *combinations*. There is practically no limit to the selections and arrangements we can make of them. This is largely due to the economy Lord Russell remarked, the speed with which each word is produced and presented and finished, making way for another word. This makes it possible for us to grasp whole groups of meanings at a time, and make a new, total, complex concept out of the separate connotations of rapidly passing words.

Herein lies the power of language to embody concepts not only of things, but of things in combination, or *situations*. A combination of words connoting a situation-concept is a descriptive phrase; if the relation-word in such a phrase is given the grammatical form called a "verb," the phrase becomes a sentence. Verbs are symbols with a double function; they express a relation, and also *assert that the relation holds*, i.e. that the symbol has a denotation.[14] Logically they combine the meaning of a function, ϕ, and an assertion-sign; a verb has the force of "assert $\phi(\ )$."

When a word is given an arbitrary denotation (which may be a simple thing, or a complex affair), it is simply a name; for instance, in a language of my invention "Moof" might mean a cat, a state of mind, or the government of a country. I may give that name to anything I like. A name may be awkward or convenient, ugly or pretty, but in itself it is never *true* or *false*. But if it already has a connotation, then it cannot be given an arbitrary denotation, nor vice versa. I cannot use the word "kitten" *with its accepted connotation* to denote an elephant. The application of *a word with its connotation* is the equivalent of a statement: "This is a

---

[14] A more detailed discussion of this double function may be found in my article, "A Logical Study of Verbs," *The Journal of Philosophy*, XXIV (1927), 5: 120–129.

such-and-such." To call an elephant "kitten," not as a proper name but as a common noun, is a mistake, because he does not exemplify the connoted concept. Similarly a word with a fixed denotation cannot be given an arbitrary connotation, for once the word is a name (common or proper), to give it a certain connotation is to *predicate* the connoted concept of whatever bears the name. If "Jumbo" denotes an elephant, it cannot be given the connotation "something furry," because Jumbo is presumably not furry.

The relation between connotation and denotation is, therefore, the most obvious seat of *truth and falsity*. Its conventional expressions are sentences asserting that something is a such-and-such, or that something has such-and-such a property; in technical language, propositions of the forms "$x \in \hat{y}(\phi y)$," and "ϕx." The distinction between these two forms lies simply in *which aspect of the name we have first determined,* its connotation or its denotation; truth and falsity have the same basis for both kinds of proposition.

In a complex symbolic structure, such as a sentence connecting several elements with each other by a verb that expresses an elaborate pattern of relations, we have a "logical picture" whose applicability depends on the denotations of many words and the connotations of many relation-symbols (word-order, particles, cases, etc.). If the names have denotations, the sentence is about *something*; then its truth or falsity depends on whether any relations actually holding among the denoted things exemplify the relational concepts expressed by the sentence, i.e. whether the pattern of things (or properties, events, etc.) denoted is analogous to the syntactical pattern of the complex symbol.

There are many refinements of logic that give rise to special symbol-situations, to ambiguities and odd mathematical devices, and to the legion of distinctions which Charles Peirce was able to make. But the main lines of logical structure in all meaning-relations are those I have just discussed; the correlation of signs with their meanings by a selective mental process; the correlation of symbols with concepts and concepts with things, which gives rise to a "short-cut" relation between names and things, known as denotation; and the assignment of elaborately patterned symbols to certain analogues in experience, the basis of all interpretation and thought. These are, essentially, the relationships we use in weaving the intricate web of meaning which is the real fabric of human life.

CHAPTER IV

Discursive and Presentational Forms

THE logical theory on which this whole study of symbols is based is essentially that which was set forth by Wittgenstein, some twenty years ago, in his *Tractatus Logico-Philosophicus*:

"One name stands for one thing, and another for another thing, and they are connected together. And so the whole, like a living picture, presents the atomic fact. (4.0311)

"At the first glance the proposition — say as it stands printed on paper — does not seem to be a picture of the reality of which it treats. But neither does the musical score appear at first sight to be a picture of a musical piece; nor does our phonetic spelling (letters) seem to be a picture of our spoken language. . . . (4.015)

"In the fact that there is a general rule by which the musician is able to read the symphony out of the score, and that there is a rule by which one could reconstruct the symphony from the line on a phonograph record and from this again — by means of the first rule — construct the score, herein lies the internal similarity between the things which at first sight seem to be entirely different. And the rule is the law of projection which projects the symphony into the language of the musical score. It is the rule of translation of this language into the language of the gramophone record." (4.0141)

"Projection" is a good word, albeit a figurative one, for the process by which we draw purely *logical* analogies. Geometric projection is the best instance of a perfectly faithful representation which, without knowledge of some logical rule, appears to be a misrepresentation. A child looking at a

map of the world in Mercator projection cannot help believing that Greenland is larger than Australia; he simply
finds it larger. The projection employed is not the usual
principle of copying which we use in all visual comparisons
or translations, and his training in the usual rule makes him
unable to "see" by the new one. It takes sophistication to
"see" the relative sizes of Greenland and Australia on a
Mercator map. Yet a mind educated to appreciate the projected image brings the eye's habit with it. After a while, we
genuinely "see" the thing as we apprehend it.

Language, our most faithful and indispensable picture of
human experience, of the world and its events, of thought
and life and all the march of time, contains a law of projection of which philosophers are sometimes unaware, so that
their reading of the presented "facts" is obvious and yet
wrong, as a child's visual experience is obvious yet deceptive
when his judgment is ensnared by the trick of the flattened
map. The transformation which facts undergo when they
are rendered as propositions is that the relations in them are
turned into something like *objects*. Thus, "A killed B"
tells of a *way* in which A and B were unfortunately combined; but our only means of expressing this way is to *name*
it, and presto! — a new entity, "killing," seems to have added
itself to the complex of A and B. The event which is "pictured" in the proposition undoubtedly involved a *succession*
of acts by A and B, but not the succession which the proposition seems to exhibit — first A, then "killing," then B. Surely
A and B were simultaneous with each other and with the
killing. But words have a linear, discrete, successive order;
they are strung one after another like beads on a rosary; beyond the very limited meanings of inflections, which can indeed be incorporated in the words themselves, we cannot
talk in simultaneous bunches of names. We must name one
thing and then another, and symbols that are not names
must be stuck between or before or after, by convention.
But these symbols, holding proud places in the chain of
names, are apt to be mistaken for names, to the detriment
of many a metaphysical theory. Lord Russell regrets that

we cannot construct a language which would express all relations by analogous relations; then we would not be tempted to misconstrue language, as a person who knows the meaning of the Mercator map, but has not used one freely enough to "see" in its terms, misconstrues the relative sizes of its areas.

"Take, say, that lightning precedes thunder," he says. "To express this by a language closely reproducing the structure of the fact, we should have to say simply: 'lightning, thunder,' where the fact that the first word precedes the second means that what the first word means precedes what the second word means. But even if we adopted this method for temporal order, we should still need words for all other relations, because we could not without intolerable ambiguity symbolize them by the order of our words." [1]

It is a mistake, I think, to symbolize things by entities too much like themselves; to let words in temporal order represent things in temporal order. If relations such as temporal order are symbolized at all, let the symbols not be those same relations themselves. A structure cannot include as *part of a symbol* something that should properly be *part of the meaning*. But it is unfortunate that names and syntactical indicators look so much alike in language; that we cannot represent objects by words, and relations by pitch, loudness, or other characteristics of speech.[2]

As it is, however, all language has a form which requires us to string out our ideas even though their objects rest one within the other; as pieces of clothing that are actually worn one over the other have to be strung side by side on the clothesline. This property of verbal symbolism is known as *discursiveness*; by reason of it, only thoughts which can be arranged in this peculiar order can be spoken at all; any idea

---

[1] *Philosophy*, p. 264.

[2] In the same chapter from which I have just quoted, Lord Russell attributes the power of language to represent *events* to the fact that, like events, it is a temporal series. I cannot agree with him in this matter. It is by virtue of *names for relations* that we can depict dynamic relations. We do not mention past events earlier in a sentence than present ones, but subject temporal order to the same "projection" as, for instance, attribution or classification; temporal order is usually rendered by the syntactical (non-temporal) device of *tense*.

which does not lend itself to this "projection" is ineffable, incommunicable by means of words. That is why the laws of reasoning, our clearest formulation of exact expression, are sometimes known as the "laws of discursive thought."

There is no need of going further into the details of verbal symbolism and its poorer substitutes, hieroglyphs, the deaf-and-dumb language, Morse Code, or the highly developed drum-telegraphy of certain jungle tribes. The subject has been exhaustively treated by several able men, as the many quotations in this chapter indicate; I can only assent to their findings. The relation between word-structures and their meanings is, I believe, one of logical analogy, whereby, in Wittgenstein's phrase, "we make ourselves pictures of facts." This philosophy of language lends itself, indeed, to great technical development, such as Wittgenstein envisaged:

"In the language of everyday life it very often happens that the same word signifies in different ways — and therefore belongs to two different symbols — or that two words, which signify in different ways, are apparently applied in the same way in the proposition. (3.323)

"In order to avoid these errors, we must employ a symbolism which excludes them, by not applying the same sign in different symbols and by not applying signs in the same way which signify in different ways. A symbolism, that is to say, which obeys the rules of *logical* grammar — of logical syntax.

"(The logical symbolism of Frege and Russell is such a language, which, however, does still not exclude all errors.)" (3.325) [3]

Carnap's admirable book, *The Logical Syntax of Language*, carries out the philosophical program suggested by Wittgenstein. Here an actual, detailed technique is developed for determining the *capacity for expression* of any given linguistic system, a technique which predicts the limit of all combinations to be made in that system, shows the equivalence of certain forms and the differences among others which might be mistaken for equivalents, and exhibits the conventions to which any thought or experience must submit in order to

[3] *Tractatus.*

become conveyable by the symbolism in question. The distinctions between scientific language and everyday speech, which most of us can feel rather than define, are clearly illumined by Carnap's analysis; and it is surprising to find how little of our ordinary communication measures up to the standard of "meaning" which a serious philosophy of language, and hence a logic of discursive thought, set before us.

In this truly remarkable work the somewhat diffuse apprehension of our intellectual age, that *symbolism* is the key to epistemology and "natural knowledge," finds precise and practical corroboration. The Kantian challenge: "What can I know?" is shown to be dependent on the prior question: "What can I ask?" And the answer, in Professor Carnap's formulation, is clear and direct. I can ask whatever language will express; I can know whatever experiment will answer. A proposition which could not, under any (perhaps ideal, impracticable) conditions, be verified or refuted, is a pseudo-proposition, it has no literal meaning. It does not belong to the framework of knowledge that we call logical conception; it is not true or false, but *unthinkable*, for it falls outside the order of symbolism.

Since an inordinate amount of our talk, and therefore (we hope) of our cerebration too, defies the canons of literal meaning, our philosophers of language — Russell, Wittgenstein, Carnap, and others of similar persuasions — are faced with the new question: What is the true function of those verbal combinations and other pseudo-symbolic structures that have no real significance, but are freely used as though they meant something?

According to our logicians, those structures are to be treated as "expressions" in a different sense, namely as "expressions" of emotions, feelings, desires. They are not symbols for thought, but symptoms of the inner life, like tears and laughter, crooning, or profanity.

"Many linguistic utterances," says Carnap, "are analogous to laughing in that they have only an expressive function, no representative function. Examples of this are cries like

'Oh, Oh,' or, on a higher level, lyrical verses. The aim of a lyrical poem in which occur the words 'sunshine' and 'clouds,' is not to inform us of certain meteorological facts, but to express certain feelings of the poet and to excite similar feelings in us. . . . Metaphysical propositions — like lyrical verses — have only an expressive function, but no representative function. Metaphysical propositions are neither true nor false, because they assert nothing. . . . But they are, like laughing, lyrics and music, expressive. They express not so much temporary feelings as permanent emotional and volitional dispositions." [4]

Lord Russell holds a very similar view of other people's metaphysics:

"I do not deny," he says, "the importance or value, within its own sphere, of the kind of philosophy which is inspired by ethical notions. The ethical work of Spinoza, for instance, appears to me of the very highest significance, but what is valuable in such a work is not any metaphysical theory as to the nature of the world to which it may give rise, nor indeed anything that can be proved or disproved by argument. What is valuable is the indication of some new way of feeling toward life and the world, some way of feeling by which our own existence can acquire more of the characteristics which we must deeply desire." [5]

And Wittgenstein:

"Most propositions and questions, that have been written about philosophical matters, are not false, but senseless. We cannot, therefore, answer questions of this kind at all, but only state their senselessness. Most questions and propositions of the philosophers result from the fact that we do not understand the logic of our language. (4.003)"

"A proposition presents the existence and non-existence of atomic facts. (4.1)"

"The totality of true propositions is the total of natural science (or the totality of the natural sciences). (4.11)"

"Everything that can be thought at all can be thought

---

[4] *Philosophy and Logical Syntax*, p. 28.
[5] "Scientific Method in Philosophy," in *Mysticism and Logic* (1918), p. 109.

clearly. Everything that can be said can be said clearly."
(4.116) [6]

In their criticism of metaphysical propositions, namely that such propositions are usually pseudo-answers to pseudo-questions, these logicians have my full assent; problems of "First Cause" and "Unity" and "Substance," and all the other time-honored topics, are insoluble, because they arise from the fact that we attribute to the world what really belongs to the "logical projection" in which we conceive it, and by misplacing our questions we jeopardize our answers. This source of bafflement has been uncovered by the philosophers of our day, through their interest in the functions and nature of symbolism. The discovery marks a great intellectual advance. But it does not condemn philosophical inquiry as such; it merely requires *every philosophical problem to be recast*, to be conceived in a different form. Many issues that seemed to concern the *sources* of knowledge, for instance, now appear to turn partly or wholly on the *forms* of knowledge, or even the forms of expression, of symbolism. The center of philosophical interest has shifted once more, as it has shifted several times in the past. That does not mean, however, that rational people should now renounce metaphysics. The recognition of the intimate relation between symbolism and experience, on which our whole criticism of traditional problems is based, is itself a metaphysical insight. For metaphysics is, like every philosophical pursuit, a study of *meanings*. From it spring the special sciences, which can develop their techniques and verify their propositions one by one, *as soon as their initial concepts are clear enough to allow systematic handling*, i.e. as soon as the philosophical work behind them is at least tentatively accomplished.[7] Metaphysics is not itself a science with fixed presuppositions, but progresses from problem to problem rather than from premise to consequence. To suppose that we have outgrown it is to suppose that all "the sciences" are finally

<hr/>

[6] *Op. cit.*
[7] I have presented a fuller discussion of philosophy as the "mother of sciences" in *The Practice of Philosophy* (1930), ch. ii.

established, that human language is complete, or at least soon to be completed, and additional facts are all we lack of the greatest knowledge ever possible to man; and though this knowledge may be small, it is all that we shall ever have.

This is, essentially, the attitude of those logicians who have investigated the limits of language. Nothing that is not "language" in the sense of their technical definition can possess the character of symbolic expressiveness (though it may be "expressive" in the symptomatic way). Consequently nothing that cannot be "projected" in discursive form is accessible to the human mind at all, and any attempt to understand anything but demonstrable fact is bootless ambition. The knowable is a clearly defined field, governed by the requirement of discursive projectability. Outside this domain is the inexpressible realm of feeling, of formless desires and satisfactions, immediate experience, forever incognito and incommunicando. A philosopher who looks in that direction is, or should be, a mystic; from the ineffable sphere nothing but nonsense can be conveyed, since language, our only possible semantic, will not clothe experiences that elude the discursive form.

But intelligence is a slippery customer; if one door is closed to it, it finds, or even breaks, another entrance to the world. If one symbolism is inadequate, it seizes another; there is no eternal decree over its means and methods. So I will go with the logisticians and linguists as far as they like, but do not promise to go no further. For there is an unexplored possibility of genuine semantic beyond the limits of discursive language.

This logical "beyond," which Wittgenstein calls the "unspeakable," both Russell and Carnap regard as the sphere of subjective experience, emotion, feeling, and wish, from which only *symptoms* come to us in the form of metaphysical and artistic fancies. The study of such products they relegate to psychology, not semantics. And here is the point of my radical divergence from them. Where Carnap speaks of "cries like 'Oh, Oh,' or, on a higher level, lyrical verses," I can see only a complete failure to apprehend a fundamental distinction. Why should we cry our feelings at such high levels that anyone would think we were *talking*? [8] Clearly, poetry means more than a cry; it has reason for being articulate; and metaphysics is more than the croon with which we might cuddle up to the world in a comfortable attitude. We are dealing with symbolisms here, and what they express is often highly intellectual. Only, the form and function of such symbolisms are not those investigated by logicians, under the heading of "language." The field of semantics is wider than that of language, as certain philosophers — Schopenhauer, Cassirer, Delacroix, Dewey, Whitehead, and some others — have discovered; but it is blocked for us by the two fundamental tenets of current epistemology, which we have just discussed.

These two basic assumptions go hand in hand: (1) That *language* [9] *is the only means of articulating thought,* and (2) That *everything which is not speakable thought, is feeling.* They are linked together because all genuine thinking *is* symbolic, and the limits of the expressive medium are, therefore, really the limits of our conceptual powers. Beyond these we can have only blind feeling, which records nothing and conveys nothing, but has to be discharged in action or self-expression, in deeds or cries or other impulsive demonstrations.

But if we consider how difficult it is to construct a meaningful language that shall meet neo-positivistic standards, it is quite incredible that people should ever *say* anything at all, or understand each other's propositions. At best, human thought is but a tiny, grammar-bound island, in the midst of a sea of feeling expressed by "Oh-oh" and sheer babble. The island has a periphery, perhaps, of mud — factual and hypothetical concepts broken down by the emotional tides into the "material mode," a mixture of meaning and nonsense. Most of us live the better part of our lives on this mudflat; but in artistic moods we take to the deep, where we flounder about with symptomatic cries that sound like propo-

---

[8] Cf. Urban, *Language and Reality*, p. 164.

[9] Including, of course, its refinements in mathematical and scientific symbolisms, and its approximations by gesture, hieroglyphics, or graphs.

sitions about life and death, good and evil, substance, beauty, and other non-existent topics.

So long as we regard only scientific and "material" (semi-scientific) thought as really cognitive of the world, this peculiar picture of mental life must stand. And *so long as we admit only discursive symbolism as a bearer of ideas, "thought" in this restricted sense must be regarded as our only intellectual activity.* It begins and ends with language; without the elements, at least, of scientific grammar, conception must be impossible.

A theory which implies such peculiar consequences is itself a suspicious character. But the error which it harbors is not in its reasoning. It is in the very premise from which the doctrine proceeds, namely that all articulate symbolism is discursive. As Lord Russell, with his usual precision and directness, has stated the case, "it is clear that anything that can be said in an inflected language can be said in an uninflected language; therefore, anything that can be said in language can be said by means of a temporal series of uninflected words. This places a limitation upon what can be expressed in words. It may well be that there are facts which do not lend themselves to this very simple schema; if so, they cannot be expressed in language. Our confidence in language is due to the fact that it . . . shares the structure of the physical world, and therefore can express that structure. But if there be a world which is not physical, or not in space-time, it may have a structure which we can never hope to express or to know. . . . Perhaps that is why we know so much physics and so little of anything else." [10]

Now, I do not believe that "there is a world which is not physical, or not in space-time," but I do believe that in this physical, space-time world of our experience there are things which do not fit the grammatical scheme of expression. But they are not necessarily blind, inconceivable, mystical affairs; they are simply matters which require to be conceived through some symbolistic schema other than discursive language. And to demonstrate the possibility of such a non-discursive pattern

[10] *Philosophy*, p. 265.

one needs only to review the logical requirements for any symbolic structure whatever. Language is by no means our only articulate product.

Our merest sense-experience is a process of *formulation.* The world that actually meets our senses is not a world of "things," about which we are invited to discover facts as soon as we have codified the necessary logical language to do so; the world of pure sensation is so complex, so fluid and full, that sheer sensitivity to stimuli would only encounter what William James has called (in characteristic phrase) "a blooming, buzzing confusion." Out of this bedlam our sense-organs must select certain predominant forms, if they are to make report of *things* and not of mere dissolving sensa. The eye and the ear must have their logic — their "categories of understanding," if you like the Kantian idiom, or their "primary imagination," in Coleridge's version of the same concept.[11] An object is not a datum, but a form construed by the sensitive and intelligent organ, a form which is at once an experienced individual thing and a symbol for the concept of it, for *this sort of thing.*

A tendency to organize the sensory field into groups and patterns of sense-data, to perceive forms rather than a flux of light-impressions, seems to be inherent in our receptor apparatus just as much as in the higher nervous centers with which we do arithmetic and logic. But this unconscious appreciation of forms is the primitive root of all abstraction, which in turn is the keynote of rationality; so it appears that the conditions for rationality lie deep in our pure animal experience — in our power of perceiving, in the elementary functions of our eyes and ears and fingers. Mental life begins with our mere physiological constitution. A little reflection shows us that, since no experience occurs more than once, so-called "repeated" experiences are really *analogous* occurrences, all fitting a form that was abstracted on the first occasion. *Familiarity* is nothing but the quality of fitting very

[11] An excellent discussion of Coleridge's philosophy may be found in D. G. James, *Skepticism and Poetry* (1937), a book well worth reading in connection with this chapter.

neatly into the form of a previous experience. I believe our ingrained habit of hypostatizing impressions, of seeing *things* and not sense-data, rests on the fact that we promptly and unconsciously abstract a form from each sensory experience, and use this form to *conceive* the experience as a whole, as a "thing."

No matter what heights the human mind may attain, it can work only with the organs it has and the functions peculiar to them. Eyes that did not see forms could never furnish it with *images*; ears that did not hear articulated sounds could never open it to *words*. Sense-data, in brief, would be useless to a mind whose activity is "through and through a symbolic process," were they not *par excellence* receptacles of meaning. But meaning, as previous considerations have shown, accrues essentially to forms. Unless the *Gestalt*-psychologists are right in their belief that *Gestaltung* is of the very nature of perception, I do not know how the hiatus between perception and conception, sense-organ and mind-organ, chaotic stimulus and logical response, is ever to be closed and welded. A mind that works primarily with meanings must have organs that supply it primarily with forms.

The nervous system is the organ of the mind; its center is the brain, its extremities the sense-organs; and any characteristic function it may possess must govern the work of all its parts. In other words, the activity of our senses is "mental" not only when it reaches the brain, but in its very inception, whenever the alien world outside impinges on the furthest and smallest receptor. All sensitivity bears the stamp of mentality. "Seeing," for instance, is not a passive process, by which meaningless impressions are stored up for the use of an organizing mind, which construes forms out of these amorphous data to suit its own purposes. "Seeing" is itself a process of formulation; our understanding of the visible world begins in the eye.[12]

----

[12] For a general account of the *Gestalt*-theory, see Wolfgang Köhler, *Gestalt Psychology* (1929), from which the following relevant passage is taken:

"It is precisely the original organization and segregation of circumscribed wholes which make it possible for the sensory world to appear so utterly

This psychological insight, which we owe to the school of Wertheimer, Köhler, and Koffka, has far-reaching philosophical consequences, if we take it seriously; for it carries rationality into processes that are usually deemed pre-rational, and points to the existence of forms, i.e. of *possible symbolic material*, at a level where symbolic activity has certainly never been looked for by any epistemologist. The eye and the ear make their own abstractions, and consequently dictate their own peculiar forms of conception. But these forms are derived from exactly the same world that furnished the totally different forms known to physics. There is, in fact, no such thing as *the* form of the "real" world; physics is one pattern which may be found in it, and "appearance," or the pattern of *things* with their qualities and characters, is another. One construction may indeed preclude the other; but to maintain that the consistency and universality of the one brands the other as *false* is a mistake. The fact that physical analysis does not rest in a final establishment of irreducible "qualities" does not refute the belief that there are red, blue, and green things, wet or oily or dry substances, fragrant flowers, and shiny surfaces in the real world. These concepts of the "material mode" are not approximations to "physical" notions at all. Physical concepts owe their origin and development to the application of *mathematics* to the world of "things," and mathematics never — even in the beginning — dealt with qualities of objects. It measured their proportions, but never treated its concepts — triangularity, circularity, etc. — as qualities of which *so-and-so much* could become an ingredient of certain objects. Even though an elliptical race-track may approximate a circle, it is not to

imbued with meaning to the adult because, in its gradual entry into the sensory field, meaning follows the lines drawn by natural organization. It usually enters into segregated wholes. . . .

"Where 'form' *exists* originally, it acquires a meaning very easily. But here a whole with its form is given first and then a meaning 'creeps into it.' That meaning automatically produces a form where beforehand there is none, has not been shown experimentally in a single case, as far as I know." (P. 208)

See also Max Wertheimer, *Drei Abhandlungen zur Gestalttheorie* (1925), and Kurt Koffka, *Principles of Gestalt Psychology* (1935).

be improved by the addition of more circularity. On the other hand, wine which is not sweet enough requires more sweetening, paint which is not bright enough is given an ingredient of more white or more color. The world of physics is essentially the real world construed by mathematical abstractions, and the world of sense is the real world construed by the abstractions which the sense-organs immediately furnish. To suppose that the "material mode" is a primitive and groping attempt at physical conception is a fatal error in epistemology, because it cuts off all interest in the developments of which sensuous conception is capable, and the intellectual uses to which it might be put.

These intellectual uses lie in a field which usually harbors a slough of despond for the philosopher, who ventures into it because he is too honest to ignore it, though really he knows no path around its pitfalls. It is the field of "intuition," "deeper meaning," "artistic truth," "insight," and so forth. A dangerous-looking sector, indeed, for the advance of a rational spirit! To date, I think, every serious epistemology that has regarded mental life as greater than discursive reason, and has made concessions to "insight" or "intuition," has just so far capitulated to *unreason*, to mysticism and irrationalism. Every excursion beyond propositional thought has dispensed with thought altogether, and postulated some inmost soul of pure feeling in direct contact with a Reality unsymbolized, unfocussed, and incommunicable (with the notable exception of the theory set forth by L. A. Reid in the last chapter of his *Knowledge and Truth*, which admits the facts of non-propositional conception in a way that invites rather than precludes logical analysis).

The abstractions made by the ear and the eye — the forms of direct perception — are our most primitive instruments of intelligence. They are genuine symbolic materials, media of understanding, by whose office we apprehend a world of *things*, and of events that are the histories of things. To furnish such conceptions is their prime mission. Our sense-organs make their habitual, unconscious abstractions, in the interest of this "*reifying*" function that underlies ordinary recognition of objects, knowledge of signals, words, tunes, places, and the possibility of classifying such things in the outer world according to their kind. We recognize the elements of this sensuous analysis in all sorts of combination; we can use them imaginatively, to conceive prospective changes in familiar scenes.

Visual forms — lines, colors, proportions, etc. — are just as capable of *articulation*, i.e. of complex combination, as words. But the laws that govern this sort of articulation are altogether different from the laws of syntax that govern language. The most radical difference is that *visual forms are not discursive*. They do not present their constituents successively, but simultaneously, so the relations determining a visual structure are grasped in one act of vision. Their complexity, consequently, is not limited, as the complexity of discourse is limited, by what the mind can retain from the beginning of an apperceptive act to the end of it. Of course such a restriction on discourse sets bounds to the complexity of speakable ideas. An idea that contains too many minute yet closely related parts, too many relations within relations, cannot be "projected" into discursive form; it is too subtle for speech. A language-bound theory of mind, therefore, rules it out of the domain of understanding and the sphere of knowledge.

But the symbolism furnished by our purely sensory appreciation of forms is a *non-discursive symbolism*, peculiarly well suited to the expression of ideas that defy linguistic "projection." Its primary function, that of conceptualizing the flux of sensations, and giving us concrete *things* in place of kaleidoscopic colors or noises, is itself an office that no language-born thought can replace. The understanding of space which we owe to sight and touch could never be developed, in all its detail and definiteness, by a discursive knowledge of geometry. Nature speaks to us, first of all, through our senses; the forms and qualities we distinguish, remember, imagine, or recognize are symbols of entities which exceed and outlive our momentary experience. Moreover, the same symbols — qualities, lines, rhythms — may occur in innumerable presentations; they are abstractable and combinatory. It is quite natural, therefore, that philosophers who have recognized the symbolical character of so-called "sense-data," especially in their highly developed uses, in science and art, often speak of a "language" of the senses, a "language" of musical tones, of colors, and so forth.

Yet this manner of speaking is very deceptive. Language is a special mode of expression, and not every sort of semantic can be brought under this rubric; by generalizing from linguistic symbolism to symbolism as such, we are easily led to misconceive all other types, and overlook their most interesting features. Perhaps it were well to consider, here, the salient characteristics of true language, or discourse.

In the first place, *every language has a vocabulary and a syntax*. Its elements are words with fixed meanings. Out of these one can construct, according to the rules of the syntax, composite symbols with resultant new meanings.

Secondly, in a language, some words are equivalent to whole combinations of other words, so that most meanings can be expressed in several different ways. This makes it possible *to define the meanings of the ultimate single words*, i.e., to construct a dictionary.

Thirdly, there may be alternative words for the same meaning. When two people systematically use different words for almost everything, they are said to speak different languages. But the two languages are roughly equivalent; with a little artifice, an occasional substitution of a phrase for a single word, etc., the propositions enunciated by one person, in his system, may be *translated* into the conventional system of the other.

Now consider the most familiar sort of non-discursive symbol, a picture. Like language, it is composed of elements that represent various respective constituents in the object; but these elements are not units with independent meanings. The areas of light and shade that constitute a portrait, a photograph for instance, have no significance by themselves. In isolation we would consider them simply blotches. Yet they are faithful representatives of visual elements composing the visual object. However, they do not represent, item for item, those elements which have *names*; there is not one blotch for the nose, one for the mouth, etc.; their shapes, in quite indescribable combinations, convey a total picture in which nameable features may be pointed out. The gradations of light and shade cannot be enumerated. They cannot be correlated, one by one, with parts or characteristics by means of which we might *describe* the person who posed for the portrait. The "elements" that the camera represents are not the "elements" that language represents. They are a thousand times more numerous. For this reason the correspondence between a word-picture and a visible object can never be as close as that between the object and its photograph. Given all at once to the intelligent eye, an incredible wealth and detail of information is conveyed by the portrait, where we do not have to stop to construe verbal meanings. That is why we use a photograph rather than a description on a passport or in the Rogues' Gallery.

Clearly, a symbolism with so many elements, such myriad relationships, cannot be broken up into basic units. It is impossible to find the smallest independent symbol, and recognize its identity when the same unit is met in other contexts. Photography, therefore, *has no vocabulary.* The same is obviously true of painting, drawing, etc. There is, of course, a technique of picturing objects, but the law governing this technique cannot properly be called a "syntax," since there are no items that might be called, metaphorically, the "words" of portraiture.

Since we have no words, there can be no dictionary of meanings for lines, shadings, or other elements of pictorial technique. We may well pick out some line, say a certain curve, in a picture, which serves to represent one nameable item; but in another place the same curve would have an entirely different meaning. It has no fixed meaning apart from its context. Also, there is no complex of other elements that is equivalent to it at all times, as "2+2" is equivalent to "4." Non-discursive symbols cannot be defined in terms of others, as discursive symbols can.

If there can be no defining dictionary, of course we have no translating dictionary, either. There are different media of graphic representation, but their respective elements cannot be brought into one-to-one correlation with each other, as in languages: *"chien"* = "dog," *"moi"* = "me," etc. There is no standard key for translating sculpture into painting, or drawing into ink-wash, because their equivalence rests on their common *total reference*, not on bit-for-bit equivalences of parts such as underlie a literal translation.

Furthermore, verbal symbolism, unlike the non-discursive kinds, has primarily a *general* reference. Only convention can assign a proper name — and then there is no way of preventing some other convention from assigning the same proper name to a different individual. We may name a child as oddly as we will, yet we cannot guarantee that no one else will ever bear that designation. A description may fit a scene ever so closely, but it takes some known proper name to refer it without possible doubt to one and only one place. Where the names of persons and places are withheld, we can never *prove* that a discourse refers — not merely applies — to a certain historic occasion. In the non-discursive mode that speaks directly to sense, however, there is no intrinsic generality. It is first and foremost a direct *presentation* of an individual object. A picture has to be schematized if it is to be capable of various meanings. In itself it represents just one object — real or imaginary, but still a unique object. The definition of a triangle fits triangles in general, but a drawing always presents a triangle of some specific kind and size. We have to abstract from the conveyed meaning in order to conceive triangularity in general. Without the help of words this generalization, if possible at all, is certainly incommunicable.

It appears, then, that although the different media of non-verbal representation are often referred to as distinct "languages," this is really a loose terminology. Language in the strict sense is essentially discursive; it has permanent units of meaning which are combinable into larger units; it has fixed equivalences that make definition and translation possible; its connotations are general, so that it requires non-verbal

acts, like pointing, looking, or emphatic voice-inflections, to
assign specific denotations to its terms. In all these salient
characters it differs from wordless symbolism, which is non-
discursive and untranslatable, does not allow of definitions
within its own system, and cannot directly convey generalities. The meanings given through language are successively
understood, and gathered into a whole by the process called
discourse; the meanings of all other symbolic elements that
compose a larger, articulate symbol are understood only
through the meaning of the whole, through their relations
within the total structure. Their very functioning as symbols depends on the fact that they are involved in a simultaneous, integral presentation. This kind of semantic may
be called "presentational symbolism," to characterize its
essential distinction from discursive symbolism, or "language" proper.[13]

The recognition of presentational symbolism as a normal
and prevalent vehicle of meaning widens our conception of
rationality far beyond the traditional boundaries, yet never
breaks faith with logic in the strictest sense. Wherever a
symbol operates, there is a meaning; and conversely, different classes of experience — say, reason, intuition, appreciation
— correspond to different types of symbolic mediation. No
symbol is exempt from the office of logical formulation, of
conceptualizing what it conveys; however simple its import,
or however great, this import is a *meaning*, and therefore
an element for understanding. Such reflection invites one
to tackle anew, and with entirely different expectations, the
whole problem of the limits of reason, the much-disputed
life of feeling, and the great controversial topics of fact and
truth, knowledge and wisdom, science and art. It brings
within the compass of reason much that has been traditionally
relegated to "emotion," or to that crepuscular depth of the
mind where "intuitions" are supposed to be born, without

---

[13] It is relevant here to note that "picture language," which uses *separate
pictures in place of words*, is a discursive symbolism, though each "word" is a
presentational symbol; and that all codes, e.g. the conventional gestures of
deaf-mutes or the drum communications of African tribes, are discursive
systems.

any midwifery of symbols, without due process of thought, to fill the gaps in the edifice of discursive, or "rational," judgment.

The symbolic materials given to our senses, the *Gestalten* or fundamental perceptual forms which invite us to construe the pandemonium of sheer impression into a world of things and occasions, belong to the "presentational" order. They furnish the elementary abstractions in terms of which ordinary sense-experience is understood.[14] This kind of understanding is directly reflected in the pattern of *physical reaction*, impulse and instinct. May not the order of perceptual forms, then, be a possible principle for symbolization, and hence the conception, expression, and apprehension, of impulsive, instinctive, and sentient life? May not a non-discursive symbolism of light and color, or of tone, be formulative of that life? And is it not possible that the sort of "intuitive" knowledge which Bergson extols above all rational knowledge because it is supposedly not mediated by any formulating (and hence deforming) symbol [15] is itself perfectly rational, but not to be conceived through language — a product of that presentational symbolism which the mind reads in a flash, and preserves in a disposition or an attitude?

This hypothesis, though unfamiliar and therefore somewhat difficult, seems to me well worth exploring. For, quite apart from all questions of the authenticity of intuitive, in-

---

[14] Kant thought that the *principles* of such formulation were supplied by a faculty of the mind, which he called *Verstand*; but his somewhat dogmatic delimitation of the field of knowledge open to *Verstand*, and the fact that he regarded the mind-engendered forms as *constitutive* of experience rather than *interpretative* (as principles must be), prevented logicians from taking serious note of such forms as possible machinery of reason. They abode by the forms of *Vernunft*, which are, roughly speaking, the forms of discourse. Kant himself exalted *Vernunft* as the special gift and glory of man. When an epistemology of medium and meaning began to crowd out the older epistemology of percept and concept, his *Verstandesformen*, in their role of *conceptual ingredients* of phenomena, were lumped with his metaphysical doctrines, and eclipsed by "metalogical" interests.

[15] See Henri Bergson, *La pensée et le mouvement* (1934), esp. essays ii ("De la position des problèmes") and iv ("L'intuition philosophique"); also his *Essai sur les données immédiates de la conscience* (1889), and *Introduction to Metaphysics* (1912).

herited, or inspired knowledge, about which I do not wish
to cavil, the very idea of a *non-rational source* of any knowledge vitiates the concept of mind as an organ of understanding. "The power of reason is simply the power of the whole
mind at its fullest stretch and compass," said Professor
Creighton, in an essay that sought to stem the great wave of
irrationalism and emotionalism following the World War.[16]
This assumption appears to me to be a basic one in any
study of mentality. Rationality is the essence of mind, and
symbolic transformation its elementary process. It is a fundamental error, therefore, to recognize it only in the phenomenon of systematic, explicit reasoning. That is a mature and
precarious product.

Rationality, however, is embodied in every mental act,
not only when the mind is "at its fullest stretch and compass." It permeates the peripheral activities of the human
nervous system, just as truly as the cortical functions.

"The facts of perception and memory maintain themselves
only in so far as they are mediated, and thus given significance
beyond their mere isolated existence. . . . What falls in any
way within experience partakes of the rational form of the
mind. As mental content, any part of experience is something
more than a particular impression having only the attributes
of existence. As already baptized into the life of the mind,
it partakes of its logical nature and moves on the plane of
universality. . . .

"No matter how strongly the unity and integrity of the
mind is asserted, this unity is nothing more than verbal if
the mind is not in principle the expression of reason. For
it can be shown that all attempts to render comprehensible
the unity of the mental life in terms of an alogical principle
fail to attain their goal." [17]

The title of Professor Creighton's trenchant little article
is "Reason and Feeling." Its central thesis is that if there
is something in our mental life besides "reason," by which

[16] J. E. Creighton, "Reason and Feeling," *Philosophical Review*, XXX
(1921), 5: 465–481. See p. 469.
[17] *Ibid.*, pp. 470–472.

he means, of course, discursive thinking, then it cannot be an alogical factor, but must be in essence cognitive, too; and since the only alternative to this reason is feeling (the author does not question that axiom of epistemology), feeling itself must somehow participate in knowledge and understanding.

All this may be granted. The position is well taken. But the most crucial *problem* is barely broached: this problem is epitomized in the word "somehow." *Just how* can feelings be conceived as possible ingredients of rationality? We are not told, but we are given a generous hint, which in the light of a broader theory of symbolism points to explanation.

"In the development of mind," he says, "feeling does not remain a static element, constant in form and content at all levels, but . . . is transformed and disciplined through its interplay with other aspects of experience. . . . Indeed, the character of the feeling in any experience may be taken as an index of the mind's grasp of its object; at the lower levels of experience, where the mind is only partially or superficially involved, feeling appears as something isolated and opaque, as the passive accompaniment of mere bodily sensations. . . . In the higher experiences, the feelings assume an entirely different character, just as do the sensations and the other contents of mind." [18]

The significant observation voiced in this passage is that *feelings have definite forms, which become progressively articulated.* Their development is effected through their "interplay with the other aspects of experience"; but the nature of that interplay is not specified. Yet it is here, I think, that cogency for the whole thesis must be sought. *What* character of feeling is "an index of the mind's grasp of its object," and by what tokens is it so? If feeling has articulate forms, what are they like? For what these are *like* determines by what symbolism we might understand them. Everybody knows that language is a very poor medium for expressing our emotional nature. It merely names certain vaguely and crudely conceived states, but fails miserably in any attempt to convey the ever-moving patterns, the ambivalences and

[18] *Ibid.*, pp. 478–479.

intricacies of inner experience, the interplay of feelings with thoughts and impressions, memories and echoes of memories, transient fantasy, or its mere runic traces, all turned into nameless, emotional stuff. If we say that we understand someone else's feeling in a certain matter, we mean that we understand why he should be sad or happy, excited or indifferent, in a general way; that we can see due cause for his attitude. We do not mean that we have insight into the actual flow and balance of his feelings, into that "character" which "may be taken as an index of the mind's grasp of its object." Language is quite inadequate to articulate such a conception. Probably we would not impart our actual, inmost feelings even if they could be spoken. We rarely speak in detail of entirely personal things.

There is, however, a kind of symbolism peculiarly adapted to the explication of "unspeakable" things, though it lacks the cardinal virtue of language, which is denotation. The most highly developed type of such purely connotational semantic is music. We are not talking nonsense when we say that a certain musical progression is significant, or that a given phrase lacks meaning, or a player's rendering fails to convey the import of a passage. Yet such statements make sense only to people with a natural understanding of the medium, whom we describe, therefore, as "musical." Musicality is often regarded as an essentially unintellectual, even a biologically sportive trait. Perhaps that is why musicians, who know that it is the prime source of their mental life and the medium of their clearest insight into humanity, so often feel called upon to despise the more obvious forms of understanding, that claim practical virtues under the names of reason, logic, etc. But in fact, musical understanding is not hampered by the possession of an active intellect, nor even by that love of pure reason which is known as rationalism or intellectualism; and *vice versa*, common-sense and scientific acumen need not defend themselves against any "emotionalism" that is supposed to be inherent in a respect for music. Speech and music have essentially different functions, despite their oft-remarked union in song. Their original relationship

lies much deeper than any such union (of which more will
be said in a subsequent chapter), and can be seen only when
their respective natures are understood.

The problem of meaning deepens at every turn. The longer
we delve into its difficulties, the more complex it appears.
But in a central philosophical concept, this is a sign of health.
Each question answered leads to another which previously
could not be even entertained: the logic of symbolism, the
possible types of representation, the fields proper to them,
the actual functions of symbols according to their nature,
their relationships to each other, and finally our main theme,
their integration in human mentality.

Of course it is not possible to study every known phenomenon in the realm of symbolism. But neither is this necessary
even in an intimate study. The logical structures underlying
all semantic functions, which I have discussed in this chapter,
suggest a general principle of division. Signs are logically
distinct from symbols; discursive and presentational patterns
show a formal difference. There are further natural divisions
due to various ways of *using* symbols, no less important than
the logical distinctions. Altogether, we may group meaning-
situations around certain outstanding types, and make these
several types the subjects of individual studies. Language,
ritual, myth, and music, representing four respective modes,
may serve as central topics for the study of actual symbolisms;
and I trust that further problems of significance in art, in
science or mathematics, in behavior or in fantasy and dream,
may receive some light by analogy, and by that most powerful human gift, the adaptation of ideas.

CHAPTER V

Language

LANGUAGE is, without a doubt, the most momentous and at the same time the most mysterious product of the human mind. Between the clearest animal call of love or warning or anger, and a man's least, trivial *word*, there lies a whole day of Creation — or in modern phrase, a whole chapter of evolution. In language we have the free, accomplished use of symbolism, the record of articulate conceptual thinking; without language there seems to be nothing like explicit thought whatever. All races of men — even the scattered, primitive denizens of the deep jungle, and brutish cannibals who have lived for centuries on world-removed islands — have their complete and articulate language. There seem to be no simple, amorphous, or imperfect languages, such as one would naturally expect to find in conjunction with the lowest cultures. People who have not invented textiles, who live under roofs of pleated branches, need no privacy and mind no filth and roast their enemies for dinner, will yet converse over their bestial feasts in a tongue as grammatical as Greek, and as fluent as French! [1]

[1] There are several statements in philological and psychological literature to the effect that certain primitive races have but a rudimentary language, and depend on gesture to supplement their speech. All such statements that I have found, however, can be traced back to one common source, namely Mary H. Kingsley's *Travels in West Africa* (1897). This writer enjoyed so high a reputation in other fields than philology that her casual and apparently erroneous observations of native languages have been accepted rather uncritically by men as learned as Sir Richard Paget, Professor G. F. Stout, and Dr. Israel Latif. Yet Miss Kingsley's testimony is very shaky. She tells us (p. 504) that "the inhabitants of Fernando Po, the Bubis, are quite unable to converse with each other unless they have sufficient light to see the accompanying gestures of the conversation." But in an earlier part of the book she writes, "I know nothing of it [the Bubi language] myself save that it

Animals, on the other hand, are one and all without speech. They communicate, of course; but not by any method that can be likened to speaking. They express their emotions and indicate their wishes and control one another's behavior by suggestion. One ape will take another by the hand and drag him into a game or to his bed; he will hold out his hand to beg for food, and will sometimes receive it. But even the highest apes give no indication of speech. Careful studies have been made of the sounds they emit, but all systematic observers agree that none of these are denotative, i.e. none of them are rudimentary words.[2] Furness, for instance, says: "If these animals have a language it is restricted to a very few sounds of a general emotional signification. Articulate speech they have none and communication with one another

---

is harsh in sound," and refers the reader to the work of Dr. Baumann for information about its words and structure; Baumann gives a vocabulary and grammar that would certainly suffice a European to carry on any ordinary conversation in the dark. (See O. Baumann, "Beiträge zur Kentniss der Bubesprache auf Fernando Póo," *Zeitschrift für afrikanische Sprachen*, I, 1888, 138–155.) It seems plausible, therefore, that the Bubis find such conversation personally or socially "impossible" for some other reason. Her other example is no surer. "When I was with the Fans they frequently said, 'We will go to the fire so we can see what they say,' when any question had to be decided after dark . . ." (p. 504). It is strange that a language in which one can make, in the dark, so complex a statement as: "We will go to the fire so we can see what they say," should require gesture to complete other propositions; moreover, where there is a question to decide, it might be awkward for the most civilized congress to take a majority vote without switching on the lights.

I am inclined, therefore, to credit the statement of Edward Sapir, that "the gift of speech and a well-ordered language are characteristic of every known group of human beings. No tribe has ever been found which is without language and all statements to the contrary may be dismissed as mere folklore." After repudiating specifically the stories just related, he concludes: "The truth of the matter is that language is an essentially perfect means of expression and communication among every known people." (From Article "Language," in *Encyclopedia of the Social Sciences*, by permission of The Macmillan Company, publishers. Cf. Otto Jespersen, *Language: its Nature, Development and Origin*, 1922, p. 413.)

[2] In 1892 R. L. Garner published a book, *The Speech of Monkeys*, which aroused considerable interest, for he claimed to have learned a monkey vocabulary of about forty words. The book, however, is so fanciful and unscientific, and its interpretations so extravagant, that I think it must be discounted *in toto*, especially as more careful observations of later scientists belie its findings.

is accomplished by vocal sounds to no greater extent than it is by dogs, with a growl, a whine, or a bark." [3] Mr. and Mrs. Yerkes, who are very reluctant to abandon the search for pre-human speech-functions in simians, come to the conclusion that "although evidence of use of the voice and of definite word-like sounds to symbolize feelings, and possibly also ideas, becomes increasingly abundant from lemur to ape, no one of the infra-human primates exhibits a systematization of vocal symbols which may approximately be described as speech." [4]

If the apes really used "definite word-like sounds to *symbolize* feelings and possibly also ideas," it would be hard to deny their power of speech. But all descriptions of their behavior indicate that they use such sounds only to *signify* their feelings, perhaps their desires. Their vocal expressions of love are *symptoms* of an emotion, not the name of it, nor any other symbol that represents it (like the heart on a Valentine). And true language begins only when a sound keeps its reference beyond the situation of its instinctive utterance, e.g. when an individual can say not only: "My love, my love!" but also: "He loves me — he loves me not." Even though Professor Yerkes' young apes, Chim and Panzee, met their food with exclamations like "Kha!" or "Nga!" these are like a cry of "Yum-yum!" rather than: "Banana, to-day." They are sounds of enthusiastic assent, of a very specialized emotional reaction; *they cannot be used between meals to talk over the merits of the feast.*

Undoubtedly one reason for the lack of language in apes is their lack of any tendency to babble. Professor and Mrs. Kellogg, who brought up a little chimpanzee, Gua, for nine months exactly as they were bringing up their own child, observed that even in an environment of speaking persons "there was no attempt on Gua's part to use her lips, tongue, teeth and mouth-cavity in the production of new utterances; while in the case of the human subject a continuous vocalized

[3] W. H. Furness, "Observations on the Mentality of Chimpanzees and Orang-Utans," *Proceedings of the American Philosophical Society*, LV (1916), 281–290.   [4] R. M. Yerkes and A. W. Yerkes, *The Great Apes* (1929), p. 569.

play was apparent from the earliest months. . . . There were no 'random' noises to compare with the baby's prattle or the spontaneous chatter of many birds. On the whole, it may be said she never vocalized without some definite provocation, that is, without a clearly discernible external stimulus or cause. And in most cases this stimulus was obviously of an emotional character." [5] She had, indeed, what they called her "food-bark," and a pathetic "Ooo-oo" of fear; the bark was extended to signify assent in general, the "Ooo" to express dissent. That is as near as she came to language. The child, too, used only a few words before the comparative experiment ended, but it is noteworthy that they were not "yes" and "no," but were *denotative words* — "din-din," "Gya" (Gua), and "Daddy." The use of true vocables for "yes" and "no" is apt to be late in children. Their interest in words centers on *names* for things and actions.

If we find no prototype of language in our nearest simian relatives, the apes, how can we conceive of a beginning for this all-important human function? We might suppose that speech is man's distinguishing instinct, that man is by nature the Linguistic Primate. Horatio Hale expressed this view in a presidential address to a learned society, many years ago.[6] He was deeply impressed with a phenomenon that occurs every so often — the invention of a spontaneous, individual language by a child or a pair of children, a language unrelated to the tongue spoken in the household. Some children will persist up to school age, or even a little beyond it, in this vagary. Such observations led him to believe that man is by nature a language-making creature, and learns his "mother tongue" merely by the overwhelming force of suggestion, when he hears a ready-made language from earliest infancy. Under the primitive conditions of nomadic family life, he thought, it might well happen that a group of young

---

[5] W. N. Kellogg and L. A. Kellogg, *The Ape and the Child* (1933), p. 281. This passage and those from the same book quoted on pp. 111, 112, and 113, below, are reproduced by permission of the McGraw-Hill Book Co., publishers.

[6] "The Origin of Languages and the Antiquity of Speaking Man," *Proceedings of the American Association for the Advancement of Science*, XXXV (1887), 279–323.

children would be orphaned, alone in the wilderness; and where the climate was warm and food abundant, such a little company might survive. The younger children's language would become the idiom of the family. Rather ingeniously he develops this notion as an explanation of the many utterly unrelated languages in the world, their distribution, and the mystery of their origin. But the interesting content of his paper in the present connection is his underlying assumption that man makes languages instinctively.

"The plain conclusion," he says, "to which all examples point with irresistible force is, that the origin of linguistic stocks is to be found in what may be termed the language-making instinct of very young children." [7]

After citing a case of two children who constructed an entirely original language, he comments: "There is nothing in the example which clearly proves that the children in question would have spoken at all if they had not heard their parents and others about them communicating by oral sounds — *though we may, on good grounds* (as will be shown), *believe that they would have done so*." [8]

The last part of his statement embodies the "instinct theory"; and that, so far as we know, is — *mere* theory. What do we know of children who, without being deaf and therefore unaware even of their own voices, have grown up without the example of people using speech around them? We know very little, but that little serves here to give us pause.

There are a few well-authenticated cases on record of so-called "wild children," waifs from infancy in the wilderness, who have managed to survive by their own precocious efforts or the motherly care of some large animal. In regions where it was (or is) customary to expose undesired infants, babes in the wood are not a nine days' wonder. Of course they usually die of neglect very soon, or are devoured; but on a few known occasions the maternal instinct of a bear or a wolf has held the foundling more sacred than did man's moral law, and a child has grown up, at least to pre-adolescence, without human influence.

[7] *Ibid.*, p. 285.   [8] *Ibid.*, p. 286. Italics mine.

The only well-attested cases are Peter the Wild Boy, found in the fields near Hanover in 1723; [9] Victor, known as "the Savage of Aveyron," captured in that district of Southern France in 1799; [10] and two little girls, Amala and Kamala, taken in the vicinity of Midnapur, India, in 1920.[11] Several other "wild children" have been reported, but all accounts of them require considerable sifting, and some — like Lukas the Baboon Boy — prove to be spurious. Even of the ones here mentioned, only Victor has been scientifically studied and described. One thing, however, we know definitely about all of them: *none of these children could speak in any tongue, remembered or invented.* A child without human companions would, of course, find no response to his chattering; but if speech were a genuine instinct, this should make little difference. Civilized children talk to the cat without knowing that they are soliloquizing, and a dog that answers with a bark is a good audience; moreover, Amala and Kamala had each other. Yet they did not talk. Where, then, is "the language-making instinct of very young children"?

It probably does not exist at all. Language, though normally learned in infancy without any compulsion or formal training, is none the less a product of sheer learning, an art handed down from generation to generation, and where there is no teacher there is no accomplishment. Despite the caprices of the children cited by Professor Hale, it is fairly certain that these little inventors would *not* have talked at all if they had not heard their elders speaking. Whatever talent it is that helps a baby to learn a language with three or four times (or any number of times!) the ease of an adult, this talent is apparently not a "speech instinct." We have no birthright to vocabularies and syntaxes.

This throws us back upon an old and mystifying problem. If we find no prototype of speech in the highest animals, and

[9] See Henry Wilson, *Wonderful Characters*, 2 vols. (1821), vol. II; also J. Burnett, Lord Monboddo, *Of the Origin and Progress of Language*, 6 vols. (1773), vol. I.

[10] See E. M. Itard, *The Savage of Aveyron* (English translation 1802).

[11] See Arnold Gesell, "The Biography of a Wolf-Child," *Harper's Magazine*, January 1941.

man will not say even the first word by instinct, then how did all his tribes acquire their various languages? Who began the art which now we all have to learn? And why is it not restricted to the cultured races, but possessed by every primitive family, from darkest Africa to the loneliness of the polar ice? Even the simplest of practical arts, such as clothing, cooking, or pottery, is found wanting in one human group or another, or at least found to be very rudimentary. Language is neither absent nor archaic in any of them.

The problem is so baffling that it is no longer considered respectable. There is a paragraph of Sapir's in the *Encyclopedia of Social Sciences*, repudiating it on excellent grounds. But in the very passage that warrants the despair of the philologists, he justifies the present philosophical study in its hopefulness, so I quote his words for their peculiar relevance:

"Many attempts have been made to unravel the origin of language but most of these are hardly more than exercises of the speculative imagination. Linguists as a whole have lost interest in the problem and this for two reasons. In the first place, it has come to be realized that there exist no truly primitive languages in a psychological sense. . . . In the second place, our knowledge of psychology, particularly of the symbolic process in general, is not felt to be sound enough to help materially with the problem of the emergence of speech. It is probable that the origin of language is not a problem that can be solved out of the resources of linguistics alone but that it is essentially a particular case of a much wider problem of the genesis of symbolic behavior and of the specialization of such behavior in the laryngeal region which may be presumed to have had only an expressive function to begin with. . . .

"The primary function of language is generally said to be communication. . . . The autistic speech of children seems to show that the purely communicative aspect of language has been exaggerated. It is best to admit that language is primarily a vocal actualization of the tendency to see reality symbolically, that it is precisely this quality which renders it a fit instrument for communication and that it is in the actual

give and take of social intercourse that it has been complicated and refined into the form in which it is known today." [12]

If it is true that "the tendency to see reality symbolically"
is the real keynote of language, then most researches into
the roots of the speech-function have been misdirected. Communication by sound is what we have looked for among the
apes; a *pragmatic use of vocables* is the only sign of word-
conception that we have interpreted to their credit, the only
thing we have tried to inspire in them, and in the "wild
children," to pave their way toward language. What we
should look for is *the first indication of symbolic behavior*,
which is not likely to be anything as specialized, conscious,
or rational as the *use* of semantic. Language is a very high
form of symbolism; presentational forms are much lower than
discursive, and the appreciation of meaning probably earlier
than its expression. The earliest manifestation of any symbol-
making tendency, therefore, is likely to be a mere *sense of
significance* attached to certain objects, certain forms or
sounds, a vague emotional arrest of the mind by something
that is neither dangerous nor useful in reality. The beginnings of symbolic transformation in the cortex must be
elusive and disturbing experiences, perhaps thrilling, but
very useless, and hard on the whole nervous system. It is
absurd to suppose that the earliest symbols could be *invented*;
they are merely *Gestalten* furnished to the senses of a creature
ready to give them some diffuse meaning. But even in such
rudimentary new behavior lies the first break with the world
of pure signs. Aesthetic attraction, mysterious fear, are probably the first manifestations of that mental function which in
man becomes a peculiar "tendency to see reality symbolically,"
and which issues in the *power of conception*, and the life-long
habit of speech.

Something very much like an aesthetic sense of import is
occasionally displayed by the anthropoid apes. It is like a
dawn of superstition — a forerunner of fetishes and demons,
perhaps. Especially in chimpanzees has this unrealistic atti-

[12] From Sapir, Article "Language," p. 159. By permission of The Macmillan
Company, publishers.

tude been observed by the most careful investigators, such as
Yerkes, Kellogg, and Köhler. Gua, the little chimpanzee who
was given the benefits of a human nursery, showed some very
remarkable reactions to objects that certainly had no direct
associations with her past experiences. For instance, the experimenters report that she stood in mortal fear of toadstools. She would run from them, screaming, or if cornered,
hide her face as though to escape the sight of them. This behavior proved to be elicited by all kinds of toadstools, and to
be based on no warning smell that might betray their poisonous properties (if, indeed, they are poisonous to apes.
Some animals, e.g. squirrels, seem to eat all kinds with im-
punity). Once the experimenters wrapped some toadstools
lightly in paper and handed her the package which, of course,
smelled of the fungi, and watched her reception of it.

"She accepts it without the slightest show of diffidence,
and even starts to chew some of the paper. But when the
package is unwrapped before her, she backs away appre-
hensively and will thereafter have none of the paper or its
contents. Apparently she is stimulated only visually by
toadstools." [13]

By way of comparison, toadstools were then offered to the
thirteen apes at the experimental station near by. Only four
of the subjects showed a similar fear, which they did not show
toward pinecones, sticks, etc. These four were two adult
females and two "children" three years old. Since the
reaction was not universal the observers concluded that it
was merely due to the chimpanzee's natural fear of the unknown. But surely pinecones are just as strange as toadstools
to a caged chimpanzee. Moreover, they say (in the very same
paragraph) that "Gua herself avoids both plucked and growing toadstools 2½ months after her original fright — or as
long as any specimens can be found in the woods. It is quite
likely that her reactions would have remained essentially
the same throughout the entire period of the research." [14]
Certainly the plants cannot have frightened her by their
novelty all summer long!

[13] Kellogg, *The Ape and the Child*, p. 177.   [14] *Ibid.*, p. 178.

The reaction on the part of the apes, limited as it was to about one subject in every three or four, has just that character of being common, yet individual, that belongs to aesthetic experiences. Some are sensitive to the sight, and the rest are not; to some of them *it seems to convey something* — to others it is just a thing, a toadstool or what you will.

Gua had other objects of unreasonable fear: a pair of blue trousers, of which she was afraid the first time she saw them and ever after; a pair of leather gloves; a flat and rusty tin can which she herself had found during her play outdoors. "It is difficult," say her observers, "to reconcile behavior of this sort with the ape's obvious preference for new toys." [15]

Yerkes and Learned have recorded similar oddities of simian behavior.

"The causes of fear or apprehension in the chimpanzees were various," they report, "and sometimes difficult to understand. Thus Panzee stood in dread of a large burlap bag filled with hay, which she was obliged to pass frequently. She would meet the situation bravely, however, holding her head high, stamping her feet, and raising her fur, as she passed with an air of injured dignity." [16]

Remembering some of the strange inanimate objects in the world of early childhood, one may wonder what sort of expression the burlap bag was showing to Panzee.

The best account of what may be termed "aesthetic frights" is given by Wolfgang Köhler, who tells, in *The Mentality of Apes*, how he showed his chimpanzees "some primitive stuffed toys, on wooden frames, fastened to a stand, and padded with straw sewn inside cloth covers, with black buttons for eyes. They were about thirty-five centimeters in height, and could in extremity be taken for oxen and asses, though most drolly unnatural. It was totally impossible to get Sultan, who at that time could be led by the hand outside,

[15] *Ibid.*, p. 179.
[16] R. M. Yerkes and B. Learned, *Chimpanzee Intelligence and its Vocal Expression* (1925), p. 143.

near these small objects, which had so little real resemblance to any kind of creature. . . . One day I entered their room with one of these toys under my arm. Their reaction-times may be very short; for in a moment a blacker cluster, consisting of the whole group of chimpanzees, hung suspended to the farthest corner of the wire roofing; each individual tried to thrust the others aside and bury his head deep among them." [17]

His comment on these events is simple and cogent.

"It is too facile an explanation of these reactions to assume that everything new and unknown appears terrible to these creatures. . . . New things are not necessarily frightful to a chimpanzee, any more than to a human child; certain inherent qualities are requisite to produce this special effect. But, as the examples cited above prove, any marked resemblance to the living foes of their species does not seem at all essential, and it almost seems as though the immediate impression of something exceptionally frightful could be conveyed in an even higher degree by *constructing* something frightful, than by any living animal (with the possible exception of snakes). For us human beings as well, many ghost-forms and specters, with which no terrible *experience* can be individually connected, are much more uncanny than certain very substantial dangers which we may easily have encountered in daily life." [18]

Not only fear, but also delight or comfort may be inspired in these animals by objects that have no biological significance for them; thus Gua, who was so attached to Mr. Kellogg that she went into tantrums of terror and grief whenever he left the house, could be comforted by being given his pair of coveralls. "This she would drag around with her," the account reads, "as a fetish of protection until his return. . . . Occasionally, if it was necessary for him to go away, the leave-taking could be accomplished without emotional display on the part of Gua if the coveralls were given her before the time of departure." [19]

Here certainly is a case where the object is *significant*.

---

[17] Page 333.   [18] Köhler, *The Mentality of Apes*, p. 334.
[19] Kellogg, *op. cit.*, p. 160.

Superficially it reminds one of a dog's recognition of his master's clothes. But whereas a dog is prompted to the action of seeking the possessor of them, Gua let the possessor go out and contented herself with the proxy. Therein lies the difference. Gua was using the coveralls even in his presence as a help to her imagination, which kept him near whether he went out or not.

Köhler describes how the chimpanzees will hoard perfectly useless objects and carry them between the lower abdomen and the upper thigh, a sort of natural trouser pocket, for days on end. Thus Tschego, an adult female, treasured a stone that the sea had rounded and polished. "On no pretext," he says, "could you get the stone away, and in the evening the animal took it with it to its room and its nest." [20]

No one knows what made the stone so valuable to Tschego; we cannot say that it was *significant*, as we can in the case of Gua's keepsake. But certainly an object which is aesthetically satisfying or horrifying is a good candidate for the office of fetish or bogie, as the case may be. An ape that can transfer the sense of her master's presence to a memento of him, and that reacts with specific emotions to the sheer quality of a perception, certainly is nervously organized above the level of purely realistic conditioned response. It is not altogether surprising, therefore, to find even more definite traces of symbolic behavior in the chimpanzee — this time a real preparation for the function of *denotation*, which is the essence of language.

This behavior is the performance of symbolic acts — acts that really seem to epitomize the creature's apprehension of a state of affairs, rather than to be just a symptom of emotion. The difference between a symbolic and a symptomatic act may be illustrated by contrasting the intentional genuflexion of a suppliant with the emotional quaver of his voice. There is a convention about the former, but not about the latter. And the *conventional expression* of a feeling, an attitude, etc., is the first, the lowest form of *denotation*. In a conventional attitude, something is summed up, understood, and

[20] Köhler, *The Mentality of Apes*, p. 99.

consciously conveyed. So it is deeply interesting that both Köhler and Kellogg have observed in their apes quite unmistakable cases of symbolic (not signific) gesture. Köhler reports that when a young chimpanzee would greet Tschego, it would put its hand into her lap. "If the movement of the arm will not go so far," he says, "Tschego, when in a good mood . . . will take the hand of the other animal, press it to her lap, or else pat it amicably. . . . She will press our hand to just that spot between her upper thigh and lower abdomen where she keeps her precious objects. She herself, as a greeting, will put her huge hand to the other animal's lap or between their legs and she is inclined to extend this greeting even to men." [21]

Here we certainly have the dawn of a conventional expression of good-will. But a still more clearly significant act is described by the Kelloggs in their account of Gua: that is the kiss of forgiveness. Kissing is a natural demonstration on the part of chimpanzees, and has an emotional value for them. In her human surroundings the little ape soon employed it in an unequivocally conscious way.

"She would kiss and offer her lips in recompense for small errors many times a day. . . . Thereafter she could be put down again and would play, but unless the ritual had been satisfactorily completed she would not be quiet or turn away until it had, or until some other climax superseded it." [22]

The upshot of all these considerations is that the tendency to a symbolic transformation of experience, the primary requisite for speech, is not entirely wanting in the ape, though it is as rudimentary as the rest of his higher functions — his perception of causal relations, for instance. If we take symbolic representation, rather than communication, as the criterion of a creature's capacity for language, we see that the chimpanzee, at least, is in some measure prepared; he has a rudimentary capacity for it.[23] Yet he definitely has no speech.

[21] *Loc. cit., infra.*   [22] Kellogg, *op. cit.,* p. 172.
[23] For a detailed study of chimpanzee behavior, see Köhler, *The Mentality of Apes, passim*; for a general evaluation of the findings, the appendix, pp. 281–342, "Some Contributions to the Psychology of Chimpanzees."

He makes no stumbling attempts at words, as he does at using tools, decorating his body, dancing and parading, and other primitive pursuits. He is conceptually not far from the supreme human achievement, yet never crosses the line. What has placed this absolute barrier between his race and ours?

Chiefly, I think, one difference of natural proclivities. The ape has no instinctive desire to babble in babyhood. He does not play with his mouth and his breath as human infants do; there is no crowing and cooing, no "goo-goo" and "ba-ba" and "do-de-da" in his otherwise uproarious nursery. Consequently there are no sounds and syllables that please or frighten him by their sheer aesthetic character, as he is pleased, frightened, or comforted by purely phenomenal sights. Oddly enough, it is just because all his utterances have *signification* — all are pragmatic or emotional — that none of them ever acquire *significance*. He does not even imitate sounds for fun, as he imitates gestures, and gravely mimics practices that have no utility for him.

This mutism of the great apes has been little realized by people who have not actually studied their habits; in fact, our satirists have made much of the supposedly simian trait of constant unsolicited chatter. "Heavens, what a genius for tongues these simians have!" said Clarence Day in one of his clever books. And assuming that we are descended from such arboreal geniuses, he comments on our political problems: "The best government for simians seems to be based on a parliament: a talk-room, where endless vague thoughts can be warmly expressed. This is the natural child of those primeval sessions that gave pleasure to apes." [24] And even Kipling, who has lived in a land where monkeys and apes are wild, did not observe that their chatter (when they do chatter) is no more imitative than the "ch-ch-ch-chee" of an angry squirrel; if he had, we might be the poorer by missing that delightful parody on human loquacity, the council-scene in Cold Lairs.

A genuine symbol can most readily originate where some

[24] *This Simian World* (1920), p. 69.

object, sound, or act is provided which has no *practical* meaning, yet tends to elicit an emotional response, and thus hold
one's undivided attention. Certain objects and gestures appear to have this phenomenological, dissociated character for
some apes, as well as for man; sounds have it for man alone.
They annoy or please him even when they are not signs of
anything further; they have an inherently interesting character. Add to this the fact that man spontaneously produces
random syllables in infancy, whereas the ape does not, and
it is immediately apparent that verbal symbols are easily
available to the one and very remote and unnatural to the
other. Man, though undoubtedly a simian, must trace his
descent from a vocalizing race — a genus of ape, perhaps, in
which the rudiments of symbolic conception, that apparently
are dawning in the chimpanzee, were coupled with an instinctive tendency to produce sounds, to play with the vocal
apparatus.

Furness succeeded in teaching a young orang-utan two
words, which it certainly appeared to use intelligently. Unfortunately for science, as well as for the ape, it died five
months after this achievement, so we do not know how much
further it might have gone on the road to Parnassus. But the
experimenter had little confidence, despite his success. His
chief obstacle was not the subject's lack of understanding,
but of instinctive response, of any tendency to imitate his
mouthings and articulations. Its lips had to be moved by
hand instead of by example. Once it learned the trick, it
soon had the words; but *the trick was something it would
never in the world have thought of by itself.*[25] For this reason,

[25] Furness' own account of this training is worth repeating here. His own
estimate of his success seems to me too modest, considering the difference
in learning-time of the first word and the second. For he says: "It seems well-
nigh incredible that in animals otherwise so close to us physically there
should not be a rudimentary speech-center in the brain which only needed
developing. I have made an earnest endeavor and am still endeavoring, but
I cannot say that I am encouraged.

"In teaching articulate speech I found the first difficulty to be overcome
in both the orang and the chimpanzee is their lack of use of lips or tongue
in making their natural emotional cries.

". . . In the case of the orang-utan it took at least six months to teach

if for no other, it is unlikely that the descendants of our great apes, ten thousand years hence, will hold parliaments (the prognosis is better for World Fairs). The apes will not evolve verbal symbolism because they do not instinctively supply themselves with verbal material, interesting little phonetic items that can acquire conventional meanings because they carry no natural messages.

The notion that the essence of language is the formulation and expression of conceptions rather than the communication of natural wants (the essence of pantomime) opens a new vista upon the mysterious problem of origins. For its beginnings are not natural adjustments, ways to means; they are purposeless lalling-instincts, primitive aesthetic reactions, and dreamlike associations of ideas that fasten on such material. The preparations for language are much lower in the rational scale than word-uses; they can be found below the evolutionary level of any communication by sounds.

---

her to say 'Papa.' This word was selected not only because it is a very primitive sound, but also because it combined two elements of vocalization to which orang-utans and chimpanzees are . . . unaccustomed, namely: the use of lips and an expired vowel. . . ." Presumably, this latter fact precluded the occurrence of the "word" by accident, and the danger of interpreting as a "word" some mere natural sound. The teacher manipulated the ape's lips, and also made the motions and sounds for her with his own mouth.

"At the end of six months, one day of her own accord, out of lesson time, she said 'Papa' quite distinctly and repeated it on command. . . . She never forgot it after that and finally recognized it as my name. When asked 'Where is Papa?' she would at once point to me or pat me on the shoulder."

Once, while being carried into the water, "she was panic-stricken; she clung with her arms about my neck; kissed me again and again and kept saying 'Papa! Papa! Papa!' Of course, I went no further after that pathetic appeal."

Her next word was "cup." The greatest art was needed to teach her the purely physical trick of pronouncing k with an open vowel, ka; but once this was learned, "after a few lessons when I showed her the cup and asked 'What is this?' she would say cup very plainly. Once when ill at night she leaned out of her hammock and said 'cup, cup, cup,' which I naturally understood to mean that she was thirsty and which proved to be the case. I think this showed fairly conclusively that there was a glimmering idea of the connection of the word with the object of her desire." (Furness, "Observations on the Mentality of Chimpanzees and Orang-Utans," pp. 281–284.)

Once *the idea of the spoken word* was awakened in the ape, which awakening took all of six months, the learning of a second word was chiefly a matter of conquering the unnaturalness of the physical process. Who knows how far this development might have gone if the subject had lived?

Moreover, this originally impractical, or better, *conceptual,* use of speech is borne out by the fact that all attempts to teach apes or the speechless "wild children" to talk, by the method of making them ask for something, have failed; whereas all cases where the use of language has dawned on an individual, simian or human, under such difficult circumstances, have been independent of the practical use of the word at the moment. Helen Keller's testimony has already been cited (pp. 62–63); after all her teacher's efforts in formal daily lessons to make the child *use* words like "cup" and "doll" to obtain the denoted objects, the significance of the word "water" suddenly burst upon her, not when she needed water, but when the stream gushed over her hand! Likewise, Yerkes' efforts to make Chim use an articulate syllable to ask for a piece of banana all failed; he articulated no "word" resembling the speech of man, nor did he seem to establish a relation between the sound and any particular object.[26] Furness, on the other hand, carefully kept all practical interests out of his experiment. He tried only to associate an impression, a visual experience, with a word, so that by constant association the two should fuse, not as sign and result, but as name and image; and he has had the greatest success on record so far as I know.[27]

But the most decisive and, at the same time, pathetic evidence that the utilitarian view of language is a mistake, may be found in the story of Victor, the Savage of Aveyron, written by the young doctor who undertook to study and educate him. Since the boy always took notice when anyone exclaimed "Oh!" and even imitated the sound, Dr. Itard undertook to

[26] See Yerkes and Learned, *op. cit.*, p. 56: "The experimenter succeeded in training him to speak for food as a dog may readily be taught to do. This he did, however, not in imitation of the trainer but to secure the food."

[27] See Furness, *op. cit.*, p. 285: "As to a comprehension of the connection of spoken words with objects and actions both the orang-utan and the chimpanzee, I think, exceed any of our domestic animals; both of my anthropoids have been able to understand what I said to them, more intelligently than any professionally trained animals I have ever seen. In their education the enticement of food has never been used as an incentive to action, and praise and petting have been the only rewards. In other words my object has been to endeavor to make them show signs of thought rather than a perfunctory performance of tricks."

make him use the word *"eau"* as a *sign* when he wanted water; but this attempt failed because he used every sign *but* the vocal one, and water could not be indefinitely withheld to force the issue. So a second attempt was made with the word *"lait,"* of which Itard gives the following account:

"The fourth day of this, my second experiment, I succeeded to the utmost of my wishes; I heard Victor pronounce distinctly, in a manner, it must be confessed, rather harsh, the word *lait*, which he repeated almost incessantly; it was the first time that an articulate sound had escaped his lips, and of course I did not hear it without the most lively satisfaction. I nevertheless made afterwards an observation, which deduced very much from the advantage which it was reasonable to expect from the first instance of success. It was not till the moment, when, despairing of a happy result, I actually poured the milk into the cup which he presented to me, the word *lait* escaped him again, with evident demonstrations of joy; and it was not till after I had poured it out a second time, by way of reward, that he repeated the expression. It is evident from hence, that the result of the experiment was far from accomplishing my intentions; the word pronounced, instead of being the sign of a want, it appeared, from the time in which it was articulated, to be merely an exclamation of joy. If this word had been uttered before the thing that he desired had been granted, my object would have been nearly accomplished: then the true sense of speech would have been soon acquired by Victor; a point of communication would have been established between him and me, and the most rapid progress must necessarily have ensued. Instead of this I had obtained only an expression of the pleasure which he felt, insignificant as it related to himself, and useless to us both. . . . It was generally only during the enjoyment of the thing, that the word *lait* was pronounced. Sometimes he happened to utter it before, and at other times a little after, but always without having any view in the use of it. I do not attach any more importance to his spontaneous repetition of it, when he happens to wake during the course of the night." [28]

[28] *The Savage of Aveyron,* pp. 93–96.

Another word which Victor acquired quite spontaneously was "Li," which Itard identifies as the name of a young girl, Julie, who stayed at the house for several weeks, to Victor's great delight; but this word he uttered to himself, all the time, and "even during the night, at those moments when there is reason to believe that he is in a profound sleep," so no importance was attached to it as a sign of reason.

Unfortunately, the young doctor was such a faithful disciple of Locke and Condillac that after his "failure" with the word *"lait"* he gave up the attempt to teach the Wild Boy spoken language, and tried to instruct him in the deaf-mutes' alphabet instead. Victor picked up a few spoken words, subsequently, by himself; but as he merely said them when he contemplated their objects with joy or sorrow, not when he *lacked* anything, no one paid much attention to these "mere exclamations" or made response to them.

Young children learn to speak, after the fashion of Victor, by constantly using words to bring things *into their minds,* not *into their hands.* They learn it fully whether their parents consciously teach them by wrong methods or right or not at all. Why did Victor not defy the doctor's utilitarian theories and learn language by the babbling method?

Because he was already about twelve years old, and the lalling-impulse of early childhood was all but completely outgrown. The tendency to constant vocalization seems to be a passing phase of our instinctive life. If language is not developed during this period, the individual is handicapped — like the apes — by a lack of *spontaneous phonetic material* to facilitate his speech experiments. The production of sounds is conscious then, and is used economically instead of prodigally. Victor did not articulate to amuse himself; his first word had to be stimulated. Wild Peter, we are told, never babbled to himself, though he sang a great deal; Kamala, the surviving little "wolf-girl" found at Midnapur, had learned about forty words at the end of six years in human surroundings, and formed sentences of two or three words; but even with this vocabulary, which would serve a three-year-old to carry on incessant conversations, Kamala *never talked unless she was spoken to.*[29] The impulse to chatter had been outgrown without being exploited for the acquisition of language.

In a social environment, the vocalizing and articulating instinct of babyhood is fostered by response, and as the sounds become symbols their use becomes a dominant habit. Yet the passing of the *instinctive phase* is marked by the fact that a great many phonemes which do not meet with response are completely lost.[30] Undoubtedly that is why children, who have not entirely lost the impulse to make random sounds which their mother tongue does not require, can so easily learn a foreign language and even master several at once, like many English youngsters born in India, who learn not only one vernacular, but speak with every native servant in whatever happens to be his dialect. A British psychologist, J. W. Tomb, has called attention to this phenomenon and concluded from it that children have a *linguistic intuition* which is lost later in life.[31]

But *intuition* is a slippery word, which has to cover, in this case, understanding, reproduction, and use — i.e. independent, analogous application — of words. It is hard to imagine any "intuition" that would bestow so many powers. It is better, perhaps, to say that there is an *optimum period of learning*, and this is a stage of mental development in which several impulses and interests happen to coincide: the

[29] The most trustworthy, because contemporary, accounts of the Midnapur children are probably the brief notes published in the *American Journal of Psychology* by Kellogg and Squires. See P. C. Squires, "'Wolf-Children' of India," XXXVIII (1927), 313–315; W. N. Kellogg, "More About the 'Wolf-Children' of India," XLII (1931), 508–509, and "A Further Note on the 'Wolf-Children' of India," XLV (1934), 149–150.

[30] Thus Israel Latif, speaking of the "lalling stage" of babyhood, says: "Many more sounds are produced by the infant during this period than are later used, at least in its own language. . . ." (To this effect he cites many authorities — Stern, Lorimer, K. C. More, Stanley Hall, Preyer, and Conradi.) "Now, out of this astonishingly rich and varied repertoire of sounds, those which are used by the child's elders are reënforced, and become habitual; the others cease to be uttered." — "The Physiological Basis of Linguistic Development and the Ontogeny of Meaning," *Psychological Review*, XLI (1934), 55–85, 153–176, 246–264. See esp. p. 60.

[31] See his article "On the Intuitive Capacity of Children to Understand Spoken Language," *British Journal of Psychology*, XVI (1925–26), 53–55.

lalling instinct, the imitative impulse, a natural interest in distinctive sounds, and a great sensitivity to "expressiveness" of any sort. Where any one of these characteristics is absent or is not synchronized with the others, the "linguistic intuition" miscarries.

The last requirement here mentioned is really the "higher function" of the mind that shines forth so conspicuously in human intercourse; yet it is the one that linguists and psychologists either overlook entirely, or certainly do not credit to early childhood. The peculiar impressionability of childhood is usually treated under the rubric of attention to exact colors, sounds, etc.; but what is much more important, I think, is the child's tendency to read a vague sort of *meaning* into pure visual and auditory forms. Childhood is the great period of synaesthesia; sounds and colors and temperatures, forms and feelings, may have certain characters in common, by which a vowel may "be" of a certain color, a tone may "be" large or small, low or high, bright or dark, etc. There is a strong tendency to form associations among sensa that are not practically fixed in the world, even to confuse such random impressions. Most of all, the over-active feelings fasten upon such flotsam material. Fear lives in pure *Gestalten*, warning or friendliness emanates from objects that have no faces and no voices, no heads or hands; for they all have "expression" for the child, though not — as adults often suppose — anthropomorphic form. One of my earliest recollections is that chairs and tables *always kept the same look*, in a way that people did not, and that I was awed by the sameness of that appearance. They *symbolized* such-and-such a mood; even as a little child I would not have judged that they *felt* it (if any one had raised such a silly question). There was just such-and-such a look — dignity, indifference, or ominousness — about them. They continued to convey that silent message no matter what you did to them.

A mind to which the stern character of an armchair is more immediately apparent than its use or its position in the room, is over-sensitive to expressive forms. It grasps analogies that a riper experience would reject as absurd. It fuses sensa that practical thinking must keep apart. Yet it is just this crazy play of associations, this uncritical fusion of impressions, that exercises the powers of symbolic transformation. To project feelings into outer objects is the first way of symbolizing, and thus of *conceiving* those feelings. This activity belongs to about the earliest period of childhood that memory can recover. The conception of "self," which is usually thought to mark the beginning of actual memory, may possibly depend on this process of symbolically epitomizing our feelings.

From this dawn of memory, where we needs must begin any first-hand record, to adolescence, there is a constant decrease in such dreamlike experience, a growing shift from subjective, symbolic, to practical associations. Sense-data now keep to their categories, and signify further events. Percepts become less weighted with irrelevant feeling and fantasy, and are more readily ranged in an objective order. But if in theory we count backward over the span which none of us recollect, and which covers the period of learning language — is it likely that the mind was realistic in its earlier phase? Is it not probable that association was even more trivial, more ready, and that the senses fused more completely in yielding impressions? No experience belongs to any class as yet, in this primitive phase. Consider, now, that the vocal play of the infant fills his world with *audible actions,* the nearest and most completely absorbing stimuli, because they are both inner and outer, autonomously produced yet unexpected, inviting that *repetition* of accidental motions which William James deemed the source of all voluntary acts; intriguing, endlessly variable noises mysteriously connected with the child himself! For a while, at least, his idle experiments in vocalization probably fill his world.

If, now, his audible acts wake echoes in his surroundings — that is to say, if his elders reply to them — there is a growth of experience; for the baby appears to recognize, gradually, that the sound which happens there and comes to him, is the *same* as his lalling. This is a rudimentary abstraction; by that sameness he becomes aware of the tone, the product of his activity, which absorbs his interest. He repeats that sound rather than another. His ear has made its first judgment. A sound (such as "da-da," or "ma-ma," probably) has been *conceived*, and his diffuse awareness of vocalizing gives way to an apparently delightful awareness of a vocable.

It is doubtful whether a child who never heard any articulate sounds but his own would ever become conscious of different phonemes. Voice and uttered syllable and the feeling of utterance would probably remain one experience to him; the babbling period might come and go without his recognizing any *product* of his own activity. If this guess is correct, it is easy to understand why Victor and Wild Peter did not invent language, and were nearly, if not entirely, past the hope of acquiring it when they were socialized.

A new vocable is an outstanding *Gestalt*. It is a possession, too, because it may be had at will, and this itself makes it very interesting. Itard tells us that when Victor pronounced his first word he repeated it "almost incessantly"; as does every baby who has learned a new syllable. Moreover, an articulate sound is an entirely *unattached* item, a purely phenomenal experience without externally fixed relations; it lies wide open to imaginative and emotional uses, synaesthetic identifications, chance associations. It is the readiest thing in the world to become a symbol when a symbol is wanted. The next sharp and emotional arrest of consciousness, the next deeply interesting experience that coincides with hearing or uttering the vocable, becomes fixed by association with that one already distinct item; it may be the personality of the mother, the concrete character of the bottle, or what not, that becomes thus identified with the recognizable, producible sound; whatever it is, the baby's mind has hold of it through the word, and can invoke a conception of it by uttering the word, which has thus become the *name* of the thing.

For a considerable time, playing with conceptions seems to be the main interest and aim in speaking. To name things is a thrilling experience, a tremendous satisfaction. Helen Keller bears witness to the sense of power it bestows. Word and conception become fused in that early period wherein both grow up together, so that even in later life they are hard to separate. In a sense, language is conception, and conception is the frame of perception; or, as Sapir has put it, "Language is heuristic . . . in that its forms predetermine for us certain modes of observation and interpretation. . . . While it may be looked upon as a symbolic system which reports or refers or otherwise substitutes for direct experience, it does not as a matter of actual behavior stand apart from or run parallel to direct experience but completely interpenetrates with it, This is indicated by the widespread feeling, particularly among primitive people, of that virtual identity or close correspondence of word and thing which leads to the magic of spells. . . . Many lovers of nature, for instance, do not feel that they are truly in touch with it until they have mastered the names of a great many flowers and trees, as though the primary world of reality were a verbal one and as though one could not get close to nature unless one first mastered the terminology which somehow magically expresses it." [32]

The fact is that our primary world of reality *is* a verbal one. Without words our imagination cannot retain distinct objects and their relations, but out of sight is out of mind. Perhaps that is why Köhler's apes could use a stick to reach a banana outside the cage so long as the banana and the stick could be seen in one glance, but not if they had to turn their eyes away from the banana to see the stick. Apparently they could not look at the one and *think of* the other.[33] A child who had as much practical initiative as the apes, turning away from the coveted object, yet still murmuring "banana," would have seen the stick in its instrumental capacity at once.

The transformation of experience into concepts, not the elaboration of signals and symptoms, is the motive of language. Speech is through and through symbolic; and only sometimes signific. Any attempt to trace it back entirely to

[32] From Sapir, Article "Language," p. 157, by permission of The Macmillan Company, publishers.   [33] Köhler, *The Mentality of Apes*, p. 37.

the need of communication, neglecting the formulative, abstractive experience at the root of it, must land us in the sort of enigma that the problem of linguistic origins has long presented. I have tried, instead, to trace it to the characteristic human activity, symbolic transformation and abstraction, of which pre-human beginnings may perhaps be attributed to the highest apes. Yet we have not found the commencement of language anywhere between their state and ours. Even in man, who has all its prerequisites, it depends on education not only for its full development, but for its very inception. How, then, did it ever arise? And why do all men possess it?

It could only have arisen in a race in which the lower forms of symbolistic thinking — dream, ritual, superstitious fancy — were already highly developed, i.e. where the process of symbolization, though primitive, was very active. Communal life in such a group would be characterized by vigorous indulgence in purely expressive acts, in ritual gestures, dances, etc., and probably by a strong tendency to fantastic terrors and joys. The liberation from practical interests that is already marked in the apes would make rapid progress in a species with a definitely symbolistic turn of mind; conventional meanings would gradually imbue every originally random act, so that the group-life as a whole would have an exciting, vaguely transcendental tinge, without any definable or communicable body of ideas to cling to. A wealth of dance-forms and antics, poses and manoeuvres might flourish in a society that was somewhat above the apes' in non-practical interests, and rested on a slightly higher development of the symbolific brain-functions. There are quite articulated play-forms, verging on dance-forms, in the natural repertoire of the chimpanzees; [34] with but a little further elaboration,

---

[34] Even at the risk of letting Köhler's apes steal the show in this chapter, I must quote his account of these plays. Tschego and Grande developed a game of spinning round and round like dervishes, which found favor with all the others. "Any game of two together," says Köhler, "was apt to turn into this 'spinning-top' play, which appeared to express a climax of friendly and amicable *joie de vivre*. The resemblance to a human dance became truly striking when the rotations were rapid, or when Tschego, for instance,

these would become most obvious material for symbolic expression. It is not at all impossible that *ritual*, solemn and significant, antedates the evolution of language.

In a vocalizing animal, such actions would undoubtedly be accompanied by purely fanciful sounds — wavering tones, strings of syllables, echoing shouts. Voice-play, which as an instinct is lost after infancy, would be perpetuated in a group by the constant stimulation of response, as it is with us when we learn to speak. It is easy enough to imagine that young human beings would excite each other to shout, as two apes excite one another to jump, rotate, and strike poses; and the shouting would soon be formalized into song. Once the vocal habits are utilized, as in speech or song, we know that they do not become lost, but are fixed as a life-long activity. In a social group, the infantile lalling-instinct would be constantly reinforced, and instead of being outgrown, would become conventionalized in social play-forms. "Never a nomadic horde in the wilderness, but must already have had its songs," says Wilhelm von Humboldt, "for man as a species is a singing creature. . . ." [35] Song, the formalization of voice-play, probably preceded speech.

Jespersen, who is certainly one of our great authorities on language, suggests that speech and song may well have sprung from the same source (as Herder and Rousseau, without

stretched her arms out horizontally as she spun round. Tschego and Chica — whose favorite fashion during 1916 was this 'spinning' — sometimes combined a forward movement with the rotations, and so they revolved slowly round their own axes and along the playground.

"The whole *group* of chimpanzees sometimes combined in more elaborate *motion-patterns*. For instance, two would wrestle and tumble near a post; soon their movements would become more regular and tend to describe a circle round the post as a center. One after another, the rest of the group approach, join the two, and finally march in an orderly fashion round and round the post. The character of their movements changes; they no longer walk, they trot, and as a rule with special emphasis on one foot, while the other steps lightly; thus a rough approximate rhythm develops, and they tend to 'keep time' with one another. . . .

"It seems to me extraordinary that there should arise quite spontaneously, among chimpanzees, anything that so strongly suggests the dancing of some primitive tribes." (*The Mentality of Apes*, pp. 326–327.)

[35] *Die sprachphilosophischen Werke Wilhelm von Humboldts* (ed. Steinthal, 1884), p. 289.

really scientific foundation, imagined long ago). "Word-tones were originally frequent, but meaningless," he observes; "afterwards they were dropped in some languages, while in others they were utilized for sense-distinguishing purposes." [36] Furthermore, he points out that in passionate speech the voice still tends to fluctuate, that civilization only reduces this effect by reducing passionate utterance, and that savages still use a sing-song manner of speaking; and in fine, he declares, "These facts and considerations all point to the conclusion that there was once a time when all speech was song, or rather when these two actions were not yet differentiated. . . ." [37]

Yet it is hard to believe that song was ever an essential form of communication. How, then, was language derived from it? He does not tell us; but the difficulty of tracing an instrument like language to a free exercise like song is minimized in his sagacious reflection: "Although we now regard the communication of thought as the main object of speaking, there is no reason for thinking that this has always been the case." [38]

Strangely enough, Professor Jespersen seems to be unacquainted with an essay by J. Donovan, "The Festal Origin of Human Speech," which appeared in the form of two articles in *Mind* as long ago as 1891–92,[39] and which develops, quite fully and logically, the very idea he advances. Probably the fact that it appeared in a philosophical journal caused it to escape the notice of philologists. Its thesis, however, is so well corroborated by Jespersen's more recent and perhaps more reliable findings, that I present it here as a very suggestive and arresting hypothesis; the sort of idea that throws light at least on the problem of human articulateness, once we accept the *Leitmotif* of symbolic activity, rather than intelligent signaling, as the key to language.

Donovan's theory is, in brief, that sound is peculiarly well

[36] *Language*, p. 418, n.
[37] *Ibid.*, p. 420.
[38] *Ibid.*, p. 437.
[39] Vol. XVI (O. S.), pp. 498–506, and vol. XVII, pp. 325–339.

adapted to become symbolic because our attention to it requires no utilitarian motive. "The passivity of the ear allowed auditory impressions to force themselves into consciousness in season and out of season, when they were interesting to the dominant desires of the animal and when they were not. These impressions got further into consciousness, so to speak, before desire could examine their right of entrance, than was possible for impressions which could be annihilated by a wink or a turn of the head." [40] Since noises have this intrinsic and commanding interest, and the ear cannot be closed, they were peculiarly well suited to become "free" items where they had no biological value, and to be utilized by the imagination in sheer play. Especially in the "play-excitement" following successful communal enterprise (one is reminded of the apes' outburst of pure *joie de vivre* culminating in a dervish-like spin), such noises as rhythmic beating and hand-clapping were used to emphasize the play-mood and keep it steady — for this primeval man was probably, like the ape, incredibly distractible. The voice could be used, like the drum, to attract attention and accentuate rhythm; and thus the force of a change of pitch to make some notes stand out (one in four, etc.) was naturally discovered. Being more variable than the drum, voices soon made patterns, and the long wandering melodies of primitive song became an integral part of communal celebration.

First the actions of the "dance" would tend to become pantomimic, reminiscent of what had caused the great excitement. They would become ritualized, and hold the mind to the celebrated event. In other words, there would be conventional modes of dancing appropriate to certain occasions, so intimately associated with *that kind of occasion* that they would presently uphold and embody the concept of it — in other words, there would emerge *symbolic gestures*.

The voice, used to accompany such ritual acts, would elaborate its own conventions; and in a babbling species, certain syllables would find favor above others and would give color to festal plays.

[40] Donovan, "The Festal Origin of Human Speech," part I, p. 499.

Now, the centering of certain festivities round particular individuals, human or other — death-dances round a corpse, triumph-dances round a captive female, a bear, a treasure, or a chief — would presently cause the articulate noises peculiar to such situations to become associated with that central figure, so that the sight of it would stimulate people to utter those syllables, or more likely *rhythmic groups of syllables*, even outside the total festive situation. "And every moment during which such objects, connected as they are with the natural appetites of the animal, could be dominated by the emotional strength of festal play, and kept, however dimly, in consciousness, without firing the train of passions natural to them (e.g. to food, females), would mean the melting away of a link in the chain which held the animals below the possibility of human development."[41]

"In the early history of articulate sounds they could make no meaning themselves, but they preserved and got intimately associated with the peculiar feelings and perceptions that came most prominently into the minds of the festal players during their excitement. Articulate sounds . . . could only wait while they entered into the order imposed on them by the players' wild imitations of actions, and then preserve them in that order.[42]

"Without the vestige of a conscious intention behind it,

[41] *Ibid.*, part II, p. 330. The importance here given to the festal as opposed to the impulsive spirit in the origination of speech stands in striking contrast to the opinion expressed by Markey, who also recognizes the probability of an emotional, perhaps ritual, source; in *The Symbolic Process* Markey writes: "Symbols must have developed only after long association had conditioned instinctive cries or sounds to specific behavior in which two or more individuals were involved. In order that the mnesic traces become sufficiently vivid and consistent to result in the necessary integration, a highly emotional state was probably necessary. While the festive group occasion of song and dance may have served as a background, it is probable that definite sex behaviour furnished the relatively similar, recurrent, and specific activity necessary for the conditioning process associated with a highly emotional facilitating state. Specific sounds being associated with this type of behaviour, would furnish a similar stimulus which could be produced and interchanged by each person" (p. 159). But specific sex behavior is just the sort of *overt* expression that obviates the need of imaginative consciousness and its symbolic expression.

[42] Donovan, *op. cit.*, part II, p. 332.

this impulse (the play) induced the players to dwell on some
sort of an image of an individual in relation to the actions
imitated, whilst rhythmic and articulate utterances were
absorbing ear and mind, and, at the same time, getting fixed
upon the perceptions which they were associated with repeatedly." Thus a rhythmic group of syllables conventionally
associated with the object or central figure of a certain type
of celebration — say, with a certain warrior — "would become
its vocal mark, and be uttered when any objects of nature
gave impressions which could, however faintly, touch the
springs of the latent mass of sensations belonging to the
festal imagining of the destroying warrior." [43]

This passage is interesting for two reasons: (1) because it
assumes that the original use of language lies in *naming,
fixating, conceiving* objects, so that the communicative use
of words is only a secondary one, a practical application of
something that has already been developed at a deeper psychological level; and (2) because it suggests the very early,
very primitive operation of *metaphor* in the evolution of
speech. The nature of metaphor is another topic which cannot be properly understood without a symbolistic rather
than a signalistic view of language; but to this matter we
will presently return.

"When particular syllables got fixed upon particular actions," Donovan continues, "they would be brought up with
them, and here two chief interests of the festal excitement
would begin to clash, the interest of significance, and that
belonging to the impulse to make the vocal apparatus produce the easiest possible enticements to the ear. . . . In the
familiar observation of travellers about 'the unmeaning inter-
jections scattered here and there to assist the metre' of savage
songs, as well as in the most polished alliterations, assonances,
rhymes, refrains and burthens, there can be no doubt that
we behold the demands for aural absorption trying to make
their way among syllables which have been fixed by significance." [44]

[43] *Ibid.*, part II, pp. 334–335.
[44] *Ibid.*, part II, p. 337.

Recent anthropological literature has certainly borne out the observations of the travellers he cites; we need only turn to Boas' statement, quoted by Jespersen,[45] that Indian song may be carried on purely rhythmic nonsense syllables, or "consist largely of such syllables, with a few interspersed words suggesting certain ideas and feelings; or it may rise to the expression of emotions connected with warlike deeds, with religious feeling, love, or even to the praises of the beauties of nature." [46]

The first symbolic value of words is probably purely connotative, like that of ritual; a certain string of syllables, just like a rite, embodies a concept, as "hallelujah" embodies much of the concept expressed in the Easter service. But "hallelujah" is not the name of any thing, act, or property; it is neither noun, verb, adjective, nor any other syntactical part of speech. So long as articulate sound serves only in the capacity of "hallelujah" or "alack-a-day," it cannot fairly be called language; for although it has connotation, it has no denotation. But denotation is the essence of language, because it frees the symbol from its original instinctive utterance and marks its deliberate *use*, outside of the total situation that gave it birth. A denotative word is related at once to a conception, which may be ever so vague, and to a *thing* (or event, quality, person, etc.) which is realistic and public; so it weans the conception away from the purely momentary and personal experience and fastens it on a permanent ele-

---

[45] Jespersen, *Language*, p. 437.

[46] The purely phonetic origin of song texts survives in our "hey-nonny-nonny" and "tralala"; Donovan remarks that such nonsense syllables have been relegated entirely to the choruses of our songs, and are no longer mixed with genuinely verbal elements; but in purely festal songs, such as drinking and cheering songs, we still find such conglomerations of words and babble as:

> "With a veevo, with a vivo,
> With a veevo-vivo-vum,
> Vum get a rat-trap bigger than a cat-trap,
> Vum get a cat-trap bigger than a rat-trap,
> Cannibal, cannibal, sizz-boom-bah,
> (College, college), rah rah rah!"

Nothing in the savages' repertoire could answer better to Boas' description, "nonsense syllables with a few interspersed words."

ment which may enter into all sorts of situations. Thus the
definiteness of sticks and stones, persons and acts and places,
creeps into the recollection and the anticipation of experience, as its symbols, with their whole load of imagery and
feeling, gradually become anchored to real objects.

The utterance of conception-laden sounds, at the sight of
things that exemplify one or another of the conceptions which
those sounds carry, is first a purely expressive reaction; only
long habit can fix an association so securely that the word
and the object are felt to belong together, so that the one is
always a reminder of the other. But when this point is
reached, the humanoid creature will undoubtedly utter the
sound in sport, and thus move the object into nearer and
clearer prominence in his mind, until he may be said to
grasp a conception of it by means of the sound; and *now the
sound is a word.*

In a sociable species this game would presumably become
a joint affair almost at once. The word uttered by one pre-
Adamite would evoke a fuzzy, individual conception in another; but if the word, besides stimulating that conception,
were tied up to the same *object* for the hearer as it was for
the speaker, the word would have a common meaning for
them both. The hearer, thinking his own thought of the
object, would be moved thereby to say the word, too. The
two creatures would look at one another with a light of
understanding dawning under their great brow-ridges, and
would say some more words, and grin at some more objects.
Perhaps they would join hands and chant words together.
Undoubtedly such a wonderful "fashion" would become
immensely popular.

Thus in a genuinely pre-human manner, and not by social
contract or practical forethought, articulate sounds with a
festal expressive value may have become *representative.* Of
course this is pure speculation; but all theory is merely
speculation in the light of significant facts. Linguists have
avowedly given it up, in this case, for lack of such facts; a
general study of symbolism may supply them, and yield at
least a plausible theory in place of the very unsatisfactory

current conviction that language simply *cannot* have begun in any thinkable way.

But another mystery remains. Given the word, and the thought of a thing through the word, how did language rise from a sheer atomic conglomeration of symbols to the state of a complex relational structure, a logical edifice, such as it is among all tribes and nations on earth? For language is much more than a set of symbols. It is essentially an organic, functioning *system*, of which the primary elements as well as the constructed products are symbols. Its forms do not stand alone, like so many monoliths each marking its one isolated grave; but instead, they tend to integrate, to make complex patterns, and thus to point out equally complex *relationships* in the world, the realm of their meanings.

This tendency is comprehensible enough if we consider the preëminence which a named element holds in the kaleidoscopic flow of sheer sense and feeling. For as soon as an object is denoted, it can be *held*, so that anything else that is experienced at the same time, instead of crowding it out, exists *with* it, in contrast or in unison or in some other definite way. If the ape who wants a banana beyond his cage could only keep "banana, banana," in his head while he looks behind him at the convenient bamboo, he could use the rod to fetch his lunch. But without language, relations are either taken for granted in action — as by a dog, for instance, who looks hopefully *inside* the garbage pail, or takes shelter from punishment *under* the sofa — or they cannot be experienced at all. The ape simply knew nothing about the relation of stick and fruit when their co-presence was not visible.

This phenomenon of *holding on to the object* by means of its symbol is so elementary that language has grown up on it. A word fixes something in experience, and makes it the nucleus of memory, an available conception. Other impressions group themselves round the denoted thing and are associatively recalled when it is named. A whole occasion may be retained in thought by the name of an object or a person that was its center. The one word "River" may bring back the excitement of a dangerous crossing, a flood, a rescue, or the thought of building a house at the water's edge. The name of a person, we all know, brings to mind any number of events in which he figured. That is to say, a mnemonic word establishes a *context* in which it occurs to us; and in a state of innocence we use it in the expectation that it will be understood with its context. A baby who says "cookie" means, and trusts his nurse to know, that he sees, or wants, or has a cookie; if he says "out" he may mean that he is going out, that someone has gone out, that the dog wants to go out, etc., and he confidently expects his utterance to be understood with its tacit context.

Carl Bühler has called this elementary stage the "empractic" use of language.[47] The context is the situation of the speaker in a setting visible to the hearer; at the point where their thinking is to converge, a word is used, to fix the crucial concept. The word is *built into* the speaker's action or situation, in a diacritical capacity, settling a doubt, deciding a response.[48]

The distinction between the novel predication in a statement and the merely qualifying situation, given by visible and demonstrable circumstance (Bühler calls it *das Zeigfeld*), or verbally by exposition (*das Symbolfeld*), was recognized fifty years ago by Philip Wegener; in a little book called *Untersuchungen über die Grundfragen des Sprachlebens* Wegener expounded the growth of explicit statement from such a matrix, such communication by mere key words, eked out by pointing and by their setting in an obvious state of affairs. He recognized two general principles of linguistic development: *emendation*, which begets syntactical forms of speech, and *metaphor*, the source of generality. The first

---

[47] See Bühler, *Sprachtheorie*, chap. iii, *passim*.

[48] "Where a diacritical verbal sign is built into the action, it frequently needs no surrounding framework or other verbal indicators. For in place of such substitute it is surrounded by that for which they are proxy, and is supported by it. That the patron of a restaurant intends to consume something . . . is thoroughly understood by his partner (the waiter). The customer uses a verbal sign . . . only at the moot point in his otherwise tacit, intelligible behavior, as a diacritical sign. He inserts it, and the ambiguity is removed; that is the *empractic* use of language." *Ibid.*, p. 158.

principle serves to solve the problem of structure, so I will briefly set it forth.

Since a word, in the elementary social use which babies and foreigners make of it, and which probably represents a primitive stage of its communicative function, is meant to convey a concept not of a mere object, but also of the part played by that object in a situation which is supposed to be "understood," such a single word is really, in meaning, a *one-word sentence*. But it requires a certain amount of good will and like-mindedness to understand the speaker of a one-word sentence. We always assume that our own attitude toward things is shared by our fellows, and needs only the "empractic" use of a vocable to designate our particular thought in that setting, until we find ourselves *misunderstood*. Then we supplement the lone verb or noun with demonstratives — little words like "da!" "his!" From such syllables, added as supplements to the one-word sentence, arise inflections, which indicate more specifically what the word-sentence asserts about the expressed concept. Wegener has traced interesting parallels between inflections and demonstratives. More and more vocables are needed to *modify* the original expression, and to accompany and emphasize gestures and attitudes; so the grammatical structure evolves by emendation of an ambiguous expression, and naturally follows quite closely the relational pattern of the situation that evokes it. In this way, the context of the primitive word-sentence is more and more adequately expressed in verbal terms. At first modifiers and identifiers follow the crucial word that expressed the required *predication* in too great haste. "Appositives and relative clauses are subsequent corrections of our deficient presentations."[49] Hence the cognate nature of relative and interrogative, or relative and demonstrative pronouns. All these auxiliary utterances Wegener calls the "exposition" of the original word, which contains the real "novelty" to be asserted. This exposition finally becomes the *verbal context* in which the assertion is made. When the speaker is fully aware of the context and

[49] Wegener, *Untersuchungen*, p. 34.

the need of stating it, his speech is full-fledged. As Wegener puts it, "Only the development of speech as an art and a science finally impresses on us the duty of rendering the exposition before the novel predication." [50]

Since language is grafted on a vocalizing tendency in immature humans and is kept up only by becoming habit, linguistic forms very easily become fixed, because they are habitual responses. The trick of accompanying all communication with words quickly becomes an ingrained custom; so that words without important meanings creep in simply to fill gaps in the vocal pattern, and utterances become *sentences* of certain standard forms. At the highest development of these language-making functions, the resultant systems are immensely inflected. Then separate items, or "roots," become conventionally attached to very bare items of conception, abstractable from the articulated whole; and the logic of language, which appears to us in our awareness of syntax, emerges as an amazing intellectual structure.

The significant feature of Wegener's theory is that it derives grammatical structure from the undifferentiated content of the one-word sentence, and the literal, fixed denotation of separate words from the total assertion by gradual crystallization, instead of trying to build the complexities of discursive speech out of supposed primitive "words" with distinctly substantive or distinctly relational connotations. No savage society of unintellectual hunters and squaws could ever *build* a language; they could only produce it by some such unconscious process as endless misunderstanding, modification, reduplication for emphasis (as we reduplicate baby words — "goody-goody," "naughty-naughty," "bye-bye," etc.) and "filling in" by force of a formal feeling based on habits.

The structure of language may, indeed, have grown up by gradual emendation, but not so its other essential value, *generality*. Even a contextual language is still primarily specific as long as the verbal exposition merely replaces the situation of an "empractically" used word, and the word is a *name*. Here we encounter the second, and I think more vital,

[50] Wegener, *Untersuchungen*, p. 40.

principle of language (and perhaps of all symbolism): Meta-phor.

Here again Wegener's study shows us a natural process, born of practical exigencies, effecting what ultimately proves to be an incomparable achievement. But to follow his reasoning it is necessary to go back to his conception of the nature of communication.

All discourse involves two elements, which may be called, respectively, the context (verbal or practical) and the novelty. The novelty is what the speaker is trying to point out or to express. For this purpose he will use any word that serves him. The word may be apt, or it may be ambiguous, or even new; the context, seen or stated, modifies it and determines just what it means.

Where a precise word is lacking to designate the novelty which the speaker would point out, he resorts to the powers of *logical analogy*, and uses a word denoting something else that is a presentational symbol for the thing he means; the context makes it clear that he cannot mean the thing literally denoted, and must mean something else symbolically. For instance, he might say of a fire: "It flares up," and be clearly understood to refer to the action of the fire. But if he says: "The king's anger flares up," we know from the context that "flaring up" cannot refer to the sudden appearance of a physical flame; it must connote the idea of "flaring up" as a *symbol* for what the king's anger is doing. We conceive the literal meaning of the term that is usually used in connection with a fire, but this concept serves us here as proxy for another which is nameless. The expression "to flare up" has acquired a wider meaning than its original use, to describe the behavior of a flame; it can be used metaphorically to describe whatever its *meaning* can symbolize. Whether it is to be taken in a literal or a metaphorical sense has to be determined by the context.

In a genuine metaphor, an image of the literal meaning is our symbol for the figurative meaning, the thing that has no name of its own. If we say that a brook is laughing in the sunlight, an idea of laughter intervenes to symbolize the spontaneous, vivid activity of the brook. But if a metaphor is used very often, we learn to accept the word in its metaphorical context as though it had a literal meaning there. If we say: "The brook runs swiftly," the word "runs" does not connote any leg-action, but a shallow rippling flow. If we say that a rumor runs through the town, we think neither of leg-action nor of ripples; or if a fence is said to run round the barnyard there is not even a connotation of changing place. Originally these were probably all metaphors but one (though it is hard to say which was the primitive literal sense). Now we take the word itself to mean *that which all its applications have in common*, namely *describing a course*. The great extent and frequency of its metaphorical services have made us aware of the basic concept by virtue of which it can function as a symbol in so many contexts; constant figurative use has generalized its sense.

Wegener calls such a word a "faded metaphor," and shows, in an argument too long and elaborate to be reproduced here, that all general words are probably derived from specific appellations, by metaphorical use; so that our literal language is a very repository of "faded metaphors."

Since the *context* of an expression tells us what is its sense — whether we shall take it literally or figuratively, and how, in the latter case, it is to be interpreted — it follows that the context itself must always be expressed literally, because it has not, in turn, a context to supplement and define its sense. Only the novel predication can be metaphorical. A discourse divorced from physical situations, i.e. a discourse in which the context is entirely expressed and not bound to "empractic" utterances, is not possible until some words have acquired fixed, general connotations, so that they may serve in a conventional, literal fashion, to render the *exposition* of the crucial assertion. "All words, therefore, which may be logical subjects (of predications) and hence expository," says Wegener, "have acquired this capacity only by virtue of their 'fading' in predicational use. And before language had any faded words to denote logical subjects, it could not render a situation by any other means than a demonstrative indication

of it in present experience. So the process of fading which
we have here adduced represents the bridge from the first
(one-word) . . . phase of language to the developed phase
of a discursive exposition." [51]

Metaphor is our most striking evidence of *abstractive seeing*, of the power of human minds to use presentational
symbols. Every new experience, or new idea about things,
evokes first of all some metaphorical expression. As the idea
becomes familiar, this expression "fades" to a new literal use
of the once metaphorical predicate, a more general use than
it had before. It is in this elementary, presentational mode
that our first adventures in conscious abstraction occur. The
spontaneous similes of language are our first record of *simi-
larities* perceived. The fact that poverty of language, need
of emphasis, or need of circumlocution for any reason whatever,[52] leads us at once to seize upon a metaphorical word,
shows how natural the perception of common form is, and
how easily one and the same concept is conveyed through
words that represent a wide variety of conceptions. The use
of metaphor can hardly be called a conscious device. It is
the power whereby language, even with a small vocabulary,
manages to embrace a multimillion things; whereby new
words are born and merely analogical meanings become
stereotyped into literal definitions. (Slang is almost entirely
far-fetched metaphor. Although much of it is conscious and
humorous in intent, there is always a certain amount of
peculiarly apt and expressive slang which is ultimately taken
into the literary language as "good usage".)

One might say that, if ritual is the cradle of language,
metaphor is the law of its life. It is the force that makes
it essentially *relational*, intellectual, forever showing up new,
abstractable *forms* in reality, forever laying down a deposit of
old, abstracted concepts in an increasing treasure of general
words.

[51] Wegener, *Untersuchungen*, p. 54.

[52] For detailed studies of motives governing the use of metaphor, see
Heinz Werner, *Die Ursprünge der Metapher* (1919); Hermann Paul, *Prin-
ciples of the History of Language* (1888; German 1880); Alfred Biese, *Die
Philosophie des Metaphorischen* (1893).

The intellectual vocabulary grows with the progress of conceptual thinking and civilized living. Technical advances make demands on our language which are met by the elaboration of mathematical, logical, and scientific terminologies. Anthropomorphic metaphors are banned, and the philological laws of word-change become almost all-important in the production of further nomenclatures and usages. Meanings become more and more precise; wherefore, as Jespersen says, "The evolution of language shows a progressive tendency from inseparable conglomerations to freely and regularly combinable short elements." [53] Speech becomes increasingly discursive, practical, prosaic, until human beings can actually believe that it was invented as a utility, and was later embellished with metaphors for the sake of a cultural product called poetry.

One more problem invites our speculation: Why do all men possess language? The answer, I think, is that all men possess it because they all have the same psychological nature, which has reached, in the entire human race, a stage of development where symbol-using and symbol-making are dominant activities. Whether there were many beginnings of language or few, or even only one, we cannot tell; but wherever the first stage of speaking, the use of any denotative symbol, was attained, there the development of speech probably occurred with phenomenal speed. For the notion of giving something a *name* is the vastest generative idea that ever was conceived; its influence might well transform the entire mode of living and feeling, in the whole species, within a few generations. We ourselves have seen how such a notion as the power-engine can alter the world, how other inventions, discoveries, and adaptations crowd in its wake. We have watched human industry change from handicraft to mass production in every phase of life, within the memory of individuals. So with the advent of language, save that it must have been more revolutionary. Once the spark was struck, the light of reason was lit; an epoch of phenomenal novelty, mutation, perhaps even cerebral evolution, was initiated, as Man succeeded to the

[53] *Op. cit.*, p. 429.

futile simian that had been himself. Once there were speaking men on earth it would take utter isolation to keep any tribe from speaking. And unless there have been many cradles of mankind, such total isolation of a society, from pre-human aeons to historic times, is hard to imagine.

The general theory of symbolism here set forth, which distinguishes between two symbolic modes rather than restricting intelligence to discursive forms and relegating all other conception to some irrational realm of feeling and instinct, has the great advantage of assimilating all mental activity to reason, instead of grafting that strange product upon a fundamentally unintellectual organism. It accounts for imagination and dream, myth and ritual, as well as for practical intelligence. Discursive thought gives rise to science, and a theory of knowledge restricted to its products culminates in the critique of science; but the recognition of non-discursive thought makes it just as possible to construct a theory of *understanding* that naturally culminates in a critique of art. The parent stock of both conceptual types, of verbal and non-verbal formulation, is the basic human act of symbolic transformation. The root is the same, only the flower is different. So now we will leave language and all its variants, and turn, for other flowers, to other fields.

CHAPTER VI

Life-Symbols: The Roots of Sacrament

IF language is born, indeed, from the profoundly sym-bolific character of the human mind, we may not be surprised to find that this mind tends to operate with symbols far below the level of speech. Previous studies have shown that even the subjective record of sense experience, the "sense-image," is not a direct copy of actual experience, but has been "projected," in the process of copying, into a new dimension, the more or less stabile form we call a picture. It has not the protean, mercurial elusiveness of real visual experience, but a unity and lasting identity that makes it an object of the mind's possession rather than a sensation. Furthermore it is not firmly and fixedly deter-mined by the pattern of natural phenomena, as real sensa-tions are, but is "free," in the same manner as the little noises which a baby produces by impulse and at will. We can call up images and let them fill the virtual space of vision between us and real objects, or on the screen of the dark, and dismiss them again, without altering the course of practical events. They are our own product, yet not part of ourselves as our physical actions are; rather might we compare them with our uttered words (save that they re-main entirely private), in that they are objects to us, things that may surprise, even frighten us, experiences that can be contemplated, not merely lived.

In short, images have all the characteristics of symbols. If they were weak sense-experiences, they would confuse the order of nature for us. Our salvation lies in that we do not normally take them for bona fide sensations, but attend to them only in their capacity of *meaning* things, being *images* of things — symbols whereby those things are conceived, re-membered, considered, but not encountered.

The best guarantee of their essentially symbolic function is their tendency to become metaphorical. They are not only capable of connoting the things from which our sense-experi-ence originally derived them, and perhaps, by the law of association, the context in which they were derived (as the sight of a bell may cause one to think of "ding-dong" and also of dinner), but they also have an inalienable tendency to "mean" things that have only a logical analogy to their primary meanings. The image of a rose symbolizes feminine beauty so readily that it is actually harder to associate roses with vegetables than with girls. Fire is a natural symbol of life and passion, though it is the one element in which nothing can actually live. Its mobility and flare, its heat and color, make it an irresistible symbol of all that is living, feeling, and active. Images are, therefore, our readiest instruments for abstracting concepts from the tumbling stream of actual im-pressions. They make our primitive abstractions for us, they are our spontaneous embodiments of general ideas.

Just as verbal symbolism has a natural evolution from the mere suggestive word or "word-sentence" of babyhood to the grammatical edifice we call a language, so presentational sym-bolism has its own characteristic development. It grows from the momentary, single, static image presenting a simple concept, to greater and greater units of successive images having reference to each other; changing scenes, even visions of things in motion,[1] by which we conceive the passage of events. That is to say, the first thing we *do* with images is to envisage a story; just as the first thing we do with words is to tell something, to make a statement.

Image-making is, then, the mode of our untutored think-ing, and stories are its earliest product. We think of things happening, remembered or imaginary or prospective; we see with the mind's eye the shoes we should like to buy, and the transaction of buying them; we visualize the drowning that

[1] Cf. M. Drummond, "The Nature of Images," *British Journal of Psychol-ogy*, XVII (1926), 1: 10–19.

almost happened by the riverbank. Pictures and stories are the mind's stock-in-trade. Those larger, more complex elements that symbolize events may contain more than merely visual ingredients, kinesthetic and aural and perhaps yet other factors, wherefore it is misleading to call them "story-images"; I will refer to them as "fantasies."

Like all symbols, fantasies are derived from specific experience; even the most elaborately monstrous ones go back to witnessed events. But the original perception — like any item that sticks in the mind — is promptly and spontaneously abstracted, and used symbolically to represent a whole *kind* of actual happening. Every process we perceive, if it is to be retained in memory, must record itself as a fantasy, an envisagement, by virtue of which it can be called up in imagination or recognized when it occurs again. For no actual process happens twice; only we may meet the same *sort* of occasion again. The second time we "know" already what the event is, because we assimilate it to the fantasy abstracted from the previous instance. It will not fit exactly, and it need not; the fantasy need only convey certain *general features*, the new case only exemplify these generalities in its own way, to make us apprehend a recurrence of a familiar event.

Suppose a person sees, for the first time in his life, a train arriving at a station. He probably carries away what we should call a "general impression" of noise and mass, steam, human confusion, mighty motion coming to heated, panting rest. Very possibly he has not noticed the wheels going round, but only the rods moving like a runner's knees. He does not instantly distinguish smoke from steam, nor hissing from squeaking, nor freight cars from windowed coaches, nor even boiler, cab, and coal car from each other. Yet the next time he watches a train pull in the process is familiar. His mind retains a fantasy which "means" the general concept, "*a* train arriving at *a* station." Everything that happens the second time is, to him, *like* or *unlike* the first time. The fantasy which we call his conception of a halting train gradually builds itself up out of many impressions; but its framework was abstracted from the very first instance, and made the later ones "familiar."

The symbolic status of fantasies (in this technical sense of action-envisagements) is further attested by the regularity with which they follow certain basic laws of symbols. Like words and like images, they have not only literal reference to concepts, but tend to convey metaphorical meanings. Events and actions, motions and emotions, are inexhaustible in our short lives; new experience overwhelms us continually; no mind can conceive in neat literal terms all the challenges and responses, the facts and acts, that crowd in upon it. Yet conception is its essential technique, and conception requires a language of some sort. Among our fantasies there is usually something, at least, that will do as a metaphor, and this something has to serve, just as the nearest word has to serve in a new verbal expression. An arriving train may have to embody nameless and imageless dangers coming with a rush to unload their problems before me. Under the pressure of fear and confusion and shrinking, I envisage the engine, and the pursuant cars of unknown content, as a first symbol to shape my unborn concepts. What the arriving train represents is the first aspect of those dangers that I can grasp. The fantasy that literally means a railroad incident functions here in a new capacity, where its literal generality, its applicability to trains, becomes irrelevant, and only those features that can symbolize the approaching future — power, speed, inevitable direction (symbolized by the track), and so forth — remain significant. The fantasy here is a figure; a metaphor of wordless cognition.

Metaphor is the law of growth of every semantic. It is not a development, but a principle. This is strikingly attested by the fact that the lowest, completely unintentional products of the human brain are madly metaphorical fantasies, that often make no literal sense whatever; I mean the riotous symbolism of dreams.

The first thing we instinctively strive to conceive is simply the experience of being alive. Life is a network of needs and fulfilments and further needs, with temporary frustrations here and there. If its basic needs are long unsatisfied, it ends. Our first consciousness is the sense of need, i.e. desire. Therefore our most elementary conceptions are of objects for desire.

The shapes and relations and names of such objects are unknown to the infant's mind. Food it knows, but not the source of food, beyond the mere touch and vague form of the mother's breast. Comfort and security, human nearness, light and motion — all these objects have neither substance nor fixed identity. The first images that sense impression begets in his mind have to serve for the whole gamut of his desires, for all things absent. Everything soft is a mother; everything that meets his reach is food. Being dropped, even into bed, is terror itself — the first definite form of insecurity, even of death (all our lives we speak of misfortune as a "fall"; we fall into the enemy's hands, fall from grace, fall upon hard times).

In the brief waking spells when his sense organs are learning to make report, when noises overcome his initial deafness and colors or light-spaces arrest his wandering focus, his infantile symbols multiply. Wish and fantasy grow up together. Since the proper function of his mind is conception, he produces ideas without number. He does not necessarily feel desire for everything he can think and dream; desire is only the power behind the mind, which goads it into action, and makes it productive. An overactive mind is uncritical, as a voracious appetite is unfastidious. Children mix dream and reality, fact and fiction, and make impossible combinations of ideas in their haste to capture *everything*, to conceive an overwhelming flood of experiences. Of course the stock of their imagery is always too small for its purpose, so every symbol has to do metaphorical as well as literal duty. The result is a dreamlike, shifting picture, a faery "world."

Something like this may be seen not only in our children, whose free fancy is somewhat hemmed by the literal logic of adults around them, but in primitive societies, where the best thought still bears a childlike stamp. Among certain peoples whom we call "savage," the very use of language exhibits a rampant confusion of metaphorical meanings clinging to every symbol, sometimes to the complete obscurance of any reasonable literal meaning. Cailliet,[2] who made a study of this phenomenon, calls this the "vegetative" stage of thought, likening the tremendous tangle of non-literal symbolism to a jungle where things choke each other in their overgrowth.[3] The cause for this sumptuous prodigality of symbols lies in the intellectual needs of an adolescent race. When new, unexploited possibilities of thought crowd in upon the human mind, the poverty of everyday language becomes acute. Apprehension outruns comprehension so far that every phrase, however homely and literal it may be in its traditional meaning, has a vague aura of further significance. Such a state of mind is peculiarly favorable to the development of metaphorical speech.[4]

It is characteristic of figurative images that their allegorical status is not recognized. Only a mind which can apprehend *both* a literal and a "poetic" formulation of an idea is in a position to distinguish the figure from its meaning. In spontaneous envisagement there is no such duality of form and content. In our most primitive presentations — the metaphorical imagery of dreams — it is the symbol, not its meaning, that seems to command our emotions. We do not know it as a symbol. In dream-experience we very often find some fairly commonplace object — a tree, a fish, a pointed hat, a staircase — fraught with intense value or inspiring the greatest terror. We cannot tell what makes the thing so important. It simply seems to be so in the dream. The emotional reaction is, of course, evoked by the idea embodied in that object, but so long as the idea lives only in this body

[2] Émile Cailliet, *Symbolisme et âmes primitives* (1936), chap. iv.

[3] The same figure was used by Jespersen (*Language*, p. 428) to describe the form-producing period of primitive language, and by Whitehead (*Symbolism*, p. 61) in speaking of undisciplined symbol-mongering.

[4] There are certain backward races which, like backward persons, seem to have become arrested in the age of their adolescence. They are no longer vigorously imaginative, yet have never outgrown the effect of that "vegetative" stage; so they have incorporated figurative speech in the genteel tradition of their social intercourse. Their metaphors are not new and revealing, they are conventional, and serve only to interfere with the progress of literal conception.

we cannot distinguish it from its symbolic incarnation which, to literal-minded common sense, seems trivial.

Primitive thought is not far removed from the dream level. It operates with very similar forms. Objects that could function as dream-symbols have a mysterious significance for the waking mind, too, and are viewed with emotion, even though they have never served a practical purpose for good or for evil. The Australian's *churinga,* the Egyptian's scarab, the charms which Greek women carried to the altar, are such objects of indescribable value, dream-symbols found and treasured in waking life. With their realistic presence, the imaginative process is carried over from dream to reality; fantasy is externalized in the veneration of "sacra."

The study of dreams gives us a clue to the deeper meaning of these bizarre holy articles: they are phallic symbols and death-symbols. We need not consult the psychoanalysts to learn this truth; any student of anthropology or archeology can assure us of it. Life and life-giving, death and the dead, are the great themes of primitive religion. Gods are at first merely emblems of the creative power; fetishes, trees, menhirs. Certain animals are natural symbols to mankind: the snake hidden in earth, the bull strong in his passion, the mysterious long-lived crocodile who metes out unexpected death. When, with the advance of civilization, their images are set up in temples or borne in processions, such images are designed to emphasize their symbolic force rather than their natural shapes. The snake may be horned or crowned or bearded, the bull may have wings or a human head.

Such sacra command a peculiar emotion, which is not the simple joy of possessing something advantageous, e.g. a strong weapon or a new slave; the "rejoicing" of a religious ceremonial is not a spontaneous delight which causes people to raise the cry of triumph, as we shout when we catch a big fish or win a game. The supposed power of the god to protect his worshipers would be no more apt to evoke cries of "hallelujah" than the tacitly accepted power of a father to protect his children. Our children live under the guarantee of our superior strength and have a sense of security in it, but they do not periodically burst into praises of it. Religious rejoicing is bound entirely to set occasions, when the god-symbol — which probably is always there, tucked away in its shrine — is brought forth and officially contemplated. Even this is not enough; someone leads the shouting and makes a demonstration of joy; gradually the feeling develops, and delight seizes the congregation. Their joy is not in an event, but in a presented idea. It centers round objects that are themselves quite passive, and useless for any other purpose than conveying the idea.

The power of conception — of "having ideas" — is man's peculiar asset, and awareness of this power is an exciting sense of human strength. Nothing is more thrilling than the dawn of a new conception. The symbols that embody basic ideas of life and death, of man and the world, are naturally sacred. But naive thinking does not distinguish between symbol and import; it sees only the physical *churinga* or the clay *thesmos*, or, where the symbol is not made by human art, but chosen among natural objects, it sees the actual snake or ibis, oak tree or *arbor vitae*. There is no explicit reason why sacredness belongs to such an object, only a strong feeling that in it the luck and hope and power of man is vested. The practical efficacy attributed to sacra is a dream-metaphor for the might of human ideation. Their "mightiness" is thought of as specific efficacy; whatever expresses Life is regarded as a source of life, whatever expresses Death as an agent of death. The savage's alleged stupidity about causal relations rests on this very profound law of mind, which is exemplified not only in primitive religions, but in our own pious beliefs, e.g. that the devil can be averted by holding up a little cross against him, or that a picture of the Virgin Mother protects a house against evil. Such notions rest on a natural identification of symbolic values with practical values, of the expressive with the physical functions of a thing. But this identification is too deeply grounded to be put aside as a "silly" mistake. It is symptomatic of our supreme and constant preoccupation with *ideas*, our spontaneous attention to expressive forms, that causes us to mix their importance with the importance of other activities by which life is carried on.

The contemplation of sacra invites a certain intellectual excitement — intellectual because it centers in a mental activity — the excitement of *realizing* life and strength, manhood, contest, and death. The whole cycle of human emotions is touched by such a contemplation. Undoubtedly the first outward show of sacred emotions is purely self-expressive, an unconscious issue of feelings into shouting and prancing or rolling on the earth, like a baby's tantrum; but soon the outburst becomes a habitual reaction and is used to *demonstrate*, rather than to relieve, the feelings of individuals. Lively demonstration makes an emotion contagious. Shout answers shout, the collective prancing becomes dancing. Even those who are not compelled by inner tension to let off steam just at this moment, fall into step and join the common cry.

But as soon as an expressive act is performed without inner momentary compulsion it is no longer *self-expressive*; it is expressive in the logical sense. It is not a sign of the emotion it conveys, but a symbol of it; instead of completing the natural history of a feeling, it denotes the feeling, and may merely bring it to mind, even for the actor. When an action acquires such a meaning it becomes a *gesture*.[5]

Genuine acts are completed in every detail unless they are forcibly interrupted, but gestures may be quite abortive imitations of acts, showing only their significant features. They are expressive forms, true symbols. Their aspect becomes fixed, they can be deliberately used to communicate an *idea* of the feelings that begot their prototypes. Because they are deliberate gestures, not emotional *acts*, they are no longer subject to spontaneous variation, but bound to an

[5] Cf. L. A. Reid, "Beauty and Significance," *Proceedings of the Aristotelian Society*, N.S. XXIX (1929), 123–154, esp. p. 144: "If an expression, which at first was automatic, is repeated for the sheer joy of expression, at that point it becomes æsthetic. . . . Anger enjoyed in being acted consciously is not mere instinctive anger, but dramatic (sometimes melodramatic) anger, a very different thing."

often meticulously exact repetition, which gradually makes their forms as familiar as words or tunes.

With the formalization of overt behavior in the presence of the sacred objects, we come into the field of *ritual*. This is, so to speak, a complement to the life-symbols; for as the latter present the basic facts of human existence, the forces of generation and achievement and death, so the rites enacted at their contemplation formulate and record man's response to those supreme realities. Ritual "expresses feelings" in the logical rather than the physiological sense. It may have what Aristotle called "cathartic" value, but that is not its characteristic; it is primarily an *articulation* of feelings. The ultimate product of such articulation is not a simple emotion, but a complex, permanent *attitude*. This attitude, which is the worshipers' response to the insight given by the sacred symbols, is an emotional pattern, which governs all individual lives. It cannot be recognized through any clearer medium than that of formalized gesture; yet in this cryptic form it *is* recognized, and yields a strong sense of tribal or congregational unity, of rightness and security. A rite regularly performed is the constant reiteration of sentiments toward "first and last things"; it is not a free expression of emotions, but a disciplined rehearsal of "right attitudes."

But emotional attitudes are always closely linked with the exigencies of current life, colored by immediate cares and desires, by specific memories and hopes. Since the sacra are consciously regarded not as symbols of Life and Death, but as life-givers and death-dealers, they are not only revered, but also besought, trusted, feared, placated with service and sacrifice. Their power is invoked for the salvation of worshipers in times of danger. They can break the drought, end famine, stay a pestilence, or turn the tide of battle. The sacred ark going up before the Children of Israel gives them their victory. Held by the Philistines, it visits disease on its captors. Its efficacy is seen in every triumph of the community, every attainment and conquest. Specific events as well as definite feelings become associated with a Holy of Holies, and seek expression round the altar.

This is the source of *mimetic* ritual. The memory of celebrated events is strong in the celebration that renders thanks
to the saving Power; it enters, perhaps quite unconsciously
at first, into the gestures and shouts traditionally conveying
such thanks. The story is retold, because it reveals the
character of the Holy One, and as the telling soon becomes
a formula, the gesticulations that accompany it become tradi-
·tional gestures, new bodily expressions that can be woven
into ritual patterns. The flourish of swords that accompanies
the recall of a great exploit is presently carried out at definite
points in the narrative, so that the congregation may join
in it, as it joins in shouts like "Hallelujah," "Iacchos," or
"Amen" at recognized periods. The gesture acquires a swing
and rhythm of its own so it can be performed in genuine
unison. At the end of the story it may be elaborated into a
long demonstration, a "sword-dance."

Another and even more obvious origin of mimetic rites
lies not in sacred story, but in supplication. Here conception
is even more vivid, more urgent than in memory; an act is
to be suggested and recommended to the only Being that
can perform it, the Holy One; the suppliants, in their eager-
ness to express their desire, naturally break into pantomime.[6]
Representations of the act mingle with gestures of entreaty.
And just as the expressive virtue of sacra is conceived as
physical virtue, so the symbolic power of mimetic rites is
presently regarded as causal efficacy; hence the world-wide
and world-old belief in sympathetic magic. It really sinks to
the inane conception of "magic" only when one assumes a
direct relation between the mimicked event and the expected
real one; in so far as the pantomime is enacted before a fetish,
a spirit, or God, it is intended to move this divine power to
act, and is simply a primitive prayer. We are often told
that savage religion begins in magic; but the chances are,
I think, that magic begins in religion. Its typical form — the

[6] Cf. W. W. Newell, "Ritual Regarded as the Dramatization of Myth,"
International Congress of Anthropology (1894), 237–245; also W. Matthews,
"Some Illustrations of the Connection between Myths and Ceremony," *ibid.*,
pp. 246–251.

confident, practical *use* of a formula, a brew, and a rite to achieve a physical effect — is the empty shell of a religious act. Confused, inferior minds may retain it, even in a society that no longer thinks in terms of hidden agency, but sees causally connected phenomena; and so we come to the absurd practice of a "magic" that is supposed to *defy* natural law.

Religion is a gradual envisagement of the essential pattern of human life, and to this insight almost any object, act, or event may contribute. There is no ingredient in ritual that may not also be found outside it. Sacred objects are not intrinsically precious, but derive their value from their religious use. Formalized expressive gesture occurs in the most casual social intercourse, in greetings, marks of deference, or mock defiance (like the grimaces school-children make behind the back of an unpopular teacher, mainly for each other's benefit). As for mimetic gestures, they are the current and often unconscious accompaniment of all dramatic imagination. It need not be of serious or important acts. Mimicry is the natural symbolism by which we represent activities to our minds. It is so obvious a semantic that even where no act is carried out, but every idea merely suggested, pantomime is universally understood. Victor the Wild Boy of Aveyron, and even Wild Peter who was less intelligent, could understand mimetic expression at once, without any training, though neither ever learned language.

Before a symbolic form is put to public religious use — before it serves the difficult art of presenting really profound ideas — it has probably had a long career in a much homelier capacity. Long before men perform *rites* which enact the phases of life, they have learned such acting in *play*. And the play of children is very instructive if we would observe the peculiarly intellectual (non-practical) nature of gesture. If its purpose were, as is commonly supposed, to *learn by imitation,* an oft-repeated enactment should come closer and closer to reality, and a familiar act be represented better than a novel one; instead of that we are apt to find no attempt at *carrying out* the suggested actions of the shared day-dreams that constitute young children's play.

"Now I go away" — three steps away from the center of the game constitute this process. "And you must be crying" — the deserted one puts her hands before her face and makes a little pathetic sound. "Now I sew your fairy dress" — a hand with all five fingertips pressed together describes little circles. But the most convincingly symbolic gesture is that of eating. Children are interested in eating, and this much-desired occasion arises often in their games. Yet their imitation of that process is perhaps their least realistic act. There is no attempt to simulate the use of a spoon or other implement; the hand that carries the imaginary food to the mouth moves with the speed of a short clock-pendulum, the lips whisper "B-b-b-b-b." This sort of imitation would never serve the purpose of learning an activity. It is an abbreviated, schematized form of an action. Whether or no the child could perform the act is irrelevant; eating is an act learned long ago, sewing is probably a total mystery. Yet the imitation of sewing, though clumsy, is not as poor as that of the banquet.

The better an act is understood and the more habitually it is associated with a symbolic gesture, the more formal and cursory may be the movement that represents it. Just as the white settlers of this country first called an Indian feast a "Pow! Wow! Wow!" and later referred to it quite off-handedly as "a pow-wow," so a child's representation of sewing, fighting, or other process will be really imitative at first, but dwindle to almost nothing if the game is played often. It becomes an act of *reference* rather than of representation.

The fact that so much of primitive religious ritual is mimetic, and that mimicry is the typical form of children's play, has misled some excellent philosophers, notably John Dewey, to believe that rites are simply a repetition of practical behavior for the fun of the action itself — a repetition which presently becomes habitual, and has to be dignified by the imputation of magical usefulness. "Men make a game of their fishing and hunting, and turn to the periodic and disciplinary labor of agriculture only when inferiors, women or slaves, cannot be had to do the work. Useful labor is, whenever possible, transformed by ceremonial and ritual accompaniments, subordinated to art that yields immediate enjoyment; otherwise it is attended to under compulsion of circumstance during abbreviated surrenders of leisure. For leisure permits of festivity, in revery, ceremonies and conversation. The pressure of necessity is, however, never wholly lost, and the sense of it led men, as if with uneasy conscience at their respite from work, to impute practical efficacy to play and rites, endowing them with power to coerce events and to purchase the favor of the rulers of events. . . . It was not conscience that kept men loyal to cults and rites, and faithful to tribal myths. So far as it was not routine, it was enjoyment of the drama of life without the latter's liabilities that kept piety from decay. Interest in rites as means of influencing the course of things, and the cognitive or explanation office of myths were hardly more than an embroidery, repeating in pleasant form the pattern which inexpugnable necessities imposed upon practice. When rite and myth are spontaneous rehearsal of the impact and career of practical needs and doings, they must also seem to have practical force." [7]

From this standpoint it is hard to understand why savage rites so often involve terrible tortures — branding, flaying, knocking out teeth, cutting off finger-joints, etc. Puberty-rites, for instance, in which boys sometimes die under the knife or the whip, can hardly be described as "enjoyment of the drama of life without the latter's liabilities." Such actions are far removed from play. Their instrumental value for bringing about victories, fertility, or general good luck is undoubtedly secondary, as Professor Dewey says; but their primary achievement is not entertainment, but *morale*. They are part of man's ceaseless quest for conception and orientation. They embody his dawning notions of power and will, of death and victory, they give active and impressive form to his demoniac fears and ideals. Ritual is the most primitive reflection of serious thought, a slow deposit, as it were, of people's imaginative insight into life. That is why it is in-

[7] *Experience and Nature* (1925), pp. 78–79.

trinsically solemn, even though some rites of rejoicing or triumph may degenerate into mere excitement, debauchery, and license.

If men's minds were essentially playful, they could have no "uneasy conscience at their respite from work." Young dogs and young children, to whom play is a necessity, have no such conscience. Only people who feel that play displaces something more vital can disapprove of it; otherwise, if the bare necessities were taken care of, work in itself could command no respect, and we would play with all the freedom in the world, if practical work and sheer enjoyment were our only alternatives.

But the driving force in human minds is fear, which begets an imperious demand for security in the world's confusion: a demand for a world-picture that fills all experience and gives each individual a definite *orientation* amid the terrifying forces of nature and society. Objects that embody such insights, and acts which express, preserve, and reiterate them, are indeed more spontaneously interesting, more serious than work.

The universality of the concepts which religion tries to formulate draws all nature into the domain of ritual. The apparently misguided efforts of savages to induce rain by dancing and drumming are not practical mistakes at all; they are rites in which the rain has a part. White observers of Indian rain-dances have often commented on the fact that in an extraordinary number of instances the downpour really "results." Others, of a more cynical turn, remark that the leaders of the dance know the weather so well that they time their dance to meet its approaching changes and simulate "rain-making." This may well be the case; yet it is not a pure imposture. A "magic" effect is one which *completes a rite*. No savage tries to induce a snowstorm in midsummer, nor prays for the ripening of fruits entirely out of season, as he certainly would if he considered his dance and prayer the physical causes of such events. He dances *with* the rain, he invites the elements to do their part, as they are thought to be somewhere about and merely irresponsive. This accounts for the fact that no evidence of past failures discourages his practices; for if heaven and earth do not answer him, the rite is simply *unconsummated*; it was not therefore a "mistake." Its failure can be redeemed by finding some extenuating circumstance, some "counter-charm" that explains the miscarriage of the usual climax. There is no evil intent in the devices of medicine men to insure, or even to simulate, answers to magical invocations; for the most important virtue of the rite is not so much its practical as its religious success. Rain-making may well have begun in the celebration of an imminent shower after long drought; that the first harbinger clouds would be greeted with entreaty, excitement, and mimetic suggestion is obvious. The ritual evolves while a capricious heaven is making up its mind. Its successive acts mark the stages that bring the storm nearer. Its real import — its power to articulate a relation between man and nature, vivid at the moment — can be recognized only in the metaphorical guise of a physical power to induce the rain.[8]

Sympathetic magic, springing from mimetic ritual, belongs mainly to tribal, primitive religion. There is, however, a type of ceremonial that runs the whole gamut from the most savage to the most civilized piety, from blind compulsive behavior, through magical conjuring, to the heights of conscious expression: that is the Sacrament.

The overt form of a sacrament is usually a homely, familiar action, such as washing, eating, drinking; sometimes a more special performance — slaughter, or sexual union — but still an act that is essentially realistic and vital. At first sight it

[8] The expressive function of ritual is properly distinguished from the practical in an article by Alfred Vierkandt, "Die entwicklungspsychologische Theorie der Zauberei," *Archiv für gesammte Psychologie*, XCVIII (1937), 420–489. Vierkandt treats the causal conception as a superimposed one. "The [mimetic] activity," he says, "appears as a means to the desired end. If this end is all that motivates the rite, then the latter has changed from a purely expressive act to a purposive act. . . . In the course of this change there may be all possible gradations of the relationship between these two structures, from the merest superimposition of a purposive activity to the complete extinction of the expressive need. At the one extreme, the practical end is a mere superstructure, an ideology, while the driving force is the desire for expression. . . . The other extreme is the genuine purposive act, in which the whole is organized according to the categories of means and ends."

seems strange that the highest symbolic import should attach
to the lowliest activities, especially as the more commonplace
and frequent of these are the most universal sacraments. But
if we consider the genesis of such profound and ancient
symbols we can understand their origin in commonplace
events.

Before a behavior-pattern can become imbued with secondary meanings, it must be definite, and to the smallest detail
familiar. Such forms are naturally evolved only in activities
that are *often repeated*. An act that is habitually performed
acquires an almost mechanical form, a sequence of motions
that practice makes quite invariable. Besides the general
repetition of *what* is done there is a repetition of the *way* it
is done by a certain person. For instance, two people putting
bread into their mouths are *doing* the same thing, but they
may do it in widely different manner, according to their respective temperaments and traditions; their behavior, though
purposive and real, contains unconsciously an element of
gesture.

This formal element offers high possibilities to the symbol-
seeking mind. Just as one person develops personal "ways,"
so a tribe develops tribal "ways," which are handed down
as unconscious mannerisms, until some breach in the usual
pattern makes people aware of them, and they are deliberately
practiced as "correct forms." As soon as they are thus abstracted, these proper gestures acquire tribal importance;
someone sees a secondary meaning in an act which has attained such a formal unity and style. It seems to have a
symbolic as well as a practical function; a new, emotional
importance attaches to it. In a society whose symbolific impulse is in the riotous, "vegetative" stage, a practical act
like dividing food, or eating the first new corn of the season,
may be so exciting as an *idea* that it actually loses its old
material interest in the new, mystical one. Many savages have
foods that may be eaten *only* ritually, and there have been
Christians who frowned on all washing and bathing that
was not incidental to a rite.

These last-named acts of cleansing and purification furnish

a good case in point. Washing away dirt is a simple, practical act; but its symbolic value is so striking that one might say the act has a "natural meaning." [9] Eating, likewise, is a daily practice, but is so easily significant of the kinship among those who eat together, and the even closer connection — identification — of the eaters with the eaten, that it has a certain sacramental character for any mind that is capable of general concepts at all. As soon as the symbolical import of (say) eating an animal dawns, the feast is conducted in a new spirit; not food, but *animal characteristics*, constitute its fare. The meat becomes a host; though the indwelling virtue may have no name of its own, and therefore may be thinkable only in terms of this eating, this gathering, this taste and smell and place. Because an *occasion* is the only symbol by which the new virtue is known, that occasion must have permanent form, that it may be repeated, the virtue recalled, reinvoked; and so the abstractable features of the occasion — the manners and mannerisms that were simply learned folkways, habitual patterns — are exalted into sacred procedure. The meat must be served in the same order, cut in the same shape and from the same part, every time it is to be eaten ritually. Gradually every detail becomes charged with meaning. Every gesture signifies some step in the acquisition of animal virtue. According to the law of all primitive symbolization, this significance is felt not as such, but as genuine efficacy; the feast not only dramatizes, but actually negotiates the desired acquisition. Its performance is magical as well as expressive. And so we have the characteristic blend of power and meaning, mediation and presentation, that belongs to sacraments.[10]

[9] Professor Urban reserves the term "true symbol" entirely for expressions whose meaning is thus "naturally" suggested, and treats all other symbols as signs (cf. *Language and Reality*, part II, esp. pp. 402–409). For reasons explained above, I cannot subscribe to this usage, as the distinction between signs and symbols seems to me to lie in a different dimension.

[10] For a modern example, consider the following statement by W. H. Frere: "The Eucharist is one homogeneous and continuous action and goes forward, if one may say so, like a drama; it has its prelude, its working up, its climax, its epilogue. . . . The Eucharist was to sum up and supersede all older rites and sacrifices; and it has been from the first the central Christian sacrament,

Whether a dim perception of sacramental forces and dangers in the routine actions of life underlies the rigid religious control that almost all primitive societies hold over daily food and drink and housekeeping, we cannot stop to investigate here. What matters in the present context is merely that meaning and magic pervade savage life to such an extent that any behavior-pattern, any striking visual form or musical rhythm, any question or announcement made often enough to become a formula, acquires some symbolic or mystical function; this stage of thinking is the creative period for religion. In it the great life-symbols are established and developed. Concepts which are far beyond the actual grasp of savage or semi-savage minds are apprehended, though not comprehended, in physical embodiments, sacred fetishes, idols, animals; human attitudes, vaguely recognized as reasonable and right, are expressed by actions which are not spontaneous emotional outlets but prescribed modes of participation and assent.

Rites of supplication and offering cannot forever be addressed to a nameless symbol, a mere bundle of sticks, jawbone, grave-mound, or monolith. The Holy One has a part, howbeit a silent part, to play in the ceremony; as the cult develops, the presiding power acquires an epithet expressing this function: "She who Harkens," "He of Appeasement," "He of Sword-play, He of the Sword." The epithet serves as a name, and soon becomes a name; the name fixes a character which gradually finds expression in new physical representations. So the pillar that was once a phallic symbol becomes a "Herm," and the rock that was itself taboo shelters a sacred snake to account for its holiness. The snake can see and hear, respond or retire, strike or spare. The snake can be a forgiver, the Herm can be a watcher.

Of course this is a step from sheer superstition toward theology, toward conceiving gods instead of mere magical cult-objects. But the envisagement of such "gods" is as yet entirely naive; "He of the Sword" may be represented as a sword,

not significant only, but efficacious." The Principles of Religious Ceremonial (1928), pp. 37–39 (italics mine).

and "She who Harkens" may not only have, but *be*, an ear.[11]
The first idea of a god is not that of an anthropomorphic being
that dwells in an object, e.g. in a certain tree; it is simply a
notion of the object itself *as a personality*, as an agent participating in the ritual. This participation is what lifts it
above mere magical potency to something like a personal will.
The might of the cult-objects, charms or sacred arks or holy
wells, is simply *efficacy*; that of gods, whether they be trees,
animals, statutes, or dead men, is *ability*. A charm is made to
operate by a correct ritual; a deity is invoked by being pleased,
either by service or flattery. The rite may persist for ages, but
when the Holy One becomes a god, the keynote of ritual
becomes prayer. One cannot simply draw "mana" from
him as from the presence of holy things; one has to ask him
to exert his talents. Therefore his worshipers recite the
catalogue of his virtues — his valor, wisdom, goodness, the
wonders of his favor, the terrors of his displeasure. In this
way his traits become very definitely and publicly accepted.
Every asset his worshipers seek is his, and in his gift. His
image tends more and more to express this enhanced character; he is the summary of a human ideal, the ideal of his tribe.

Herein lies the rationale of animal worship, which seems
to have preceded, almost universally, the evolution of higher
religions. A god who symbolizes moral qualities does well to
appear in animal form; for a human incarnation would be
confusing. Human personalities are complex, extremely
varied, hard to define, hard to generalize; but animals run
very true to type. The strength of the bull, the shiftiness of
the rabbit, the sinuous mobility of the snake, the solemnity
of the owl, are exemplified with perfect definiteness and
simplicity by every member of their respective species. Before men can find these traits clearly in themselves they can
see them typified in animals. The beast that symbolizes a
virtue, physical or moral, is divine to men who see and envy
that virtue in it. It is the possessor, hence the possible dis-
penser, of its peculiar quality. Therefore it is honored, wooed,

[11] See Jane Harrison, *Prolegomena to the Study of Greek Religion* (1908),
p. 187.

placated, and sometimes sacramentally eaten by its worshipers.

The man who sees his ideal in an animal calls himself by its name, because, exemplifying his highest aspirations as it does, it is his "true self." We who have higher gods still describe our enemies as the beasts we despise — they are "perfect asses," "just pigs," or on extreme provocation "skunks." Men who still look up to animals bestow analogous titles on human beings in a reverent spirit. Those to whom the swift, intensely vital and prolific hare is a symbol of life and fertility, think of themselves as hares, and attribute even more harishness to their venerated, beatified ancestors. They were the "Great Hares." A civilized man would mean this epithet metaphorically, but the primitive mind is always losing its way between symbol and meaning, and freely changes "My earliest ancestor was a 'Hare,' " into "A hare was my first ancestor."

Here is probably the genesis of totemism. The fact that totems feature all kinds of animals and even plants does not preclude such an origin; for once a tribe has adopted an animal form to express its essence, other tribes will follow suit by sheer imitation, without the same motive, choosing different animals to distinguish them from their neighbors. They may have no original notion of any ideal. A tribal ideal is then formed in keeping with the symbol, if at all. But the primary conception of a totem must have sprung from some insight into the human significance of an animal form; perhaps a purely sexual significance, perhaps a sublimer notion of savage virtue.

Such speculation is borne out by the fact that it is the animal *form* rather than any living representative of the species that is preëminently holy. Émile Durkheim, who has made a close study of totemism in *Les formes élémentaires de la vie religieuse*, warns against the fallacy of seeing a simple animal worship in its practices; for in the course of such study, he says, "One comes to the remarkable conclusion that *images of the totem-creature are more sacred than the totem-creature itself.*" [12]

[12] *Op. cit.*, p. 189.

"Here is the real nature of the totem: it is nothing but the material form by which human minds can picture that immaterial substance, that energy diffused throughout all sorts of heterogeneous things, that power which alone is the true object of the cult." [13] Moreover, it is this Power concentrated in the character of the clan — the social influence and authority — which, in M. Durkheim's opinion, is the real divinity.

"The totem is the banner of the clan," he says; and further, "Since the religious Power is nothing else than the collective and nameless Power of the clan, and since this is not capable of representation except through the totem, the totemic emblem is like the visible body of the god. . . . This explains why, in the hierarchy of things sacred, it holds the highest place. . . .

"Why is it forbidden to kill and eat the totem-animal, and why has its flesh these positive virtues which give it its part in ritual? Because this animal resembles the tribal emblem, namely its own image. And as of course it resembles it more closely than man, it has a higher rank than he in the hierarchy of holies." [14]

Durkheim's whole analysis of totemism bears out the contention that it is, like all sacraments, a form of *ideation*, an expression of concepts in purely presentational metaphor.

"Religion is, first and foremost, a system of ideas by means of which individuals can envisage the society of which they are members, and the relations, obscure yet intimate, which they bear to it. That is the primordial task of a faith. And though it be metaphorical and symbolical, it is not therefore untrue. On the contrary, it conveys all that is essential in the relations it claims to portray. . . ." [15]

"The believer is not deceiving himself when he puts his faith in the existence of a moral potency, on which he is dependent, and to which he owes his better part; this Power exists, it is Society. . . . Doubtless, he is mistaken when he believes that the enhancement of his vital strength is the work of a Being that looks like an animal or a plant. But his error lies only in the literal reading of the symbol by

[13] *Ibid.*, p. 270.
[14] *Ibid.*, pp. 315-318.   [15] *Ibid.*, p. 323.

which this Being is presented to his mind, the external aspect under which his imagination conveys it, and does not touch the fact of its existence. Behind these figures and metaphors, however gross or refined they may be, there lies a concrete and living reality." [16]

From such primitive sacramentalism to a real theology, a belief in Olympians who lie on beds of asphodel, or in a heavenly Jerusalem where a triune God sits enthroned, may seem so far a call that one may incline to doubt whether human imagination could have passed continuously from one to the other. The mentalities of Australian aborigines and of European worshipers, ancient and modern, appear to be just worlds apart; the Sacred Emu does not give any promise of a future Zeus, nor does a lizard in a cave appear to foreshadow the Christian God of Love. Yet when we trace the histories of such high divinities back to their antecedents in earlier ages, there is an astonishing kinship between those antecedents and the local deities of Australian, African, or American savages. We have no evidence that genuine totemism ever existed in Europe; but of animal cults we have convincing proof. Luck has it that one of the most civilized religions of all time, namely the Greek, has inscribed the whole course of its evolution for us on the places where it flourished — on the temples and households, cemeteries and libraries that tell the story of Hellas from its dawn to its slow destruction; and that a classical scholar with patience and insight has traced that evolution from its earliest recoverable phases to its last decadent forms. For, as Professor Gilbert Murray has said, "In this department as in others, ancient Greece has the triumphant if tragic distinction of beginning at the very bottom and struggling, however precariously, to the very summits. There is hardly any horror of primitive superstition of which we cannot find some distant traces in our Greek record. There is hardly any height of spiritual thought attained in the world that has not its archetype or its echo in the stretch of Greek literature that lies between Thales and Plotinus. . . ." [17]

[16] *Ibid.*, p. 322.   [17] *Five Stages of Greek Religion* (1925), pp. 15–16.

The scholar to whom we are most indebted for a truly coherent picture of religious origins is Jane Harrison, whose *Prolegomena to the Study of Greek Religion* sets forth with all detail the evolution of Olympian and Christian divinities from their humble, zoölatrous beginnings in tombs and snake-holes and chimney-corners. This evolution is a long story. It has been briefly retold by Professor Murray in the book from which the above quotation is taken,[18] and here I can do no more than indicate its beginning, direction, and moral.

Its beginning — contrary to our traditional ideas of the Greek mind — is not at all in bright fancies, lovely anthropomorphic conceptions of the sun, the moon, and the rainbow. Professor Murray remarks this at the outset.

"The things that have misled us moderns in our efforts towards understanding the primitive stage in Greek religion," he says, "have been first the widespread and almost ineradicable error of treating Homer as primitive, and more generally our unconscious insistence on starting with the notion of 'Gods.' . . . The truth is that this notion of a god far away in the sky — I do not say merely a First Cause who is 'without body parts or passions,' but almost any being that we should naturally call a 'god' — is an idea not easy for primitive man to grasp. It is a subtle and rarefied idea, saturated with ages of philosophy and speculation." [19]

The Olympian gods, who seem like free inventions of an innocent, delighted imagination, "are imposed upon a background strangely unlike themselves. For a long time their luminous figures dazzled our eyes; we were not able to see the half-lit regions behind them, the dark primaeval tangle of desires and fears and dreams from which they drew their vitality. The surest test to apply in this question is the evidence of actual cult. Miss Harrison has here shown us the right method. . . ." [20]

Her findings by this method were, in brief, that in the great Greek festivals the Olympian gods played no role at

---

[18] See esp. chaps. i and ii.
[19] *Ibid.*, p. 24.   [20] *Ibid.*, p. 28.

all; their names were quite externally associated with these occasions, and were usually modified by an epithet, to make the connection at least reasonable. Thus the Athenian Diasia is held in honor of "Zeus Meilichios," or "Zeus of Placation."

"A god with an epithet," says Murray, "is always suspicious, like a human being with an 'alias.' Miss Harrison's examination shows that in the rites Zeus has no place at all. Meilichios from the beginning has a fairly secure one. On some of the reliefs Meilichios appears not as a god, but as an enormous, bearded snake, a well-known representation of underworld powers or dead ancestors. . . .

"The Diasia was a ritual of placation, that is, of casting away various elements of pollution or danger and appeasing the unknown wraths of the surrounding darkness. The nearest approach to a god contained in this festival is Meilichios. . . . His name means 'He of appeasement,' and he is nothing else."

"The Thesmophoria formed the great festival of Demeter and her daughter Korê, though here again Demeter appears with a clinging epithet, Thesmophoros. We know pretty clearly the whole course of the ritual. . . . The Olympian Demeter and Persephone dwindle away as we look closer, and we are left with the shadow Thesmophoros, 'She who carries Thesmoi,' not a substantive personal goddess, but merely a personification of the ritual itself; an imaginary charm-bearer generated by so much charm-bearing, just as Meilichios in the Diasia was generated from the ritual of appeasement." [21]

The first entirely anthropomorphic conception seems to have come into Greece with the conquering Achaeans, whose Olympian Zeus, a mountain god,[22] had attained human form, at a time when the native Pelasgian gods still retained their animal shapes or were at best monstrous hybrids; Athena still identified with an owl, or figured as the Diver-Bird or bird-headed "Diver-Maid" of Megara.[23] The effect of this personified Achaean god on the barbarian worship then current

[21] *Ibid.*, pp. 28–31.
[22] *Ibid.*, p. 66. "It ['Olympus'] is a pre-Greek word applied to Mountains."
[23] Harrison, *Prolegomena*, p. 304.

in Aegean lands was probably spectacular; for a single higher conception can be a marvellous leaven in the heavy, amorphous mass of human thought. The local gods took shape in the new human pattern, so obvious once it had been conceived; and it is not surprising that this Achaean mountain-god, or rather mountain-dwelling sky-god, became either father or conqueror of those divinities who grew up in his image.

"He had an extraordinary power of ousting or absorbing the various objects of aboriginal worship which he found in his path," says Professor Murray. "The story of Meilichios [whose cult he usurped] is a common one." [24]

But even this great Olympian could not attain his perfect form, his definite relations to the heavens, the gods, and the human world, until he became a figure in something more than ritual; it is in the great realm of *myth* that human conceptions of divinity really become articulated. A symbol may give identity to a god, a mimetic dance may express his favors, but what really fixes his character is the tradition of his origin, actions, and past adventures. Like the hero of a novel or a drama, he becomes a personality, not by his sheer appearance, but by his story. Moloch, however widely worshiped, has never become an independent being apart from his rites, because if he had any myth, it never became coherent in any systematic account. But Zeus and all his family had their genealogist in Homer, to mention only the greatest mythmaker we know. Herodotus was probably not far from the truth when he said that Homer gave the Greek gods their names and stations and even their shapes.[25] Divinities are born of ritual, but theologies spring from myth. Miss Harrison, in describing the origin of a *Korê* or primitive earthgoddess, says: "The May-pole or harvest-sheaf is half-way to a harvest Maiden; it is thus . . . that a goddess is made. A song is sung, a story told, and the very telling fixes the outline of the personality. It is possible to worship long in the spirit, but as soon as the story-telling and myth-making

[24] Murray, *op. cit.*, p. 70.
[25] Harrison. *Prolegomena*, p. 64.

instinct awakes you have anthropomorphism and theology." [26]

The "myth-making instinct," however, has a history of its own, and its own life-symbols; though it is the counterpart of sacrament in the making of higher religion, it does not belong to the lower phases; or, at least, it has little importance below the level of dawning philosophic thought, which is the last reach of genuine religion, its consummation and also its dissolution.

[26] Harrison, *op. cit.*, p. 80.

CHAPTER VII

Life-Symbols: The Roots of Myth

WHILE religion grows from the blind worship of Life and magic "aversion" of Death to a definite totem-cult or other sacramentalism, another sort of "life-symbol" develops in its own way, starting also in quite unintentional processes, and culminating in permanent significant forms. This medium is myth. Although we generally associate mythology with religion, it really cannot be traced, like ritual, to an origin in anything like a "religious feeling," either of dread, mystic veneration, or even festal excitement. Ritual begins in motor attitudes, which, however personal, are at once externalized and so made public. Myth begins in fantasy, which may remain tacit for a long time; for the primary form of fantasy is the entirely subjective and private phenomenon of *dream*.

The lowest form of story is not much more than a dream-narrative. It has no regard whatever for coherence or even consistency of action, for possibility or common sense; in fact, the existence of such yarns as for instance the Papuans tell, in a society which is after all intelligent enough to gauge the physical properties of clubs and arrows, fire and water, and the ways of animals and men, shows that primitive story has some other than literal significance. It is made essentially of dream-material; the images in it are taken from life, they are things and creatures, but their behavior follows some entirely unempirical law; by realistic standards it is simply inappropriate to them.

Roland Dixon, in his *Oceanic Mythology*,[1] cites a story from Melanesia, in which two disputants, a buffalo and a

[1] Vol. ix of *The Mythology of All Races* (1916).

crocodile, agree to ask "the next to come down the river"
to arbitrate their quarrel; their request for a judgment is
refused successively by a leaf-plate, a rice-mortar, and a mat,
before the Mouse-Deer finally acts as judge.[2] There is another tale which begins: "One day an egg, a snake, a centi-
pede, an ant, and a piece of dung set out on a head-hunting
expedition. . . ."[3] In yet another narrative, "while two
women were sleeping in a house, a *tapa*-beater transformed
itself into a woman resembling one of the pair, and waking
the other, said to her, 'Come, it is time for us to go fishing.'
So the woman arose, and they took torches and went out to
sea in a canoe. After a while she saw an island of driftwood,
and as the dawn came on, perceived that her companion had
turned into a *tapa*-beater, whereupon she said: 'Oh, the *tapa*-
beater has deceived me. While we were talking in the evening
it stood in the corner and heard us, and in the night it came
and deceived me.' Landing her on the island, the *tapa*-beater
paddled away and abandoned her. . . ." After a miraculous
rescue and return, "the woman told her parents how the
tapa-beater had deceived and kidnapped her; and her father
was angry, and building a great fire, he threw the *tapa*-beater
into it and burned it up."[4]

In these stories we have certainly a very low stage of human
imagination; one cannot call them "myths," let alone "religious myths." For the leaf-plate which refused to arbitrate
a quarrel (it was peeved, by the way, because it had been
thrown out when it was still perfectly good), the equally
unobliging mortar and mat, the piece of dung that went head-
hunting, and the deceitful *tapa*-beater, are not "persons" in
a strange disguise; despite their humanoid activities they are
just domestic articles. In fact, the *tapa*-beater is in disguise
when it resembles a woman, and when the rising sun breaks
the spell it must return to its *real* form. But even as a *tapa*-
beater it has no trouble in paddling the canoe home, and
returning alone to the house.

[2] Dixon, *Oceanic Mythology*, p. 198.
[3] *Ibid.*, p. 202.
[4] *Ibid.*, pp. 141–142.

No sane human being, however simple, could really "suppose" such events to occur; and clearly, in enjoying this sort of story nobody is trying to "suppose" anything. To imagine the assorted hunting-party really on its way through the jungle is perhaps just as impossible for a Papuan as for us. The only explanation of such stories is, then, that nobody cares whether their *dramatis personae* act in character or not. The act is not really proper to its agent, but to *someone its agent represents*; and even the action in the story may merely *represent* the deeds of such a symbolized personality. In other words, the psychological basis of this remarkable form of nonsense lies in the fact that the story is a fabrication out of subjective symbols, not out of observed folkways and nature-ways. The psychoanalysts, who have found such unconscious metaphor to be the rationale of our otherwise inexplicable dreams, can give us ample illustration of this sort of fantasy. It is entirely bound to feelings and wishes of its author, cast in its bizarre or monstrous mold by his unavowed fears and reticences, formulated and told and retold as a means of *self-expression*. As we meet it in these Melanesian stories, it is really only a cut above genuine dream. But even so, the story is an improvement on mere dream, because the very telling of it requires a little more coherence than our nightmares usually have. There must be a thread of logic; a *tapa*-beater who is *also* a woman must, in one capacity or the other, be "in disguise"; the head-hunting dung, egg, and animals must set out together, and — though the head-hunt is forgotten before the end of the story — they must either do *something* together or get separated. Characters have to be generally accounted for, which is more than we do in dreaming.

So long as a story is told to a very uncritical audience by the person who made it up, it may be ever so silly without giving offense. Anyone who has heard young children telling yarns to each other can corroborate this. But as soon as the story goes abroad, it meets with more rigorous demands for significance. If it survives in a larger sphere, it undergoes various modifications, in the interests of coherence and public appeal. Its purely personal symbols are replaced by more

universal ones; animals, ghosts, and witches take the place of
tapa-beaters and suchlike in the villain's role. Just as sacra
change their form, and become gradually personified with
the growth of ritual action, so the development and integration of story-action makes the symbols of fantasy take on more
and more reasonable outward form to fit the role in which
they are cast. A higher fictional mode emerges — the animal
fable, the trickster story, or the orthodox ghost story.[5] Often
the theme is quite ephemeral — merely the homecoming of a
strayed person, the theft of a cocoanut, or somebody's meeting
with a cannibalistic ghoul in the bush — but such simple plots
grow, with the advancing arts of life and social organization,
into the well-known *genre* of fairytale.

Here we have a literary product belonging to the civilized
races of Europe just as much as to the savage cultures of
darker continents. Aristocratic beings, chiefs or princes, now
play the leading role; dragons and ogres and wicked kings,
or beautiful witches of great power, replace the monkeys,
crocodiles, angry dead men, or local cannibals of the older
tradition. The wishful imagination of man has been disciplined, by public exposure and realistic reflection, into a
genuine art-form, as far removed from personal dreaming
as the ritual dance from self-expressive bouncing and shouting.

Yet this high development of fantasy has brought us nowhere in the direction of mythology. For although fairy-story
is probably an older form than myth, the latter is not simply
a higher development of the former. It, too, goes back to
primitive fantasy, but the point of its origin from that source
lies far back in cultural history, long before the evolution of
our modern fairytale — of *Kunstmärchen*, as the Germans
say, or even *Volksmärchen*. It required not a higher stage of
story-telling, but a *thematic shift*, to initiate what Miss Harrison called "the myth-making instinct."

The difference between the two fictional modes — many

---

[5] It must be borne in mind here that the primitive animal fable has no
conscious allegorical import, as Aesop's or La Fontaine's fables have, and
that the ghost story has no naturalistic "explanation," because ghosts are
accepted beings in the savage's cosmos.

scholars to the contrary notwithstanding [6] — is a crucial one. For the fairytale is irresponsible; it is frankly imaginary, and its purpose is to gratify wishes, "as a dream doth flatter." Its heroes and heroines, though of delightfully high station, wealth, beauty, etc., are simply individuals; "a certain prince," "a lovely princess." The end of the story is always satisfying, though by no means always moral; the hero's heroism may be slyness or luck quite as readily as integrity or valor. The theme is generally the triumph of an unfortunate one — an enchanted maiden, a youngest son, a poor Cinderella, an alleged fool — over his or her superiors, whether these be kings, bad fairies, strong animals (e.g. Red Riding Hood's wolf), stepmothers, or elder brothers. In short, the fairytale is a form of "wishful thinking," and the Freudian analysis of it fully explains why it is perennially attractive, yet never believed by adults even in the telling.

Myth, on the other hand, whether literally believed or not, is taken with religious seriousness, either as historic fact or as a "mystic" truth. Its typical theme is tragic, not utopian; and its personages tend to fuse into stable *personalities* of supernatural character. Two divinities of somewhat similar type — perhaps miraculously born, prodigious in strength, heroically defeated and slain — become identified; they are one god under two names. Even those names may become mere epithets linking the god to different cults.

This sets the hero of myth strikingly apart from the fairytale hero. No matter how closely the Prince Charming of Snow White's story resembles the gentleman who wakens Sleeping Beauty, the two characters do not become identified. No one thinks that the trickster "Little Claus" is the little tailor who slew "seven at a stroke," or that the giant whom Jack killed was in any way related to the ogre defeated by Puss in Boots, or that he figured elsewhere as Bluebeard. Fairy stories bear no relation to each other. Myths, on the

---

[6] See esp. P. Ehrenreich, *Die allgemeine Mythologie und ihre ethnologischen Grundlagen* (1910); E. Mudrak, "Die deutsche Heldensage," *Jahrbuch für historische Volkskunde,* VII (1939); and Otto Rank, *Psychoanalytische Beiträge zur Mythenforschung* (1922).

other hand, become more and more closely woven into one fabric, they form cycles, their *dramatis personae* tend to be intimately connected if not identified. Their stage is the actual world — the Vale of Tempe, Mount Olympus, the sea, or the sky — and not some ungeographical fairyland.

Such radical dissimilarities between two kinds of story lead one to suspect that they have fundamentally different functions. And myth has, indeed, a more difficult and more serious purpose than fairytale. The elements of both are much alike, but they are put to quite different uses. Fairytale is a personal gratification, the expression of desires and of their imaginary fulfilment, a compensation for the shortcomings of real life, an escape from actual frustration and conflict. Because its function is subjective, the hero is strictly individual and human; for, although he may have magic powers, he is never regarded as divine; though he may be an oddity like Tom Thumb, he is not considered supernatural. For the same reason — namely that his mission is merely to represent the "self" in a day-dream — he is not a savior or helper of mankind. If he is good, his goodness is a personal asset, for which he is richly rewarded. But his humanitarian role is not the point of the story; it is at best the setting for his complete social triumph. The beneficiary of his clever acts, his prowess, or his virtue is he himself, not mankind forever after. And because an individual history is what the fairytale fancies, its interest is exhausted with the "happy ending" of each finished story. There is no more mutual reference between the adventures of Cinderella and those of Rapunzel than between two separate dreams.

Myth, on the other hand, at least at its best, is a recognition of natural conflicts, of human desire frustrated by non-human powers, hostile oppression, or contrary desires; it is a story of the birth, passion, and defeat by death which is man's common fate. Its ultimate end is not wishful distortion of the world, but serious envisagement of its fundamental truths; moral orientation, not escape. That is why it does not exhaust its whole function in the telling, and why separate myths cannot be left entirely unrelated to any others. Because it presents, however metaphorically, a world-picture, an insight into life generally, not a personal imaginary biography, myth tends to become systematized; figures with the same poetic meaning are blended into one, and characters of quite separate origin enter into definite relations with each other. Moreover, because the mythical hero is not the subject of an egocentric day-dream, but a subject greater than any individual, he is always felt to be superhuman, even if not quite divine. He is at least a descendant of the gods, something more than a man. His sphere of activity is the real world, because what he symbolizes belongs to the real world, no matter how fantastic its expression may be (this is exactly contrary to the fairytale technique, which transports a natural individual to a fairyland outside reality).

The material of myth is, indeed, just the familiar symbolism of dream — image and fantasy. No wonder psychologists have discovered that it is the same material as that of fairytale; that both have symbols for father and son, maiden and wife and mother, possession and passion, birth and death.[7] The difference is in the two respective *uses* of that material: the one, primarily for supplying vicarious experience, the other essentially for understanding actual experience.[8] Both interests may be served in one and the same fiction; their complete separation belongs only to classic cases. Semi-mythical motives occur in sheer day-dream and even night-dream, and an element of compensation-fantasy may persist in the most universalized, perfected myths. That is inevitable, because the latter type has grown at some point out of the former,

[7] Cf. Sigmund Freud, *Collected Papers*, vol. IV (1925), Essay ix (pp. 173–183), "The Relation of the Poet to Day-Dreaming"; also Otto Rank, *op. cit.*, esp. essays vi (pp. 119–145), "Das Brüdermärchen," and vii (pp. 146–184), "Mythus und Märchen."

[8] This distinction was made fairly long ago by E. Bethe, in his monograph, *Mythus — Sage — Märchen* (1905), in which he writes: "Myth, legend, and fairytale differ from one another in origin and purpose. Myth is primitive philosophy, the simplest presentational (*anschauliche*) form of thought, a series of attempts to understand the world, to explain life and death, fate and nature, gods and cults. Legend is primitive history, naively formulated in terms of love and hate, unconsciously transformed and simplified. But fairytale has sprung from, and serves, no motive but entertainment." Cf. also A. Thimme, *Das Märchen* (1909).

as all realistic thinking springs from self-centered fancy. There is no clean dividing line. Yet the two are as distinct as summer and winter, night and day, or any other extremes that have no exact zero-point between them.

We do not know just where, in the evolution of human thought, myth-making begins, but it begins somewhere with the recognition of *realistic significance* in a story. In every fantasy, no matter how utopian, there are elements that represent real human relations, real needs and fears, the quandaries and conflicts which the "happy ending" resolves. Even if the real situation is symbolized rather than stated (a shocking condition may well be disguised, or a mysterious one strangely conceived), a certain importance, an emotional interest, attaches to those elements. The ogre, the dragon, the witch, are intriguing figures in fairy-lore. Unlike the hero, they are usually ancient beings, that have troubled the land for many generations. They have their castles or caves or hermitages, their magic cook-pots and sorcerer's wands; they have evil deeds laid up against them, and extremely bad habits, usually of a cannibalistic turn. Their records are merely suggested in the story, which hastens to get on with the fortunes of the hero; but the suggestion is enough to activate a mind which is, after all, committed to some interests besides dream-spinning. Because they represent the realistic setting from which the dream starts its fanciful escape, they command a serious sort of contemplation.

It is significant that people who refuse to tell their children fairytales do not fear that the children will believe in princes and princesses, but that they will believe in witches and bogeys. Prince or princess, to whom the wish-fulfulment happens, we find in ourselves, and need not seek in the outer world; their reference is subjective, their history is our dream, and we know well enough that it is "make-believe." But the incidental figures are material for superstition, because their meanings are in the real world. They represent those same powers that are conceived, first perhaps through "dreadful" objects like corpses or skulls or hideous idols, as ghosts, keres, hoodoos, and similar spooks. The ogres of literature and the ghouls of popular conception embody the same mysterious Powers; therefore the fairytale, which even most children will not credit as a narrative, may carry with it a whole cargo of ideas, purely secondary to its own purpose, that are most convincing elements for superstition. The awful ancestor in the grave goes abroad as the goblin of story: that is the god of superstition. The world-picture of spook-religion is a reflection of fairytale, a dream whose nightmare elements become attached to visible cult objects and thus taken seriously.

There is nothing cosmological about the being such a symbol can embody. Deities in the classical sense cannot be born of tales whose significance is personal, because the setting of such tales is necessarily a *genre* picture, a local, temporal, human environment, no matter how distorted and disguised. The forces that play into an individual's dream are social forces, not world-powers. So long as the hero is the self, the metaphorical dragons he slays are his elders, his rivals, or his personal enemies; their projection into the real world as sacred beings can yield only ancestors, cave-monsters, manitos, and capricious demigods.

It is noteworthy that when these secondary characters of day-dream or story are incorporated into our picture of the external world as objects of superstition, they represent a generalized, heightened conception of the social forces in question: not a man's father, but his *fathers*, the paternal power in all generations, may be seen in the fabulous animal-ancestor he reveres; not his brother, but a "Great Brother," in the manito-bear that is his familiar of the forest. The process of symbolization, while it often obscures the origin of our ideas, enhances their conceptual form. The demon, therefore, presents to us not a specific person, but the human estate of such a person, by virtue of which we are oppressed, challenged, tempted, or triumphant. Though he is born of a purely self-centered imagination, he is super-personal; a product not only of particular experience, but of *social insight*. He is the envisagement of a vital factor in life; that is why he is projected into reality by the symbolism of religion.

The great step from fairytale to myth is taken when not only social forces — persons, customs, laws, traditions — but also cosmic forces surrounding mankind, are expressed in the story; when not only relationships of an individual to society, but of mankind to nature, are conceived through the spontaneous metaphor of poetic fantasy.

Perhaps this transition from subjectively oriented stories, separate and self-contained, to the organized and permanent envisagement of a world-drama could never be made if creative thought were not helped by the presence of permanent, obvious symbols, supplied by nature: the heavenly bodies, the changes of day and night, the seasons, and the tides. Just as the social framework of personal life, first conceived in dream-like, inchoate forms, is gradually given enduring recognition through religious symbols, so the cosmic setting of man's existence is imponderable, or at best a mere nightmare, until the sun and the moon, the procession of stars, the winds and waters of earth, exhibit a divine rule, and define the realm of human activity. When these gods arrive, whose names connote heavenly powers and natural processes, the deities of local caves and groves become mere vassals and lesser lights.

It has often been asked, not without justification, how men of sane observant minds — however unschooled or innocent — can be led to identify sun, moon, or stars with the anthropomorphic agents of sacred story. Yet the interpretation of gods and heroes as nature-symbols is very ancient; it has been variously accepted and rejected, disputed, exploded, and reëstablished, by Hellenic philosophers, medieval scholars, modern philologists, archeologists, and theologians, over a period of twenty-five hundred years. Mystifying as it is to psychology, it challenges us as a fact. Demeter was certainly an earth-goddess, and the identity of Olympian Zeus with the heavens, Apollo with the sun, Artemis with the moon, etc., is so authentic that it has long been considered a truism to declare these gods "personifications" of the corresponding natural phenomena. Yet such a process of personification seems like an unnatural flight of fancy. It is a fairly safe rule not to impute to the savage mind processes that never even threaten to arise in our own minds. The difference between savage and civilized mentality is, after all, one of naive versus critical thinking; bizarre and monstrous imagery pops into our heads, too, but is rejected almost instantly by the disciplined reason. But I do not think that either in dream or in childhood we are prone to think of the sun as a man. As for the stars, it takes a sophisticated literary tradition to make them people, or even Lady Moon's sheep.

How then did heroic adventures become attached to these most impersonal actors, as they almost universally did? The process, I believe, is a natural phase of the evolution of mythology from fairy-story, and indeed represents a potent factor in that development. The change is a gradual one, and has necessarily its intermediate steps; one of these is marked by the introduction of the first cosmic symbols. This transitional stage between the egocentric interest of folktale, focussed on a human hero, and the emergence of full-fledged nature-mythology dealing with divine characters of highly general import, is the so-called *legend*, which produces the "culture-hero."

This widely represented fictional character is a hybrid of subjective and objective thinking; he is derived from the hero of folktale, representing an individual psyche, and consequently retains many of that personage's traits. But the symbolic character of the other beings in the fairytale has infected him, too, with a certain supernaturalism; he is more than an individual wrestling with powers of society. Just what else he is, must be gathered from his personality as it reveals itself in the legendary mode.

He is half god, half giant-killer. Like the latter, he is often a Youngest Son, the only clever one among his stupid brothers. He is born of high parentage, but kidnapped, or exposed and rescued, or magically enslaved, in his infancy. Unlike the dream-subject of fairytale, however, his deeds only begin with his escape from thraldom; they go on to benefit mankind. He gives men fire, territory, game, teaches them agriculture, ship-building, perhaps even language;

he "makes" the land, finds the sun (in a cave, in an egg, or in a foreign country), and sets it in the sky, and controls wind and rain. But despite his greatness he slips back frequently into his role of folktale hero, and plays the trickster, outwitting human enemies, local ghosts, or even a venerable ancestor just for mischief.

The status of the culture-hero is thus very complex. His activities lie in the real world, and their effects are felt by real men forever after; he therefore has a somewhat vague, yet unmistakable historical relation to living men, and a tie to the locality on which he has left his mark. This alone would suffice to distinguish him from the hero of fairyland, whose acts are bound up entirely with a story, so that he can be dispensed with at the end of it, and a new hero introduced for the next story. The historical and local attachments of the culture-hero give his being a certain permanence. Stories gather round him, as they gather round real heroes of history whose deeds have become legendary, such as Charlemagne, Arthur, or Kubla Khan. But whereas these princes are credited with enhanced and exaggerated human acts, the primitive culture-hero interferes with the doings of nature rather than of men; his opponents are not Saracens or barbarians, but sun and moon, earth and heaven.

A perfect example of such a demigod is the Indian Manabozho or Michabo, also known as Hiawatha.[9] He is at once a supernatural being, and a very human character. The fact that he is a manito who can take whole mountain ranges at a couple of strides, that he chastises his father the West Wind for the indignities inflicted on his moon-descended mother, does not put him above feeling the pinch of hunger in winter, or getting stung in robbing a bee-tree.

Brinton, one of the earliest systematic collectors of Indian folk-lore, looking for "natural theology" in the Red Man, was baffled and distressed by the character of Manabozho;

---

[9] The first printed source of the Hiawatha legend seems to be J. V. Clark's *History of Onondaga* (1849), from which Longfellow drew the materials for his version. H. R. Schoolcraft's *The Myth of Hiawatha* (1856) is fuller and more coherent, but less authentic.

for "He is full of pranks and wiles, but often at a loss for a meal of victuals; ever itching to try his arts magic on great beasts and often meeting ludicrous failure therein; envious of the powers of others, and constantly striving to outdo them in what they do best; in short, little more than a malicious buffoon delighting in practical jokes, and abusing his super-human powers for selfish and ignoble ends." At the same time, "From a grain of sand brought from the bottom of the primaeval ocean he fashioned the habitable land and set it floating on the waters. . . . One of his footsteps measured eight leagues, the Great Lakes were the beaver dams he built, and when the cataracts impeded his progress he tore them away with his hands." [10] He invented picture writing and made the first fishing-nets. Obviously he is a deity; yet his name, in every dialect that varies or translates it, means "Great Hare" or "Spirit Hare." Brinton was convinced that the popular stories about him are "a low, modern, and corrupt version," and that his name rests on a philological mistake which all the Indians made, confusing *wabo*, "hare," with *wapa*, "the dawn"; that his various names originally desig-nated a sun-god, but led to his representation as a hare, by an accident of language." [11]

Manabozho is in all likelihood not a degraded Supreme God, but an enhanced, exalted fictional hero. He still bears the marks of his human origin, though he has established rela-tions to the great forces which encompass human life, the heavens, the seasons, and the winds. His superhuman deeds

[10] D. Brinton, *The Myths of the New World* (1896), pp. 194–195.

[11] *Ibid.*, p. 194 ff. On Brinton's theory, one might suppose that the Sacred Cod of Massachusetts, enshrined in the State House, and sometimes pictured, totem-like, on Massachusetts number-plates, had originated through a little confusion in the Puritan mind between "Cod" and "God." The Indian is no more likely than the white man to mistake even exact homonyms for each other where their meanings are so diverse that their interchange is patently absurd. The same objection holds against every attempt to rest mythology on verbal errors or garbled versions of fact, as Max Müller and Herbert Spencer proposed to do. We do not learn religious thinking, on the one hand, nor on the other turn gospel into bed-time stories, just by mistake — by reading "son" for "sun," or confusing Simon called Peter with Peter Rabbit; and presumably right-minded Indians don't, either.

have raised him to a comradeship with these powers; and
his pseudo-historic relation to mankind leads to his identification with the totem-animal, the mystic ancestor of his
people. Therefore he is at once the son of the West Wind,
grandson of the Moon, etc., and the Great Hare; and at the
same time the clever trickster, the great chief, the canoe-
builder, and the superman.

We meet the culture-hero again, in all his glory, as Maui,
the Polynesian demigod.[12] He, too, combines the buffoon,
trickster, or naughty boy with heroic and even divine qualities. Like Manabozho, he is of cosmological descent, though
his normal shape is human. Maui is too widely claimed to
bear the marks of any totem, but can change himself into
fish, bird, or beast at will. He is, indeed, everything from
a troll to a deity, because he belongs to all stages of culture —
he is known as a prankster in Papuan fairytale, the fire-stealer
and dragon-killer ("hero" in a classical sense) in more advanced legends, the demiurge who shapes earth and sky in
Hawaiian cosmology, and in the mythology of New Zealand
he actually becomes a benevolent patron of humanity, self-
sacrificed in an attempt to bestow immortality on men.

Yet Maui, like Manabozho, is not worshiped. He has no
cult, his name is not sacred, nor do men feel or fear his
power as a factor in current events. He has died, or gone
west, or otherwise ended his local career; one may see his
footprints in the lava, his handiwork in the arrangements of
heaven and earth, but he no longer presides over these. His
old adversary the Sun still runs the course Maui bade him
follow; his ancestress and murderess, the Moon, still vaunts
her immortality in one resurrection after another. These
are visible powers, deities to be entreated or honored. Why
is their son, grandson, conqueror, or playmate, the culture-
hero, not an eternal god, set as a star in the sky, or imagined
as a king of the sea?

---

[12] See Roland Dixon, *Oceanic Mythology*; E. Shortland, *Maori Religion and
Mythology* (1882); J. C. Andersen, *Maori Life in Ao-tea* (no date; c. 1907);
W. D. Westervelt, *Legends of Maui, a Demigod of Polynesia, and of his
Mother Hina* (1910).

Because he is not as seriously "believed in" as gods and spirits are. Like the hero of fairytale, the culture-hero is a vehicle of human wishes. His adventures are fantasies. But, whereas the story-hero is an individual overcoming personal opponents — father, master, brothers, or rivals — *the culture-hero is Man, overcoming the superior forces that threaten him.* A tribe, not a single inventor, is unconsciously identified with him. The setting of his drama is cosmic; storm and night are his foes, deluge and death his ordeals. These are the realities that inspire his dream of deliverance. His task is the control of nature — of earth and sky, vegetation, rivers, season — and the conquest of death.

Just as the fairytale served to clarify a personal environment and human relations in its secondary characters, its kings, witches, ghosts, and fairies (which were often identified with real beings and so abstracted from the mere tale), so the culture-hero's story furnishes symbols of a less personal encircling reality. The hero's exploits are largely make-believe even to their inventors; but the forces that challenge him are apt to be taken seriously. They belong to the real world, and their symbols mean something beyond the pipe dream in which they were formulated. Maui is a superman, a wishful version of human power, skill, and importance; but his place among the forces of nature is Man's own place. Where did he come from? From nature, from heaven and earth and sea. In cosmic terms, he came "out of the Night." In human terms he came out of Woman. In his myth, therefore, he is descended from Hine-nui-te-po, Great Woman of Night.[13]

The Polynesian word "Hine" (variants "Hina," "Ina") has an interesting etymology. By itself, it seems to be always either a proper noun or an adjective connoting either light (e.g. white, pale, glimmering) or falling, declining; in composite words it usually refers to woman.[14] As a name, it denotes the

---

[13] See Dixon, *op. cit.*, p. 52; Shortland, *op. cit.*, p. 23; Westervelt, *op. cit.*, p. 133; for complete genealogy see Andersen, *op. cit.*, p. 182.

[14] The general word for "woman" is "wahine." See H. R. Hitchcock, *English-Hawaiian Dictionary* (1887); E. Tregear, *The Maori-Polynesian Com-*

woman or maiden of such-and-such character, somewhat like the Greek *Korê*. The mixture of common and proper meaning gives the word a *generalizing* function; therefore it applies with special aptness to supernatural beings which, as we have seen, are generalized personalities.[15] But when several personages bear the same name because they have essentially the same symbolic value, they naturally tend to merge. Since every "Great Woman," "Mountain Maid," "Mother," or "She" is Woman, we find a great confusion of Hinas.

In Polynesian mythologies the various Hina characters are developed mainly as secondary figures in the story of Maui. They appear as his mother, sister, grandmother, or very first ancestress. As few English readers are familiar with the legend, I will sketch briefly the most important tales of this powerful, mischievous, and brilliant hero.

1. THE QUEST OF FIRE

Maui was the youngest of four or five brothers, all named Maui with various epithets. The Mauis were all stupid except this youngest son, who was miraculous from his infancy. He had been prematurely born, and his mother Hina, not interested in such a weakling, threw him into the sea. But a jellyfish nursed him, and the elements returned him to his home, where consequently he was received as a foundling. He was full of power and mischief, always in trouble with his brothers and his elders.

Maui's mother slept in a hut with her children, like any Polynesian mother. But when the first dawn light appeared she would depart, and keep herself in some mysterious retreat all day. Young Maui, determined to find her out, blocked all the chinks and window-holes of the hut, so that no ray of light wakened her until it was full day; then, when she

---

parative Dictionary (1891); L. Andrews, *Dictionary of the Hawaiian Language* (1865).

[15] Shortland (*op. cit.*, chap. ii) gives the following translations:
Hine-ahu-one — the Earth-formed Maid (first created woman).
Hine-a-tauira — the Pattern Maid (first begotten woman).
Hine-tu-a-maunga — the Mountain Maid.
Hine-nui-te-po — Great Woman of Night.

woke and hastily fled, he followed her, and discovered the path she took to the Underworld, where she was wont to spend the day with her dead ancestors. Maui, in the form of a bird, joined this company of chthonic gods, who gave him his first taste of cooked food. Here he found the ancestress in whose custody was the precious secret of fire.

There are many versions of his Promethean exploit. In one of these, the ancestress gives him one of her fingers, in which the principle of fire dwells; sometimes he wrests it from her, and sometimes he learns the secret of fire-making from the Alae, "the bird of Hina," a mud-hen sacred to that ancestral fire-woman. But in every case, an ancient Hina, living in a volcano, in a cave, or simply in the earth, possesses the treasure, and Maui obtains it by trickery, cajoling, or violence.

2. THE MAGIC FISH-HOOK

This story, current in New Zealand, tells how Maui was sent to take food to one of his aged progenitors; "but when he came to his ancestress he found her very ill, one half of her body being already dead, whereupon he wrenched off her lower jaw, made from it a fish-hook, which he concealed about him, and then returned to his home." [16] With this hook he went fishing, and drew up a huge fish, which proved to be the dry land. Had his foolish brothers who were in the canoe with him not cut up the fish, there would have been a continent; as it was, the land fell apart into several islands.

3. THE HINA OF HILO, AND MAUI'S DEED OF SNARING THE SUN [17]

"The Wailuku river, which flows through the town of Hilo, has its own peculiar and weird beauty. For miles it is a series of waterfalls and rapids. . . . By the side of this river Hina's son Maui had his lands. In the very bed of the river, in a cave under one of the largest falls, Hina made her home. . . . By the side of this river, the legends say, she pounded her tapa

[16] Dixon, *Oceanic Mythology*, p. 43 ff.
[17] An excerpt from Westervelt, *Legends of Maui*, pp. 140–145.

and prepared her food. . . . The days were very short and there was no time for rest while making tapa-cloth. . . . Although Hina was a goddess and had a family possessing miraculous power, it never entered the mind of the Hawaiian legend tellers to endow her with ease in producing wonderful results. . . .

"The Hina of Hilo was grieved as she toiled because after she had pounded the sheets out so thin that they were ready to be dried, she found it almost impossible to secure the necessary aid of the sun in the drying process. . . . The sun always hurried so fast that the sheets could not dry. . . . Hina found her incantations had no influence with the sun. She could not prevail upon him to go slower and give her more time for the completion of her task. Then she called on her powerful son, Maui-ki-i-ki-i, for aid.

". . . He took ropes made from the fibre of trees and vines [in another version, his sister Ina-Ika's hair] [18] and lassoed the sun while it climbed the side of the mountain and entered the great crater which hollows out the summit. The sun came through a large gap in the eastern side of the crater, rushing along as rapidly as possible. Then Maui threw his lassoes one after the other over the sun's legs (the rays of light), holding him fast and breaking off some of them. With a magic club Maui struck the face of the sun again and again. At last, wounded and weary, and also limping on its broken legs, the sun promised Maui to go slower forevermore."

4. THE DEATH OF MAUI

This story belongs to New Zealand, and has a tragic, ethical ring that really suggests a more epic phase of mythology than the Oceanic. For here the mischievous, wily hero appears in a serious mood, contemplating the unhappy fate of mankind, whereby every man must sooner or later go through the gate of death, and never return. Maui, in the pride of his magic power, tries to undo this fate, to find life beyond death and bring it to men on earth.

[18] *Ibid.*, p. 54. Ina-Ika is another "Hina," for "Ina" = "Hina."

Maui, after his many successful exploits, came home to his parents in high spirits. His father, though duly admiring the hero's feats, warned him that there was one who might yet overcome him.

When Maui asked incredulously by whom he could be overcome, "His father answered him, 'By your great ancestress, by Hine-nui-te-po, who, if you look, you may see flashing, and as it were, opening and shutting there, where the horizon meets the sky. . . . What you see yonder shining so brightly are her eyes, and her teeth are as sharp and hard as volcanic glass; her body is like that of man, and as for the pupils of her eyes, they are jasper; and her hair is like the tangles of long seaweed, and her mouth is like that of a barracouta.' " [19]

Maui, despite all warnings, set forth to find the dreadful ancestress Hina, and to creep through her gaping mouth into her belly, where Eternal Life was hidden in her womb. He took his friends the little birds with him — presumably for moral support, since they certainly offered no other aid — on his way down the shining path to the horizon; and he adjured them to make no noise that might wake the monster before he was safely out of her mouth again. Then he crept into her, past her obsidian teeth that were the gates of death. He found the treasure of Eternal Life, and started to make his escape. But just as he was between the sharp gates once more, one of the silly small birds could no longer contain itself at the sight of his undignified exit, and burst into loud, chirping laughter. Hine-nui-te-po awoke, and Maui was bitten in two. So his great ancestress conquered him, as she conquers all men — for through her jaws they must all go in the end.

Maui is the same person in various poses throughout these stories; but it is certainly bewildering to find so many strange females bearing the name of Hina, and claiming to be Maui's

[19] From Sir George Grey, *Polynesian Mythology and Ancient Traditional History of the New Zealand Race, as Furnished by their Priests and Chiefs,* quoted by Dixon, *op. cit.,* p. 52.

mother, grandmother, first begotten ancestress, first divine ancestress, sister, or other relative. Between his mother who lived in a hut, and threw him away for a useless weakling — a very true Polynesian lady, we may assume — and the terrible giantess Hine-nui-te-po, there seems to be little likeness. Why do all these mythical women merge their weird personalities in one name?

The mystery lightens when we consider that *Hina also means the moon.*[20] In the various Hinas of Polynesian myth we have just so many stages of "personification" of the moon, from the luminous, hollow woman on the horizon at the end of the shining path, to the mother who spends the nights with her children but goes down beneath the earth by day. The ancestress who is alive on one side and dead on the other, who appears to be the same Hina that owned the fire-secret, is clearly a lunar deity; [21] the Hina of Hilo, emerging from a cave to spread her tapa-cloth, seems to be a transitional figure.

If the gods of mythology really arose by a process of "personification," then Maui's mother who threw him away and later re-adopted him must be regarded as the end-result of a process beginning with a mere animistic conception of the moon. But in view of the fairytale character of all primitive story, the complete lack of cosmic interest in the truly savage mind, and the clear nature-symbolism in the higher mythologies, I believe the process of development to be exactly the contrary: Hina is not a symbol of the moon, but *the moon is a symbol of Hina, Woman.*

The moon, by reason of its spectacular changes, is a very expressive, adaptable, and striking symbol — far more so than the sun, with its simple career and unvarying form. A little contemplation shows quite clearly why the moon is so apt a feminine symbol, and why its meanings are so diverse that it may present many women at once — Hina in many, often incompatible forms, mother and maid and crone, young and

[20] Cf. Westervelt, *op. cit.*, p. 165; also Martha Beckwith, *Hawaiian Mythology* (1940), p. 220 ff.

[21] Cf. Dixon, *op. cit.*, p. 43; Westervelt, *op. cit.*, p. 23.

old. The human mind has an uncanny power of recognizing symbolic forms; and most readily, of course, will it seize upon those which are presented again and again without aberration. The eternal regularities of nature, the heavenly motions, the alternation of night and day on earth, the tides of the ocean, are the most insistent repetitious forms outside our own behavior-patterns (the symbolic value of which was discussed in the previous chapter). They are the most obvious metaphors to convey the dawning concepts of life-functions — birth, growth, decadence, and death.

Woman is, to primitive reflection, one of the basic mysteries of nature. In her, life originates; only the more enlightened societies know that sexual union initiates it. To naive observation, her body simply waxes and wanes with it for a certain length of years. She is the Great Mother, the symbol as well as the instrument of life.

But the actual process of human conception and gestation is too slow to exhibit a pattern for easy apprehension. One needs a symbol, to think coherently about it. Long before discursive thought could frame propositions to this purpose, men's minds probably recognized that natural symbol of womanhood, the waxing and waning moon.

It is a characteristic of presentational symbolism that many concepts may be telescoped into one total expression, without being severally presented by its constituent parts. The psychoanalysts, who discovered this trait in dream-symbolism, call it "condensation." The moon is a typical "condensed" symbol. It expresses the whole mystery of womankind, not only in its phases, but in its inferiority to the sun, its apparent nearness to the clouds that veil it like garments; perhaps the element of mystery that moonlight invariably creates, and the complicated time-cycle of its complete withdrawal (women, in tribal society, have elaborate schedules of taboo and ritual, of which a man cannot keep track), are not to be underestimated as symbolical factors.

But just as life grows to completeness with every waxing phase, so in the waning period one can see the old moon take possession, gradually, of the brilliant parts; life is swallowed

by death in a graphic process, and the swallowing monster
was ancestor to the life that dies. The significance of the
moon is irresistible. Ages of repetition hold the picture of
life and death before our eyes. No wonder if men learn to
contemplate it, to form their notions of an individual life
on the model of that cycle, and conceive death as a work of
ghostly forbears, the same who gave life — Hina the ancestress
is image of them all; nor that notions of resurrection or re-
incarnation should arise from such contemplation.

All this may explain why the name Hina should be bestowed on the moon, and why that luminary should be
deified. But since savage ideation does not require human
form to embody a power, why should this Hina be personified?

It is a generally accepted doctrine, almost a truism, that
a savage thinks everything that acts on him must be a person
like himself, and attributes human forms, needs, and motives
to inanimate objects because he cannot explain their activities in any other way. Again and again we read how primitive men, the makers of mythology, believed the sun, moon,
and stars to be people like themselves, with houses and fami-
lies, because the untutored mind could not distinguish between heavenly bodies and human bodies, or between their
respective habits. Almost any book on primitive myth that
one picks up repeats this credo, expounded long ago in the
classic work of Tylor:

"To the lower tribes of man, sun and stars, trees and
rivers, winds and clouds, become personal animate creatures,
leading lives conformed to human or animal analogies, and
performing their special functions with the aid of limbs like
beasts or of artificial instruments like men." [22] Or, in the
words of Andrew Lang:

"The savage draws no hard and fast line between himself
and the things in the world. . . . He assigns human speech
and feelings to sun and moon and stars and wind, no less
than to beasts, birds and fishes." [23]

[22] Tylor, *Primitive Culture*, I, 285.
[23] Lang, *Myth, Ritual and Religion*, I, 47.

Now, there is no doubt that Maui was said to have cut off the sun's legs,[24] and that the god Tane saw daylight under the armpit of his father Rangi, the sky; [25] these natural elements were certainly anthropomorphized in their full-fledged myths. What I do not believe, however, is that savages originally and spontaneously see the sun as a man, the moon as a woman, etc., else cosmological fantasy would be found much lower in the scale of human mentality than it is; nor do I think that nature-myths are originally attempts to explain astronomical or meteorological events. Nature-myths are originally stories of a superman hero, Maui, Hiawatha, Balder, or Prometheus, who is a superman because he is felt to be more than a man — he is Mankind in a single human figure. He battles with the forces of nature, the very same forces that made him and still sustain him. His relation to them is both filial and social; and *it is his incarnation that leads his elemental ancestors, brethren, and opponents to be personified.* In his story, he has a mother who is human enough; but, as he is Man, so she is Woman. Now the symbol of womanhood is the moon; and as a myth-making mentality does not keep symbol and meaning apart, the moon not only *represents*, but *presents*, Woman, the mother of Maui. Not personification of the moon, but a *lunarization of Hina*, gives rise to Polynesian cosmology.

Here we have the genesis of myth from legend. The savage does not, in his innocence, "think" the moon is a woman because he cannot tell the difference; he "thinks" it is a round fire, a shining disk; but *he sees Woman in it*, and names it Woman, and all its acts and relationships that interest him are those which carry out that significance. The connection of the culture-hero with the moon helps to humanize and define the functions of that deity, because the culture-hero is unequivocally human; so the lunar changes of light and form and place, nameless and difficult as mere empirical facts, acquire importance and obviousness from their analogy to human relations and functions: conceiving,

[24] Cf. Westervelt, *Legends of Maui*, p. 46.
[25] Cf. Shortland, *Maori Religion and Mythology*, p. 20.

bearing, loving, and hating, devouring and being devoured. The moon lends itself particularly to such interpretations, because it can present so many phases of womanhood. A host of different Hinas are lunar deities. Yet the unity of the underlying symbol reacts on the theological conception to make the various distinct Hinas *all of one blood*, the "mother" with her "daughters." This calls for mythological elaboration, and gives rise to genuine nature-myths.

The apparently irrational genealogies of gods and demi-gods spring from the fact that family relationships in myth may represent many different physical or logical relationships in nature and in human society. Night "gives birth" to Hanging Night, Drifting Night, Moaning Night; Morn, by a different logic, to Abiding Day, Bright Day, and Space.[26] And Man, in yet a different sense, is descended from the family of all these Powers.[27] The moon's "daughters" owe their filial status to a very different source than Maui his sonship, yet they are, by reason of both relations, unquestionably his sisters. Thus it is that one may find a personage who is clearly a moon-goddess taking part in one of Maui's fishing adventures.[28]

I have dwelled so long on the personification of the moon because it is, in the first place, the most convincing example of myth-making, and in the second place it may well have been the original inspiration to that age-long and world-wide process. There is a school of mythologists who maintain that not only the first, but *all*, mythology is moon-mythology.[29] I doubt whether this sweeping assumption is justified, since analogous treatment would most naturally be accorded the sun, stars, earth, sea, etc., as soon as human mentality advanced to the conception of an anthropomorphic lunar deity. Such an epoch-making stride of creative imagination could hardly have been limited to one subject or one symbol. Once we envisage Man's status in nature as that of a hero among cosmic gods, we cannot fail to see a host of gods all

[26] *Ibid.*, p. 12.   [27] Cf. Dixon, *Oceanic Mythology*, pp. 26–27.
[28] Cf. Westervelt, *op. cit.*, p. 156.
[29] *Gesellschaft für vergleichende Mythenforschung.*

round us; one would naturally expect, at this point, a "vegetative period" of religious fantasy.

The term *"religious* fantasy" is deliberately used here, although many mythologists quite explicitly reject it. Lessmann, of the afore-mentioned school, points out as a peculiar fact that "Greek mythology creates an impression as though religion and mythology were two closely related phenomena," [30] and explains the origin of that deceptive appearance through a confusion of Greek mythological gods with the Babylonian cultus-gods. The gods of ritual are related to ancestral spooks, devils, and local deities; but "at bottom," he says, "demonology is nothing but a low state of religion, and has no more than the latter to do with mythology." [31] I have tried to show how this "confusion" is the normal meeting point of ritual gods and story gods, how the harvest sheaf who becomes a harvest maid takes over the story of some maiden of mythology, whereby the story becomes theology, and enters into genuine religious thought.

In a book called *La genèse des mythes*, A. H. Krappe declares categorically that myths are made up out of whole cloth by poets, are purely aesthetic productions, and are not believed unless they happen to be incorporated in some sacred book.[32] But this is to confuse the myth-making stage of thought with the literal stage. Belief and doubt belong essentially to the latter; the myth-making consciousness knows only the appeal of ideas, and uses or forgets them. Only the development of literal-mindedness throws doubt upon them and raises the question of religious *belief.* Those great conceptions which can only dawn on us in a vast poetic symbolism are not propositions to which one says yea or nay; but neither are they literary toys of a mind that "knows better." The Homeric Greeks probably did not "believe in" Apollo as an American fundamentalist "believes in" Jonah and the whale, yet Apollo was not a literary fancy, a pure figment, to Homer, as he was to Milton. He was

[30] H. Lessmann, *Aufgaben und Ziele der vergleichenden Mythenforschung* (1907–1908), p. 7.
[31] *Loc. cit.*   [32] See p. 23 ff.

one of the prime realities — the Sun, the God, the Spirit from which men received inspirations. Whether anyone "believed" in all his deeds and amours does not matter; they were expressions of his character and seemed perfectly rational. Surely the Greeks believed in their gods just as we believe in ours; but they had no dogma concerning those gods, because in the average mind no matter-of-fact doubts of divine story had yet arisen, to cloud the significance of those remote or invisible beings. Common sense had never asserted itself *against* such stories, to make them look like fairytales or suggest that they were figures of speech. They were *figures of thought*, and the only figures that really bold and creative thought knew.

Yet there is something to be said for the contention that mythology is made by the epic poets. The great dreams of mankind, like the dreams of every individual man, are protean, vague, inconsistent, and so embarrassed with the riches of symbolic conception that every fantasy is apt to have a hundred versions. We see this in the numberless variants in which legends are handed down by peoples who have no literature. One identical hero has quite incompatible adventures, or one and the same adventure is ascribed to several heroes, gods, or ogres. Sometimes one cannot tell a maiden from a bird, or from her own mother, whose "attributive animal" may be that same bird; and this bird-mother-daughter may be the Earth-Goddess and the Moon and the First Woman. Mythological figures in their pristine stages have no fixity, either of form or meaning; they are very much like dream images, elusive, over-determined, their stories condensations of numberless ideas, their names often the only evidence of any self-identity.[33] As soon as their imaginative growth is accomplished, traditions become mean-

---

[33] Miss Harrison has given recognition to this fact, and it was this very insight which led her to find the primitive sources of religion behind the civilized forms of Greek antiquity which she knew as a scholar.

"Our minds are imbued with classical mythology," she says, "our imagination peopled with the vivid personalities, the clear-cut outlines of Olympian gods; it is only by a severe mental effort that we realize . . . that *there were no gods at all*, . . . but only conceptions of the human mind, shifting and

ingless and corrupt. Disconnected fragments of great primitive world-concepts survive in superstitions or in magic formulae, which the skilled mythologist may recognize as echoes of a more ancient system of thought, but which the average intelligent mortal can only view as bizarre and surprising forms of foolishness.

The great mythologies which have survived both the overgrowth of mystic fable and the corruption of popular tradition are those that have become fixed in national poems, such as the Iliad, the Eddas, the Ramayana, the Kalevala. For an epic may be fantastic, but it cannot be entirely inconsistent; it is a narrative, its incidents have temporal order, its world is geographical and its characters personal. Just as the introduction of nature-symbols gave fantasy a certain dominant pattern by seeing its monsters and personages exemplified in the behavior of sun and moon and stars, so the great vehicle of mythological tradition, the epic, places its peculiar restrictions on the rampant imagination and disciplines it further into consistency and coherence. For it demands not only personification, not only some sort of rise and fall in heroic action, but *poetic form*, a unity above the separate incidents, a beginning, climax, and solution of the entire mythical drama. Such formulation requires a radical handling of the story-material which tradition is apt to supply in prodigal quantities and utter confusion; therefore the principle of poetic form is a powerful agent in the refashioning of human ideas. This has given rise to the belief, stated in somewhat doctrinaire and exaggerated terms by Krappe, that mythology is *essentially* the work of epic poets. "Without the epic, no mythology. Homer is the author of the Hellenic mythology, the Norwegian and Icelandic Skalds have created the mythology of Scandinavia. The same phenomenon may be seen in India, in Ireland, and in Japan." [34]

changing colour with every human mind that conceived them. Art which makes the image, literature which crystallizes attributes and functions, arrest and fix this shifting kaleidoscope; but, until the coming of art and literature and to some extent after, the formulary of theology is 'all things are in flux.' "
Prolegomena, p. 164.
[34] Krappe, *La génèse des mythes*, p. 57.

Indeed, the mythologies of Hellas and of the Eddas seem very remote from the crazy dreamlike yarns of savages. For the great epics may move against a background of divine powers and cosmic events, but their heroes are human, not mystical, and the most wonderful deeds arc logically motivated and accomplished. Ulysses or Siegfried or Beowulf sets out on a definite quest, and the story ends with its success or frustration; the whole structure presents the career of a superhuman personage, a representative of the race in its strength and pride, definitely oriented in a world of grand forces and conflicts, challenges, and destinies. When we look from these perfected cosmic and social conceptions in the great epics to the fantasies of Iroquois and South Sea Islanders, we may well be tempted to say that savages have no mythology worthy of the name, and that the poets are the creators of that vast symbolic form.

Yet this is not true. The "making" of mythology by creative bards is only a metamorphosis of world-old and universal ideas. In the finished works of Homer and Hesiod we may see only what looks like free invention for the sake of the story, but in the poetry of ruder tribes the popular, religious origin of myth is still clearly apparent despite the formative influence of a poetic structure.

The Finnish *Kalevala* is a classic example of the transition from mystical nature-theology and immemorial legend, to a national treasure of philosophical beliefs and historical traditions embodied in permanent poetic form. It is probably the most primitive — though by no means the oldest — of all epics; and it is quite obviously a transcript of savage mythology, more concerned with cosmic origins, conflicts of nature-deities, incantations, feats and contests of magic, than with the exploits of brave men and the good or evil ways of women. It knows no Trojan wars, no planned campaigns of vengeance; neither lifelong quests, nor founding of cities and temples. In its first "rune," or canto, the Water-Mother swims in the sea for seven hundred years; at last she lets the blue teal nest on her lifted knee, until from the fragments of its broken eggs the land, the shallows, the deeps and the sky are fashioned; after this creation she carries the hero in her womb for thirty years, whereupon he is born an old man full of magic. The Queen of Night supplies him with Rainbow Maidens and Air Princesses for unwilling lady-loves whom he never actually manages to marry. Waina-moinen, this strangely old and unsuccessful hero, plants forests and fells them, supervises the creation of grain, invents the steam bath, builds boats by sheer magic, and makes the first harp. He is no fairytale prince beloved of women, but is purely a culture-hero. When he conquers an adversary he does so by magic songs, and his rash young enemies and rivals challenge him not to armed combat, but to singing-contests.

The whole story really reads more like Polynesian mythology than like European epic poetry. Animals are men's messengers or servants, heroes are custodians of sun, moon, fire and water, maidens go to live with fishes, their mothers are Night Queens and their brothers Frost Giants. *Kalevala* is essentially a string of magic fishings and plantings and strange encounters, like a told dream, patched together with such human episodes as sledge-building, broom-binding, and the Finns' inevitable baths, to hold heroes and spirits somehow to the local scene. How far a call to Helen and Mene-laus and Paris, the Achaean armies encamped, the death of Hector, the sorrow of Andromache!

Yet there are culture-heroes in Greek legend, too, who steal fire from the gods, and youths who would contend with the sun; and in the *Kalevala* there are sudden passages of human import set in its strange mystical frame. When ancient Wainamoinen seeks the Rainbow Maid, the daughter of the Night Woman, that very real and lovely little girl throws herself into a lake rather than give herself to the weird magician who was old when he was born. The maiden Aino is too childlike, too human for him. She sits on a rock above the water, bewailing her youth and freedom and the cruel decree of her parents. Her plight is realistic and touching, and her suicide quite naturally taboos the lake for the family, the tribe, and the unhappy lover.

There is nothing in Polynesian or Indian mythology that comes as near to real life as the lament and desperate act of the Rainbow Maiden Aino. Every nature mythology treats the rainbow as an elusive maiden, but it requires the thoughtful formulation of poetry to see the rainbow's ephemeral beauty in a girl too wayward and beautiful for her aged lover, to put the human story first and incorporate the heavenly phenomenon merely in her symbolic name. Here is the beginning of that higher mythology wherein the world is essentially the stage for human life, the setting of the true epic, which is human and social. This development in fantasy depends on the clarifying and unifying medium of conscious composition, the discipline of the compact metrical verse, which inevitably sets up standards of coherence and continuity such as the fragmentary dream-mode does not know or require.

The effect of this poetic influence is incomplete in the *Kalevala*, but it is there, and lets us see the process by which mythology is "made" in the epic. The embodiment of mythology in poetry is simply its perfected and final form; because it has no subsequent higher phases, we regard this formulation as the "true" mythical imagination. And because the symbolic forms stand forth so clearly as pure articulations of fantasy, we see them only as fictions, not as the supreme concepts of life which they really represent, and by which men orient themselves religiously in the cosmos.

It is a peculiar fact that every major advance in thinking, every epoch-making new insight, springs from a new type of symbolic transformation. A higher level of thought is primarily a new activity; its course is opened up by a new departure in semantic. The step from mere sign-using to symbol-using marked the crossing of the line between animal and man; this initiated the natural growth of language. The birth of symbolic gesture from emotional and practical movement probably begot the whole order of ritual, as well as the discursive mode of pantomime. The recognition of vague, vital meanings in physical forms — perhaps the first dawn of symbolism — gave us our idols, emblems, and totems; the primitive function of dream permits our first envisagement of events. The momentous discovery of nature-symbolism, of the pattern of life reflected in natural phenomena, produced the first universal insights. Every mode of thought is bestowed on us, like a gift, with some new principle of symbolic expression. It has a logical development, which is simply the exploitation of all the uses to which that symbolism lends itself; and when these uses are exhausted, the mental activity in question has found its limit. Either it serves its purpose and becomes truistic, like our orientation in "Euclidean space" or our appreciation of objects and their accidents (on the pattern of language-structure, significantly called "logic"); or it is superseded by some more powerful symbolic mode which opens new avenues of thought.

The origin of myth is dynamic, but its purpose is philosophical. It is the primitive phase of metaphysical thought, the first embodiment of *general ideas*. It can do no more than initiate and present them; for it is a non-discursive symbolism, it does not lend itself to analytic and genuinely abstractive techniques. The highest development of which myth is capable is the exhibition of human life and cosmic order that epic poetry reveals. We cannot abstract and manipulate its concepts any further *within the mythical mode*. When this mode is exhausted, natural religion is superseded by a discursive and more literal form of thought, namely philosophy.

Language, in its literal capacity, is a stiff and conventional medium, unadapted to the expression of genuinely new ideas, which usually have to break in upon the mind through some great and bewildering metaphor. But bare denotative language is a most excellent instrument of exact reason; it is, in fact, the only general precision instrument the human brain has ever evolved.[35] Ideas first adumbrated in fantastic form become real intellectual property only when discursive language rises to their expression. That is why myth is the indispensable forerunner of metaphysics; and metaphysics is the literal formulation of basic abstractions, on which our

[35] I regard mathematical symbolism as a linguistic form of expression.

comprehension of sober facts is based. All detail of knowledge, all exact distinction, measure, and practical manipulation, are possible only on a basis of truly abstract concepts, and a framework of such concepts constitutes a philosophy of nature, literal, denotative, and systematic. Only language has the power to effect such an analysis of experience, such a rationalization of knowledge. But it is only where experience is already presented — through some other formative medium, some vehicle of apprehension and memory — that the canons of literal thought have any application. We must have ideas before we can make literal analyses of them; and really new ideas have their own modes of appearance in the unpredictable creative mind.

The first inquiry as to the literal truth of a myth marks the change from poetic to discursive thinking. As soon as the interest in factual values awakes, the mythical mode of world-envisagement is on the wane. But emotional attitudes that have long centered on a myth are not easily broken; the vital ideas embodied in it cannot be repudiated because someone discovers that the myth does not constitute a *fact*. Poetic significance and factual reference, which are two entirely different relations in the general symbol-and-meaning pattern, become identified under the one name of "truth." People who discover the obvious discrepancy between fantasy and fact deny that myths are true; those who recognize the truth of myths claim that they register facts. There is the silly conflict of religion and science, in which science must triumph, not because what it says about religion is just, but because religion rests on a young and provisional form of thought, to which philosophy of nature — proudly called "science," or "knowledge" — must succeed if thinking is to go on. There must be a rationalistic period from this point onward. Some day when the vision is totally rationalized, the ideas exploited and exhausted, there will be another vision, a new mythology.

The gods have their twilight, the heroes are forgotten; but though mythology has been a passing phase in man's mental history, the epic lives on, side by side with philosophy and science and all the higher forms of thought. Why? What is the epic, the apotheosis of myth, to those who have repudiated that metaphorical view of life?

The epic is the first flower — or one of the first, let us say — of a new symbolic mode, the mode of *art*. It is not merely a receptacle of old symbols, namely those of myth, but is itself a new symbolic form, great with possibilities, ready to take meanings and express ideas that have had no vehicle before. What these new ideas are to which art gives us our first, and perhaps our only, access, may be gathered from an analysis of that perfectly familiar yet cryptic notion, "musical significance," to which we proceed in the next chapter.

CHAPTER VIII

On Significance in Music

WHAT distinguishes a work of art from a "mere" artifact? What distinguishes the Greek vase, as an artistic achievement, from the hand-made bean pot of New England, or the wooden bucket, which cannot be classed as a work of art? The Greek vase is an artifact, too; it was fashioned according to a traditional pattern; it was made to hold grain or oil or other domestic asset, not to stand in a museum. Yet it has an artistic value for all generations. What gives it that preëminence?

To reply, "Its beauty," is simply to beg the question, since artistic value *is* beauty in the broadest sense. Bean pots and wooden buckets often have what artists call "a good shape," i.e., they are in no wise offensive to the eye. Yet, without being at all ugly, they are insignificant, commonplace, *non*-artistic rather than *in*artistic. What do they lack, that a work of art — even a humble, domestic Greek vase — possesses?

In the words of a well-known critic, Mr. Clive Bell, " 'Significant Form' is the one quality common to all works of visual art." [1] Professor L. A. Reid, a philosopher well versed in the problems of aesthetics, extends the scope of this characteristic to all art whatsoever. For him, "Beauty is just expressiveness," and "the true aesthetic form . . . is expressive form." [2] Another art critic, Mr. Roger Fry, accepts the term "Significant Form," though he frankly cannot define its meaning. From the contemplation of (say) a beautiful

[1] *Art* (1914), p. 8.
[2] *A Study in Aesthetics* (1931). See esp. pp. 43 and 197. See also *Knowledge and Truth* (1923), esp. the final chapter, and "Beauty and Significance," *Proceedings of the Aristotelian Society*, N.S. XXIX (1928–29), pp. 123–154.

pot, and as an effect of its harmony of line and texture and color, "there comes to us," he says, "a feeling of purpose; we feel that all these sensually logical conformities are the outcome of a particular feeling, or of what, for want of a better word, we call an idea; and we may even say that the pot is the expression of an idea in the artist's mind." [3] After many efforts to define the notion of artistic expressiveness, he concludes: "I seem to be unable at present to get beyond this vague adumbration of significant form. Flaubert's 'expression of the idea' seems to me to correspond exactly to what I mean, but alas! he never explained, and probably could not, what he meant by the 'idea.' " [4]

There is a strong tendency today to treat art as a *significant* phenomenon rather than as a pleasurable experience, a gratification of the senses. This is probably due to the free use of dissonance and so-called "ugliness" by our leading artists in all fields — in literature, music, and the plastic arts. It may also be due in some measure to the striking indifference of the uneducated masses to artistic values. In past ages, these masses had no access to great works of art; music and painting and even books were the pleasures of the wealthy; it could be assumed that the poor and vulgar would enjoy art if they could have it. But now, since everybody can read, visit museums, and hear great music at least over the radio, the judgment of the masses on these things has become a reality, and has made it quite obvious that *great art is not a direct sensuous pleasure*. If it were, it would appeal — like cake or cocktails — to the untutored as well as to the cultured taste. This fact, together with the intrinsic "unpleasantness" of much contemporary art, would naturally weaken any theory that treated art as pure pleasure. Add to this the current logical and psychological interest in symbolism, in expressive media and the articulation of ideas, and we need not look far afield for a new philosophy of art, based upon the concept of "significant form." [5]

[3] *Vision and Design* (1925), p. 50.   [4] *Ibid.*, p. 302.
[5] This tendency was recognized long ago by the author of an article on symbolism, which opens with the words: "An exhaustive treatise on the

But if forms in and of themselves be significant, and indeed must be so to be classed as artistic, then certainly the kind of significance that belongs to them constitutes a very special problem in semantics. What is artistic significance? What sort of meaning do "expressive forms" express?

Clearly they do not convey propositions, as literal symbols do. We all know that a seascape (say) represents water and rocks, boats and fish-piers; that a still-life represents oranges and apples, a vase of flowers, dead game or fish, etc. But such a content is not what makes the paint-patterns on the canvas "expressive forms." The mere notion of rabbits, grapes, or even boats at sunset is not the "idea" that inspires a painting. The artistic idea is always a "deeper" conception.

Several psychologists have ventured to unmask this "deeper" significance by interpreting pictures, poems, and even musical compositions as symbols of loved objects, mainly, of course, of a forbidden nature. Artistic activity, according to the psychoanalysts who have given it their attention, is an expression of primitive dynamisms, of unconscious wishes, and uses the objects or scenes represented to embody the secret fantasies of the artist.[6]

---

symbol is an aesthetic in miniature; for in recent years symbolism has acquired such a central position in aesthetics that one can hardly take a step in that wide domain without stumbling upon some sort of symbolic relation." R. M. Wernaer, "Das aesthetische Symbol," *Zeitschrift für Philosophie und philosophische Kritik*, CXXX (1907), 1: 47–75.

[6] See Ch. Badouin, *Psychanalyse de l'art* (1929); A. M. Bodkin, "The Relevance of Psycho-Analysis to Art Criticism," *British Journal of Psychology*, XV (1924–25), part II, 174–183; J. W. Brown, "Psychoanalysis in the Plastic Arts," *International Journal of Psychoanalysis*, X, part I (January 1929); J. Landquist, "Das künstlerische Symbol," *Imago*, VI (1920), 4: 297–322; Hanns Sachs, "Kunst als Persönlichkeit," *Imago*, XV (1929), 1: 1–14; the same author's bibliographical essay, "Aesthetics and Psychology of the Artist," *International Journal of Psychoanalysis*, II (1921), part I, 94–100; George Whitehead, *Psychoanalysis and Art* (1930). With special reference to music, see A. Elster, *Musik und Erotik* (1925); Max Graf, *Die innere Werkstatt des Musikers* (1910); K. Eggar, "The Subconscious Mind and the Musical Faculty," *Proceedings of the Musical Association*, XLVII (1920–21), 23–38; D. Mosonyi, "Die irrationalen Grundlagen der Musik," *Imago*, XXI (1935), 2: 207–226; A. van der Chijs, "Ueber das Unisono in der Komposition," *Imago*, XII (1926), 1: 23–31. This list is not exhaustive, but representative.

This explanation has much to recommend it. It accounts for the fact that we are inclined to credit works of art with *significance*, although (by reason of the moral censorship which distorts the appearance of basic desires) we can never say what they signify. It does justice to the emotional interest, the seriousness with which we receive artistic experience. Above all, it brings this baffling department of human activity into the compass of a general psychological system — the so-called "dynamic psychology," based on the recognition of certain fundamental human needs, of the conflicts resulting from their mutual interference, and of the mechanism whereby they assert, disguise, and finally realize themselves. The starting-point of this psychology is the discovery of a previously unrecognized *symbolic mode*, typified in dream, and perfectly traceable in all works of fantasy. To assimilate art to the imaginative life in general is surely not a forced procedure. It seems, moreover, to bring the problem of aesthetic experience into the symbol-centered philosophy that constitutes the theme of this book.

These are strong recommendations for the psychoanalytic theory of aesthetics. But despite them all, I do not think this theory (though probably valid) throws any real light on those issues which confront artists and critics and constitute the philosophical problem of art. For the Freudian interpretation, no matter how far it be carried, never offers even the rudest criterion of *artistic* excellence. It may explain why a poem was written, why it is popular, what human features it hides under its fanciful imagery; what secret ideas a picture combines, and why Leonardo's women smile mysteriously. But *it makes no distinction between good and bad art*. The features to which it attributes the importance and significance of a great masterpiece may all be found just as well in an obscure work of some quite incompetent painter or poet. Wilhelm Stekel, one of the leading Freudian psychologists interested in artistic productions as a field for analysis, has stated this fact explicitly: "I want to point out at once," he says, "that it is irrelevant to our purpose whether the poet in question is a great, universally acknowledged poet, or whether we are dealing with a little poetaster. For, after all, we are investigating only the impulse which drives people to create." [7]

An analysis to which the artistic merit of a work is irrelevant can hardly be regarded as a promising technique of art-criticism,[8] for it can look only to a hidden *content* of the work, and not to what every artist knows as the real problem — the *perfection of form*, which makes this form "significant" in the artistic sense. We cannot evaluate this perfection by finding more and more obscure objects represented or suggested by the form.

Interest in represented objects and interest in the visual or verbal structures that depict them are always getting hopelessly entangled. Yet I believe "artistic meaning" belongs to the sensuous construct as such; this alone is beautiful, and contains all that contributes to its beauty.

The most obvious approach to the formal aspect of art would be, of course, through the study of pure design. But in poetry pure design is non-existent, and in the plastic arts

[7] *Die Träume der Dichter* (1912), p. 32.

[8] Oddly enough, this fact is overlooked by so excellent a literary critic as J. M. Thorburn, who says: "The poet must, I think, be regarded as striving after the simplicity of a childish utterance. His goal is to think as a child, to understand as a child. . . .

"When he has written, and the work is good, the measure of his genius is the depth to which he has gone back, the originality of his idiom and the degree of its antiquity." (*Art and the Unconscious*, pp. 70–71.)

"If art be symbolic, it is the artist who discovers the symbol. But he need not — though of course he may — recognize it as a symbol. We, the appreciative recipients of his work, must so recognize it." (*Ibid.*, p. 79.)

This makes artistic judgment a special development of psychoanalytic technique. "We try to reconstruct his [the artist's] personality from whatever sources we may." (*Ibid.*, p. 21.) The more dreamlike and subjective the work, the more primitive is its language; the greatest poets should then be the most graphic dreamers. Stekel has pointed out, however, that at the level of symbol production the poet does not differ from the most prosaic soul. After analyzing three dreams — one reported by a woman under his care, one by Goethe, and one by that poet's friend and henchman, Eckermann — he observes: "Is it not remarkable that the great poet Goethe and the unknown little woman . . . should have constructed such similar dreams? And were one to award a prize for poetic excellence, Eckermann and the deserted woman would both win over Goethe." (*Die Träume der Dichter*, p. 14.)

it has played but a minor role until very recent times. It is carried to considerable heights in textiles, and occurs as decoration in conjunction with architecture and ceramics. But the world's greatest artists have rarely worked in these media; sculptures and paintings are their high achievements. If we would really restrict ourselves to pure perceptible forms, the plastic arts offer but a sparse field for research, and not a central one.

Music, on the other hand, is preëminently non-representative even in its classical productions, its highest attainments. It exhibits pure form not as an embellishment, but as its very essence; we can take it in its flower — for instance, German music from Bach to Beethoven — and have practically nothing but tonal structures before us: no scene, no object, no fact. That is a great aid to our chosen preoccupation with form. There is no obvious, literal content in our way. If the meaning of art belongs to the sensuous percept itself apart from what it ostensibly represents, then such purely artistic meaning should be most accessible through musical works.

This is not to say that music is the highest, the most expressive, or the most universal art. Sound is the *easiest* medium to use in a purely artistic way; but to work in the safest medium is not at all the same thing as to achieve the highest aim. Furthermore, we should take warning against the fallacy of hasty generalization — of assuming that through music we are studying all the arts, so that every insight into the nature of music is immediately applicable to painting, architecture, poetry, dance, and drama; and above all, that propositions which do not have obvious analogues in all these departments are not very valuable in their restricted musical context.[9] A basic unity of purpose and even of general method

[9] An artistic principle may be obvious in just one special field, and prove to be generally applicable only after development in that field; for instance, Edward Bullough's excellent notion of "psychical distance" (of which more will be said later) would probably not have been recognized as an important principle in music or ceramic art, but the peculiar problems of drama required such a concept. Even if it had not proved to be universally applicable, it would be valid in its original domain. (See " 'Psychical Distance'

for all the arts is a very inviting hypothesis, and may well be demonstrable in the end; but as a foregone conclusion, a dogmatic premise, it is dangerous because it discourages special theories and single-minded, technical study. General theories should be constructed *by generalization* from the principles of a special field, known and understood in full detail. Where no such systematic order exists to serve as a pattern, a general theory is more likely to consist of vague generalities than of valid generalizations.

Therefore let us concern ourselves, at present, with the significance of music alone. A great deal of philosophical thought has been bestowed on this subject, if not since Winkelmann and Herder, at least since Schopenhauer; and not only from the general standpoint of the aesthetician, which those early writers took, but from the more specialized one of the musician and the musical critic. The history of musical aesthetics is an eventful one, as intellectual histories go, so it is unavoidable that a good many theories have to be weighed in considering it. In the course of all this reflection and controversy, the problem of the nature and function of music has shifted its center several times; in Kant's day it hinged on the conception of the arts as cultural agencies, and concerned the place of music among these contributions to intellectual progress. On this basis the great worshiper of reason naturally ranked it lowest of all art-forms.[10] The Darwinians of later days sought the key to its importance in its origins; if it could be proved — or at least, imagined — to have survival value, or even to be the residue of some formerly useful instinct or device, its dignity was saved, even if our interest in it now were only what William James took it to be — "a mere incidental peculiarity of the nervous system, with no teleological significance." [11] Helmholtz,

---

as a Factor in Art and as an Aesthetic Principle," *British Journal of Psychology*, V (1912), part II, 87–118.)

[10] See the excerpt from Kant's *Kritik der Urteilskraft* in F. M. Gatz's source-book, *Musik-Aesthetik* (1929), p. 53.

[11] *Principles of Psychology*, 2 vols. (1890). See vol. II, p. 419. His words refer directly to fear-reactions in high places, which, he says, in this respect resemble "liability to sea-sickness, or love of music."

Wundt, Stumpf, and other psychologists to whom the existence and persistence of music presented a problem, based their inquiries on the assumption that music was a form of *pleasurable sensation*, and tried to compound the value of musical compositions out of the "pleasure-elements" of their tonal constituents. This gave rise to an aesthetic based on liking and disliking, a hunt for a sensationist definition of beauty, and a conception of art as the satisfaction of taste; this type of art theory, which of course applies without distinction to all the arts, is "aesthetic" in the most literal sense, and its exponents today are rather proud of not overstepping the limits of the field so defined.[12] But beyond a description of tested pleasure-displeasure reactions to simple sounds or elementary sound-complexes, and certain observations on people's tastes in musical selections, this approach has not taken us; it seems to be an essentially barren adventure.

Another kind of reaction to music, however, is more striking, and seems more significant: that is the *emotional* response it is commonly supposed to evoke. The belief that music arouses emotions goes back even to the Greek philosophers. It led Plato to demand, for his ideal state, a strict censorship of modes and tunes, lest his citizens be tempted by weak or voluptuous airs to indulge in demoralizing emotions.[13] The same principle is often invoked to explain the use of music in tribal society, the lure of the African drum, the clarion call and the "Pibroch" calling armies or clans to battle, the world-old custom of lulling the baby to sleep with slumber songs. The legend of the sirens is based on a belief in the narcotic and toxic effect of music, as also the story of Terpander's preventing civil war in Sparta, or of the Danish King Eric, who committed murder as a result

[12] Thus Clive Bell, having proposed the concept of "significant form" as the keynote of art criticism, says: "At this point a query arises . . .: 'Why are we so profoundly moved by forms related in a particular way?' The question is extremely interesting, but irrelevant to aesthetics. In pure aesthetics we have only to consider our emotion and its object."

If questions about the *relation* between emotion and object are irrelevant, what is there to "consider" about these factors?

[13] *Republic*, bk. iii.

of a harpist's deliberate experiment in mood-production.[14] Despite the fact that there is, to my knowledge, not a single authentic record of any specific change of disposition or intention, or even the inhibition of a practical impulse in any person by the agency of music, this belief in the physical power of the art has come down to modern times. Music is known, indeed, to affect pulse-rate and respiration, to facilitate or disturb concentration, to excite or relax the organism, *while the stimulus lasts*; but beyond evoking impulses to sing, tap, adjust one's step to musical rhythm, perhaps to stare, hold one's breath or take a tense attitude, music does not ordinarily influence behavior.[15] Its somatic influences seem to affect unmusical as well as musical persons (the selections usually employed in experimentation would be more likely to irritate than to soothe or inspire a musical person), and to be, therefore, functions of *sound* rather than of *music*.[16] Experiments made with vocal music are entirely unreliable, since words and the pathos of the human voice are added to the musical stimulus. On the whole, the behavior of concert audiences after even the most thrilling performances makes the traditional magical influence of music on human actions very dubious. Its somatic effects are transient, and its moral hangovers or uplifts seem to be negligible.

Granting, however, that the effects do not long outlive their causes, the proposition that music arouses emotions in

[14] These and other stories are cited by Irmgard Otto in an essay, "Von sonderbahrer Würckung und Krafft der Musik," *Die Musik*, XXIX (1937), part II, 625–630.

[15] For an exhaustive treatment of the physical and mental effects of music, see the dissertation by Charles M. Disserens, *The Influence of Music on Behavior* (1926). Dr. Disserens accepts much evidence that I would question, yet offers no report of practical acts inspired by music, or even permanent effects on temperament or disposition, such as were claimed for it in the eighteenth century. (Cf., e.g., *Reflections on Antient and Modern Musick, with Application to the Cure of Diseases* (Anon., 1749); or Albrecht's *De Effectu Musices in Corpus Animatum*.)

[16] An often neglected distinction pointed out in Ernst Kurth's *Musikpsychologie*, p. 152. Kurth observes that Stumpf, working deliberately with unmusical rather than musical persons, gave us a *Tonpsychologie* but not a *Musikpsychologie*.

the listener does not seem, offhand, like a fantastic or mythical assertion. In fact, the belief in the affective power of music is respectable enough to have led some very factual-minded modern psychologists to conduct tests for the emotional effects of different compositions and collect the reported data. They have compiled lists of possible "effects," such as:

Sad	Rested
Serious	Amused
Like dancing	Sentimental
Stirred, excited	Longing
Devotional	Patriotic
Gay, happy	Irritated

The auditors of certain musical selections, which were usually of the so-called "semi-popular" sort (e.g. MacDowell's *To a Wild Rose*, Sousa's *Volunteer March*), were given prepared data-sheets and asked to check their musically stimulated feelings with the rubrics there suggested.[17]

The results of such experiments [18] add very little to the well-known fact that most people connect feelings with music, and (unless they have thought about the precise nature of that connection) believe they *have* the feelings while they are under the influence of the music, especially if you ask them which of several feelings the music is giving them. That quick, lilting tunes are said to make one feel happy or "like dancing," hymns to make one solemn, and funeral marches sad, is hardly surprising; nor that *Love's*

[17] See Esther Gatewood, "The Nature of Musical Enjoyment," in *The Effects of Music*, edited by Max Schoen (1927).

[18] These results were, of course, not spontaneous, since the questionnaire directed the subjects' expectations to a special kind of experience which is popularly supposed to result from hearing music, and moreover dictated a *choice*, which made it necessary to attribute some particular feeling wholly, or preëminently, to any given piece. Fleeting affects, superseded by others, could not be checked off without creating a wrong impression; only general states of feeling were supposed to result, and were therefore dutifully reported.

Essentially the same technique is employed by Kate Hevner; see her "Expression in Music: Discussion of Experimental Studies and Theories," *Psychological Review*, XLII (1935), 2: 186–204, and "Experimental Studies of the Elements of Expression in Music," *American Journal of Psychology*, XLVIII (1936), 2: 246–268.

Old Sweet Song was generally said to stir "tender memories."
The whole inquiry really took for granted what Charles
Avison, a British musicologist and organist, said without
experimental evidence in 1775: that "the force of sound
in alarming the passions is prodigious," and that music "does
naturally raise a variety of passions in the human breast,
similar to the sounds which are expressed; and thus, by the
musician's art, . . . we are by turns elated with joy, or
sunk in pleasing sorrow, rouzed to courage, or quelled by
grateful terrors, melted into pity, tenderness, and love, or
transported to the regions of bliss, in an extacy of divine
praise." [19]

The terms "pleasing sorrow" and "grateful terrors" present
something of a puzzle. If music really grieves or frightens
us, why do we listen to it? The modern experimenters are
not disturbed by this question, but Avison felt called upon
to meet it. The sorrows and terrors of music, he explained,
are not our own, but are sympathetically felt by us; "There
are certain sounds natural to joy, others to grief or de-
spondency, others to tenderness and love; and by hearing
these, we naturally sympathize with those who either enjoy
or suffer." [20]

But if we are moved by sympathy, with whom are we
sympathizing? Whose feelings do we thus appreciate? The
obvious answer is: the musician's. He who produces the
music is pouring out the real feelings of his heart. Music is
his avenue of self-expression, he confesses his emotions to an
audience, or — in solitude — just works them off to relieve
himself. In an age when most performers offered their own
compositions or even improvisations, this explanation of
music was quite natural. Rousseau, Marpurg, Mattheson,
C. Ph. E. Bach, were all convinced that (as Bach put it)
"since a musician cannot otherwise move people, but he be
moved himself, so he must necessarily be able to induce in
himself all those affects which he would arouse in his auditors;
he conveys his feelings to them, and thus most readily moves

---

[19] *An Essay on Musical Expression* (1775), pp. 3–4.
[20] *Loc. cit.* See also p. 5, n.

them to sympathetic emotions." [21]   The problem was somewhat complicated by the growing distinction between composers and performers toward the end of the century; but here the reciprocity of expression and impression came to the rescue. The composer is, indeed, the original subject of the emotions depicted, but the performer becomes at once his confidant and his mouthpiece. He transmits the feelings of the master to a sympathetic audience.

In this form the doctrine has come down to our day, and is widely accepted by musicians and philosophers alike. From Rousseau to Kierkegaard and Croce among philosophers, from Marpurg to Hausegger and Riemann among music critics, but above all among musicians themselves — composers, conductors, and performers — we find the belief very widely disseminated that music is an emotional catharsis, that its essence is self-expression. Beethoven, Schumann, Liszt, to mention only the great, have left us testimonials to that effect. Moreover, it is the opinion of the average sentimental music-lover that all moving and poignant music must translate some personal experience, the longing or ecstasy or despair of the artist's own *vie amoureuse*; and most musical amateurs will accept without hesitation the statement of Henri Prunières, who says categorically that whatever feelings a composer may convey, "we may rest assured that he will not express these sentiments with authority unless he has experienced them at some given moment of his existence." [22]   Most likely they will even go so far as to agree that, in the case of a theme which Beethoven used ten years after he had first jotted it down, "It is probable that such a theme, translating an impression of keenest sorrow, came to him during a day of suffering." [23]   The self-expression theory, which classes music with "such expressions as 'oh-oh,'

[21] *Versuch ueber die wahre Art, das Klavier zu spielen* (1925, reprint from 2nd ed.; 1st ed., part I, 1753, part II, 1762). See part I, p. 85. For a detailed study of this early theory, see Wilhelm Caspari's dissertation, *Gegenstand und Wirkung der Tonkunst nach der Ansicht der Deutschen im 18. Jahrhundert* (1903). For extensive source-material, see Gatz, *Musik-Aesthetik*.

[22] "Musical Symbolism," *Musical Quarterly*, XIX (1933), 1: 18–28. See p. 20.   [23] *Ibid.*, p. 21.

or at a higher level, lyrical verses," as Carnap says, is the
most popular doctrine of the significance and function of
music.[24] It explains in a very plausible way the undeniable
connection of music with feeling, and the mystery of a work
of art without ostensible subject-matter; above all, it brings
musical activity within the compass of modern psychology —
behavioristic, dynamic, genetic, or what not.

Yet the belief that music is essentially a form of self-
expression meets with paradox in very short order; philosophically it comes to a stop almost at its very beginning. For
the history of music has been a history of more and more
integrated, disciplined, and articulated *forms,* much like the
history of language, which waxes important only as it is
weaned from its ancient source in expressive cries, and becomes denotative and connotative rather than emotional.
We have more need of, and respect for, so-called "pure
music" than ancient cultures seem to have had; [25] yet our
counterpoints and harmonic involutions have nothing like
the expressive abandon of the Indian "Ki-yi" and "How-
how," the wailing primitive dirge, the wild syncopated shouts
of African tribesmen. *Sheer self-expression requires no
artistic form.* A lynching-party howling round the gallows-
tree, a woman wringing her hands over a sick child, a lover
who has just rescued his sweetheart in an accident and stands
trembling, sweating, and perhaps laughing or crying with
emotion, is giving vent to intense feelings; but such scenes
are not occasions for music, least of all for composing. Not
even a theme, "translating an impression of keenest sorrow,"
is apt to come to a man, a woman, or a mob in a moment
when passionate self-expression is needed. The laws of
emotional catharsis are natural laws, not artistic. Verbal

[24] Even our leading psychologists subscribe to this conviction: "To be
successful, the musician must carry his audience on a wave of emotion often
bordering on the point of ecstasy." This from Carl Seashore, who prides
himself on his strict investigation of facts, not "the rehashing of semi-
scientific knowledge under the name of philosophy in aesthetics"! (See *Psychology of Music,* 1938, pp. 174 and 377.)

[25] Cf. Eduard Hanslick, *Vom Musikalisch-Schönen* (5th ed. 1876; 1st ed.
1854), p. 103; also Ferruccio Busoni, *Entwurf einer neuen Aesthetik der Tonkunst* (1907), p. 5.

responses like "Ah!" "Oh-oh!" are not creations, but speech-habits; even the expressiveness of oaths rests not on the fact that such words were invented for psycho-cathartic purposes, but that they are taboo, and the breaking of a taboo gives emotional release. Breaking a vase would do better still.

Yet it may well be argued that in *playing* music we seek, and often find, self-expression. Even Hanslick, to whom emotive *meanings* in a composition were anathema, granted the possibility of relieving one's feelings at the keyboard; [26] and anyone who has a voice or an instrument can verify the relief of musical outpourings, from his own experience. Surely, at some time, he has been moved to vent his excitement in song or rhapsody or furious tarantelle, and felt better for the manic outburst; and, being "keyed up," he probably sang or played unusually well. He chose the piece because it seemed to "express" his condition. It seemed to him, at least at the time, that the piece was designed to speak his feelings, and not impossibly he may believe forever after that these must be the very feelings the composer intended to record in the score.

The great variety of interpretations which different players or auditors will give to one and the same piece — differences even of such general feeling-contents as sad, angry, elated, impatient — make such confidence in the author's intentions appear somewhat naive. He could not possibly have been feeling all the different emotions his composition seems to be able to express. The fact is, that we can *use* music to work off our subjective experiences and restore our personal balance, but this is not its primary function. Were it so, it would be utterly impossible for an artist to announce a program in advance, and expect to play it well; or even, having announced it on the spot, to *express himself* successively in *allegro, adagio, presto,* and *allegretto,* as the changing moods of a single sonata are apt to dictate. Such mercurial passions would be abnormal even in the notoriously capricious race of musicians!

[26] *Op. cit.,* pp. 78–79.

If music has any significance, it is semantic, not sympto-matic. Its "meaning" is evidently not that of a stimulus to evoke emotions, nor that of a signal to announce them; if it has an emotional content, it "has" it in the same sense that language "has" its conceptual content — *symbolically.* It is not usually derived *from* affects nor intended *for* them; but we may say, with certain reservations, that it is *about* them. Music is not the cause or the cure of feelings, but their *logical expression*; though even in this capacity it has its special ways of functioning, that make it incommensurable with language, and even with presentational symbols like images, gestures, and rites.

Many attempts have been made to treat music as a language of emotions. None has been really satisfactory, though some of them are both searching and well-directed. An extraordi-nary amount of able thinking has been expended on the philosophy of music, and the only stumbling-block which has held up the progress of this central problem of "significant form" has been, I think, a lack of understanding of the ways in which logical structures may enter into various types of "significance." Practically all the work has been done; the anomalies and puzzles that remain, though very baffling, are mainly due to logical misconceptions, or slightly naive as-sumptions which only a logician could be expected to recog-nize as such. Here we run into a difficulty inherent in the scholarship of our time — the obstacle of *too much knowledge*, which forces us to accept the so-called "findings" of specialists in other fields, "findings" that were not made with reference to our searchings, and often leave the things that would be most important for us, unfound. Riemann, for instance, de-clared with perfect confidence that musical aesthetics may and must accept the laws of logic and the doctrines of logicians as given.[27]

But it happens that just in musical aesthetics the vital problem with which we are faced is one that involves the entire logic of symbolism. It is a *logical problem of art*, and no logician would be likely to search, in his own interest,

[27] Hugo Riemann, *Die Elemente der musikalischen Aesthetik* (1903), p. 3.

for the "findings" that are relevant to it. It concerns the logical structure of a type of symbol that logicians do not use, and would therefore not even stumble upon as an interesting freak. In short, we are dealing with a *philosophical* problem, requiring logical study, and involving music: for to be able to define "musical meaning" adequately, precisely, but *for an artistic, not a positivistic context and purpose*, is the touchstone of a really powerful philosophy of symbolism.

For the sake of orientation, let us now explicitly abandon the problems of music as stimulus and music as emotive symptom, since neither of these functions (though both undoubtedly exist) would suffice to account for the importance we attach to it; and let us assume that its "significance" is *in some sense* that of a symbol. The challenge to our theory, then, is to determine *in what sense* this can be said; for it is certainly not true in every sense. The question takes us back to Chapter III, to the logic of symbols and the various possibilities of meaning that symbolic structures may contain. Here we should find the conditions for a "language of music" if such there be, or of "significant form" of any other sort than language.

The assumption that music is a kind of language, not of the here-and-now, but of genuine conceptual content, is widely entertained, though perhaps not as universally as the emotive-symptom theory. The best-known pioneer in this field is Schopenhauer; and it has become something of an accepted verdict that his attempt to interpret music as a symbol of the irrational aspect of mental life, the Will, was a good venture, though of course his conclusion, being "metaphysical," was quite bad. However that may be, his novel contribution to the present issue was certainly his treatment of music as an impersonal, negotiable, real semantic, a symbolism with a content of ideas, instead of an overt sign of somebody's emotional condition. This principle was quickly adopted by other thinkers, though there was considerable debate as to what ideational content was embodied in the language of tones. Indeed, one author lists no less than sixteen interpretations, including "the expression of the Freedom of the Will" and "the expression of Conscience." [28]

The most obvious and naive reading of this "language" is the onomatopoetic one, the recognition of natural sounds in musical effects. This, as everybody knows, is the basis of "program music," which deliberately imitates the clatter and cries of the market place, hoof-beats, clanging hammers, running brooks, nightingales and bells and the inevitable cuckoo. Such "sound-painting" is by no means modern; it goes back as far as the thirteenth century, when the cuckoo's note was introduced as a theme in the musical setting of "Sumer is acumen in." [29] An eighteenth-century critic says disapprovingly, "Our intermezzi . . . are full of fantastic imitations and silly tricks. There one can hear clocks striking, ducks jabbering, frogs quacking, and pretty soon one will be able to hear fleas sneezing and grass growing." [30] But its early uses were frankly tricks, like Bach's fugue on the letters of his name, B-A-C-H (to a German, B♭-A-C-B♮). Only with the development of opera and oratorio, the orchestra was called upon to furnish *sounds* appropriate to certain scenes. In Haydn's *Creation* the prancing horses and sinuous worms merely furnish musical figures with technical possibilities, like the traditional cuckoos and cocks, but the waters over the earth are certainly used with the serious intent of building up a thought with the sound-effect. In Bach's *Passion According to St. Matthew* the orchestra registers the rending of the temple curtain in midst of an unmistakable musical storm. From this time onward, sound-painting increases until the romantic symphony may require a whole outfit of wooden rattles, cowbells, whistles, even sound-recordings and a wind-machine.[31] A veritable code of "effects" grew up, helped by

[28] Colin McAlpin, *Hermaia: A Study in Comparative Esthetics* (1915). See his table of contents.

[29] Cf. Richard Aldrich, *Musical Discourse* (1928), p. 25.

[30] J. A. Hüller, "Abhandlung von der Nachahmung der Natur in der Musik," in Marpurg's *Historisch-kritische Beyträge zur Aufnahme der Musik*, 5 vols. (1754–1760). See vol. I, p. 532.

[31] Respighi's *The Pines of Rome* features a phonograph record of a nightingale's song; Strauss' *Alpine Symphony* calls for the "wind-machine."

the more and more detailed and indispensable program notes. Finally, as an eminent *New York Times* critic says, "Strauss, in the heyday of his programmatic frenzy, went so far as to declare that a day would come when a composer could compose the silverware on the table so that the listener could distinguish the knives from the forks." [32]

But not all conceptions of musical semantic were thus naive and literal. Side by side with the evolution of sound-painting runs the development of "dramatic" music in a more subjective sense — music that is intended, and taken, to be a *language of feeling*. Not silverware, nor even parades and thunderstorms, are the objects of musical representation here, but love and longing, hope and fear, the essence of tragedy and comedy. This is not "self-expression"; it is *exposition* of feelings which may be attributed to persons on the stage or fictitious characters in a ballad. In pure instrumental music without dramatic action, there may be a high emotional import which is not referred to any subject, and the glib assurance of some program writers that this is the composer's protest against life, cry of despair, vision of his beloved, or what not, is a perfectly unjustified fancy; for if music is really a language of emotion, it expresses primarily the composer's *knowledge of human feeling*, not how or when that knowledge was acquired; as his conversation presumably expresses his knowledge of more tangible things, and usually not his first experience of them.

This is the most persistent, plausible, and interesting doctrine of meaning in music, and has lent itself to considerable development; on the theoretical side by Kretschmar, E. v. Hartmann, more recently Schweitzer and Pirro, and on the practical side by Schumann, Wagner, Liszt, Berlioz (who have all left us theoretical statements as well), and many others. From Wagner I take what may be the most explicit rendering of the principle:

"What music expresses, is eternal, infinite and ideal; it does not express the passion, love, or longing of such-and-such an individual on such-and-such an occasion, but pas-

sion, love or longing in itself, and this it presents in that
unlimited variety of motivations, which is the exclusive and
particular characteristic of music, foreign and inexpressible
to any other language." [33]

Despite the romantic phraseology, this passage states quite
clearly that music is not self-expression, but *formulation
and representation* of emotions, moods, mental tensions and
resolutions — a "logical picture" of sentient, responsive life,
a source of insight, not a plea for sympathy. Feelings revealed in music are essentially *not* "the passion, love or
longing of such-and-such an individual," inviting us to put
ourselves in that individual's place, but are presented directly
to our understanding, that we may grasp, realize, comprehend
these feelings, without pretending to have them or imputing
them to anyone else. Just as words can describe events we
have not witnessed, places and things we have not seen, so
music can present emotions and moods we have not felt,
passions we did not know before. Its subject-matter is the
same as that of "self-expression," and its symbols may even
be borrowed, upon occasion, from the realm of expressive
symptoms; yet the borrowed suggestive elements are *formalized*, and the subject-matter "distanced" in an artistic perspective.

The notion of "psychical distance" as the hall-mark of
every artistic "projection" of experience, which Edward
Bullough has developed, does not make the emotive contents typical, general, impersonal, or "static"; but it makes
them *conceivable*, so that we can envisage and understand
them without verbal helps, and without the scaffolding of an
occasion wherein they figure (as all self-expression implies
an occasion, a cause — true or imaginary — for the subject's
temporary feelings). A composer not only indicates, but
articulates subtle complexes of feeling that language cannot
even name, let alone set forth; he knows the forms of emotion
and can handle them, "compose" them. We do not "compose" our exclamations and jitters.

[33] Richard Wagner, "Ein glücklicher Abend," reprinted by Gatz, in *Musik-
Aesthetik*, from the *Gazette Musicale*, nos. 56–58 (1841).

The actual opposition between the two emotive theories of musical meaning — that of self-expression and that of logical expression — is best summed up by contrasting the passage from C. Ph. E. Bach, already quoted on page 214, to the effect that "a musician cannot otherwise move people, but he be moved himself," and always "conveys his feelings to them, and thus most readily moves them to sympathetic emotion," with Busoni's statement:

"Just as an artist, if he is to move his audience, must never be moved himself — lest he lose, at that moment, his mastery over the material — so the auditor who wants to get the full operatic effect must never regard it as real, if his artistic appreciation is not to be degraded to mere human sympathy." [34]

This degradation is what Bullough would call a loss of "psychical distance." It is, in fact, a confusion between a symbol, which lets us *conceive* its object, and a sign, which causes us to *deal with* what it means.

"Distance . . . is obtained by separating the object and its appeal from one's own self, by putting it out of gear with practical needs and ends. But . . . distance does not imply an impersonal, purely intellectually interested relation. . . . On the contrary, it describes a *personal* relation, often highly emotionally colored, but *of a peculiar character.* Its peculiarity lies in that the personal character of the relation has been, so to speak, filtered. It has been cleared of the practical, concrete nature of its appeal. . . ." [35]

The content has been *symbolized* for us, and what it invites is not emotional response, but *insight.* "Psychical Distance" is simply the experience of apprehending through a symbol what was not articulated before. The content of art is always real; the mode of its presentation, whereby it is at once revealed and "distanced," may be a fiction. It may also be music, or, as in the dance, motion. But if the content be the life of feeling, impulse, passion, then the symbols

[34] Busoni, *Entwurf einer neuen Aesthetik der Tonkunst,* here quoted from Gatz, *op. cit.*, p. 498.
[35] Bullough, "Psychical Distance," p. 91.

which reveal it will not be the sounds or actions that normally would *express* this life; not associated signs, but *symbolic forms* must convey it to our understanding.

Very few writers who assign significance of any sort to music have kept these several kinds of meaning strictly apart. Literal meanings — the renderings of birds and bells and thunder and the Twentieth Century Limited by orchestral instruments — are usually mixed up in a vague way with emotive meanings, which they are supposed to support, or even to inspire by suggestion. And emotions, in turn, are treated now as effects, now as causes, now as contents of so-called "emotive music." Even in Wagner, who stated explicitly the abstractive, generalizing function of music in depicting feelings, there is plenty of confusion. In describing his own *furor poeticus* he presents himself as expressing his personal sentiments and upheavals. In *Oper und Drama* he says that operatic music must express the sentiments *of the speaker and actor* ("*des Redenden und Darstellenden*," not "*des redend Dargestellten*").[36] Yet it is perfectly clear that the "poetic intention" ("*die dichterische Absicht*") which is the *raison d'être* of the work is not to give the actors self-expression, nor the audience an emotional orgy, but is to *put over*, to make conceivable, a great insight into human passional nature. And again, in the same work, he refers to the tragic fate of Beethoven as an inability to communicate his private feelings, *his* sufferings, to the curious but unmoved listener who could not understand him.[37]

So it was that, when Hanslick wrote his famous little book *Vom Musikalisch-Schönen*, which attempted to blast the growing romantic conception of a "language of music," he found himself called upon to combat not only the use of onomatopoeia, the hoofbeats of Wagner's riding Valkyries and the thunder-peals that announce the wreck of the Flying Dutchman, but also the production, exhibition, or symbolic representation of emotions — the moan and tremolo of the orchestra, the surging outbursts of Tristan and Isolde. Against

[36] Here quoted from Gatz, *op. cit.*, p. 166.
[37] *Ibid.*, p. 172.

all these alleged "expressive functions" of music the great purist mustered his arguments. Vehemently he declared that music conveys no meanings whatever, that the content of music is nothing but dynamic sound-patterns ("*tönend bewegte Formen*"),[38] and that "the theme of a musical composition is its proper content." [39] But especially the true Wagnerian aim — the *semantic* use of music, the *representation* of emotive life — aroused his opposition.

"It is no mere fencing with words," he declares at the very outset, "to protest most emphatically against the notion of 'representation,' because this notion has given rise to the greatest errors of musical aesthetics. To 'represent' something always involves the conception (*Vorstellung*) of two separate, distinct things, one of which must first be given, by a specific act, an explicit relation of reference to the other." [40] Music, in his estimation, can never be used in this degrading fashion.

His statement of the conditions for representation can, of course, be challenged in the light of a better knowledge of symbolism. What he says applies generally to literal, especially to scientific, expression; but it is not true of some other modes, which serve rather to formulate knowledge than to communicate its finished products. Yet there is justice in his protest, too; for the claim of his adversaries to a *language of music* is indeed a misleading one, which may well do mischief among musicians and audiences alike.

Those claims, just like Hanslick's counter-claims, invite logical criticism. So, instead of wrangling over this or that alleged "meaning," let us look at music from the purely logical standpoint as a possible symbolic form of some sort. As such it would have to have, first of all, formal characteristics which were analogous to whatever it purported to symbolize; that is to say, if it represented anything, e.g. an event, a passion, a dramatic action, it would have to exhibit a *logical form* which that object could also take. Everything

[38] Hanslick, *Vom Musikalisch-Schönen*, p. 45.
[39] *Ibid.*, p. 136.
[40] *Ibid.*, introd., p. viii.

we conceive is conceived in some form, though there are alternative forms for every content; but the musical figure which we recognize as such must be *a* figuration under which we could apprehend the thing referred to.

That musical structures logically resemble certain dynamic patterns of human experience is a well-established fact. Even Hanslick admitted as much, perhaps with less scientific backing than our modern theorists can claim; for what in his day was a psychological assumption for the sake of musical understanding, has become, in ours, a psychological doctrine aptly illustrated by musical examples. Wolfgang Köhler, the great pioneer of Gestalt psychology, remarks the usefulness of so-called musical "dynamics" to describe the forms of mental life. "Quite generally," he says, "the inner processes, whether emotional or intellectual, show types of development which may be given names, usually applied to musical events, such as: *crescendo* and *diminuendo, accelerando* and *ritardando.*" He carries these convenient terms over into the description of overt behavior, the reflection of inner life in physical attitudes and gestures. "As these qualities occur in the world of acoustical experiences, they are found in the visual world too, and so they can express *similar* dynamical traits of inner life in directly observable activity. . . . To the increasing inner tempo and dynamical level there corresponds a *crescendo* and *accelerando* in visible movement. Of course, the same inner development may express itself acoustically, as in the *accelerando* and *reforzando* of speech. . . . Hesitation and lack of inner determination become visible . . . as *ritardando* of visible or audible behavior. . . ." [41]

This is just the inverse of Jean D'Udine's description of music, which treats it as a kind of gesture, a tonal projection of the forms of feeling, more directly reflected in the mimic "dance" of the orchestral conductor. "All the expressive gesticulations of the conductor," says that provocative and readable book, *L'art et le geste,* "is really a dance . . . all music is dancing. . . . All melody is a series of attitudes." [42]

[41] Köhler, *Gestalt Psychology,* pp. 248–249.
[42] Jean D'Udine, *L'art et le geste* (1910), p. xiv.

And again: "Every feeling contributes, in effect, certain special gestures which reveal to us, bit by bit, the essential character- istic of Life: movement. . . . All living creatures are con- stantly consummating their own internal rhythm." This rhythm, the essence of life, is the steady background against which we experience the special articulations produced by feeling; "and even the most uneventful life exhibits some such breaks in its rhythm, sources of joys and sorrows without which we would be as inert as the pebbles of the highway." [43] And these rhythms are the prototypes of musical structures, for all art is but a projection of them from one domain of sense to another, a symbolic transformation. "Every artist is a transformer; all artistic creation is but a transmutation." [44]

Just as Köhler uses the language of musical dynamics to express psychological phenomena, on the basis of their for- mal analogy, so D'Udine makes movement the prototype of vital forms and thus reduces all the arts to "a kind of dance" (this analogy with life-functions, both lower and higher, was made long ago by Havelock Ellis in *The Dance of Life*); and so the musicologist von Hoeslin likens dance, plastic art, thought, and feeling to music by reason of that same analogy. The fundamental relationships in music, he says, are *tensions and resolutions*; and the patterns generated by these functions are the patterns exemplified in all art, and also in all emotive responses. Wherever sheer contrasts of ideas produce a re- action, wherever experiences of pure form produce mental tension, we have the essence of *melody*; and so he speaks of *Sprachmelodien* in poetry and *Gedankenmelodien* in life.[45] More naturalistically inclined critics often mediate the com- parison between the forms of music and those of feeling, by assuming that music exhibits patterns of excitation occurring in the nervous tissues, which are the physical sources of emotion; [46] but it really all comes to the same thing. The

[43] *Ibid.*, p. 6.
[44] *Ibid.*, p. xii.
[45] J. K. v. Hoeslin, *Die Melodie als gestaltender Ausdruck seelischen Lebens* (1920).
[46] Both Köhler and Koffka subscribe to this notion of the "physiological picture," of which we see, according to them, not some external duplicate,

upshot of all these speculations and researches is, that there are certain aspects of the so-called "inner life" — physical or mental — which have formal properties similar to those of music — patterns of motion and rest, of tension and release, of agreement and disagreement, preparation, fulfilment, excitation, sudden change, etc.

So the first requirement for a connotative relationship between music and subjective experience, a certain similarity of logical form, is certainly satisfied. Furthermore, there is no doubt that musical forms have certain properties to recommend them for symbolic use: they are composed of many separable items, easily produced, and easily combined in a great variety of ways; in themselves they play no important practical role which would overshadow their semantic function; they are readily distinguished, remembered, and repeated; and finally, they have a remarkable tendency *to modify each other's characters in combination*, as words do, by all serving each as a context.[47] The purely structural requirements for a symbolism are satisfied by the peculiar tonal phenomenon we call "music."

Yet it is not, logically speaking, a language, for it has no vocabulary. To call the tones of a scale its "words," harmony its "grammar," and thematic development its "syntax," is a useless allegory, for tones lack the very thing that distinguishes a word from a mere vocable: fixed connotation, or

but the actual outward aspects of a total bodily state or activity. The same standpoint was already defined by C. Beauquier in his *Philosophie de la musique* in 1865, and by subsequent authors too numerous to cite.

[47] A. Gehring carried this principle of *contextual function* even beyond the compass of the individual composition. "Unrelated compositions," he said, "will affect one another as inevitably as those which are related. The whole realm of music may be regarded as a single huge composition, in which every note that is written exerts its influence throughout the whole domain of tones. To speak with Guyau, . . . it changes the very conditions of beauty.

"This explains the different effects produced by the same composition at different times. The harmonies which sound novel today will be familiar in a few decades; the volume and richness of sound which pleased our ancestors are inadequate today." (*The Basis of Musical Pleasure* [1910], p. 34.)

Gehring's observation bears out the similarity with language, where every word that is used even in a narrow context contributes its meaning, as there established, to the living and growing language.

"dictionary meaning." Moreover, a tone has many aspects that enter into the notion of musical significance, but not of harmony. These aspects have been minutely and seriously studied from a psychological standpoint, in ways that fairly well exclude non-musical factors such as personal associations with tunes, instruments, styles (e.g. church music, military music), or programmatic suggestions. In a remarkably able and careful work,[48] Dr. Kurt Huber has traced the successive emergence of expressive factors in the apprehension of the simplest possible tonal patterns — bare pitch-patterns of two to three tones, stripped of all contextual elements of timbre, rhythm, volume, etc., by their uniform production on an electrical instrument, in timed succession and equal strength. The subjects were instructed to describe their experiences in any terms they chose: by their qualities, relations, meanings, emotional characters, somatic effects, associations, suggestions, or what-not. They were asked to report any images or memories evoked, or, failing such experiences, simply to convey their impressions as best they could. This form of experiment is certainly much more controlled and decisive than the Schoen and Gatewood questionnaires on the influence of musical selections; and the results of Huber's experiments, which might be expected to be poorer, by reason of the simplicity of the material and lack of specific instructions, are actually much more significant and more capable of systematic arrangement than the emotive-value statistics. They may be briefly summarized as follows:

(1) The lowest stage of tone-apprehension yields merely an impression of *tone-color* of the whole tonal complex, or of a difference between tone-colors of the separate tones.

(2) Meanings conveyed by such a mere impression of tonal brightness always involve states or qualities or their changes, i.e. *passive* changes. Imagination of an *event* does not occur without an impression of *tonal movement*.

(3) The most primitive factor in the perception of tonal

[48] *Der Ausdruck musikalischer Elementarmotive. Eine experimental-psychologische Untersuchung* (1923).

movement is a sense of its *direction*. This, according to the author, "constitutes the point of departure of that psychological symbolism of figures (*psychische Gestaltsymbolik*) which we encounter in the tendency to relate musical motives to sentiments."

(4) The apprehension of a *width of tonal intervals* is independent of this sense of direction; and "all spatial symbolism in the interpretation of motives has its roots in this impression of inter-tonal distance."

(5) The idea of a *musical step* requires a joint perception of tonal distance and direction. "We are not saying too much if we make all the higher psychical interpretation directly dependent on the grasping of *interval-forms*, or at least view them as mediately related to these."

(6) Impressions of consonance, dissonance and relatedness (*Zusammengehörigkeit*) require the notion of a musical step, or progression (simultaneous tones were not given; the inquiry rested on *melodic* elements).

(7) Tones taken as related may then be referred to a tonic, either chosen among them or "understood," i.e. imaginatively supplied by the auditor (this orientation is most forcibly suggested by the perfect fourth, e.g.

 , which connotes almost irresistibly the setting:

).

(8) Reference to a tonic determines the feeling of modality; for instance, [musical notation] connotes a different modality if taken as [musical notation] from what it would as

 .

(9) A subjective accent may simply fall upon the tone

which is harmonically more important as the hearer has organized the interval; it may, but need not, suggest a rhythmic structure.

(10) Subjective rhythmatization, when it occurs, is built upon mental accentuation.

Since such mental accentuation may occur without any actual emphasis (as in these experiments it necessarily did), the problem of rhythm in music as we know it is immensely complicated, and cannot be solved by mere reference to the drum and footfall of dancing hordes. In fact, Huber distinguishes between such purely temporal *measure*, and "musical rhythm," which latter results from the internal, tonal organization of the motif.[49]

The entire study shows effectively how many factors of possible expressive virtue are involved in even the simplest musical structure, how many things beside the acknowledged materials of composition have crucial functions in conveying a musical message. One may argue that voice-inflections enter into the "expressiveness" of speech, too; but the fact is that the verbal message may be understood apart from these. They do not alter the content of a statement, which is uniquely determined by vocabulary and syntax, but at most they may affect one's reaction to the statement. Musical semantic factors, however, have never been isolated; even the efforts of Schweitzer [50] and Pirro [51] to trace the "emotional vocabulary" of Bach by correlating musical figures with the words he usually sets to them, interesting though they are, show us certain associations in Bach's mind, perhaps also accepted conventions of his day or his school, rather than

[49] "So it appears," he says, "upon this view (which is shared, incidentally, by Ohmann) that musical rhythm, in contrast with the mere temporal rhythm of *measures*, grows out of the inner *Gestalt*-relations of the motif itself." (*Ibid.*, p. 179.) This conclusion corroborates by scientific evidence the doctrines of Heinrich Schenker concerning meter and rhythm, namely that rhythm is a function of *tonal motion*, not of time-division; such motion depends as much on melodic and harmonic tension and direction as on tempo. (See Schenker's *Neue musikalische Theorien und Phantasien*, 3 vols. [1935], esp. vol. III, *Der freie Satz*, ch. xii, pp. 191–206.)

[50] Albert Schweitzer, *J. S. Bach, le musicien-poète* (2nd ed. 1905).

[51] André Pirro, *L'esthétique de Jean-Sebastien Bach* (1907).

musical laws of expression. Such precise interpretations of separate figures are inconclusive because, as Huber remarked in his direct psychological study, "It is impossible to determine the absolute expressive value of separate intervals (third, fifth, etc.) because their absolute pitch affects the brightness of their constituents and therewith their qualities of contrast, apprehensibility, etc." [52] That there are tonal figures derived from natural rhythms, that upward and downward direction, pendular motion, etc., may be musically "imitated," that melodic lines may suggest sobs, whimpers, or yodelers, need not be reiterated here; such general classifications [53] do not give us a vocabulary of music; and even if we accept the more ambitious dictionary of Schweitzer or Pirro, what is usually called the "grammar" of music, i.e. harmony, does not recognize such "words" as elements at all. The analogy between music and language breaks down if we carry it beyond the mere semantic function in general, which they are supposed to share.[54] Logically, music has not the characteristic properties of language — separable terms with fixed connotations, and syntactical rules for deriving complex connotations without any loss to the constituent elements. Apart from a few onomatopoetic themes that have become conventional — the cuckoo, the bugle-calls, and possibly the church-bell — music has no literal meaning.

Yet it may be a presentational symbol, and present emotive experience through global forms that are indivisible as the elements of chiaroscuro. This view has indeed been suggested.[55] But it seems peculiarly hard for our literal minds to grasp the idea that anything can be *known* which cannot be *named*. Therefore philosophers and critics have repeatedly denied the musical symbolization of emotion on the ground that, as Paul Moos puts it, "Pure instrumental music is unable to render even the most ordinary feelings, such as love,

[52] Huber, *Der Ausdruck musikalischer Elementarmotive*, p. 182.

[53] A perfect example may be found in E. Sorantin's *The Problem of Musical Expression* (1932).

[54] Cf. Siegfried F. Nadel, *Der duale Sinn der Musik* (1931), p. 78.

[55] Cf. Julius Bittner, "Die Grenzen des Komponierbaren," *Der Merker*, II (1910), part I, pp. 11–14.

loyalty, or anger, unambiguously and distinctly, by its own unaided powers." [56] Or Heinrich, in the same vein: "There are many musical works of high artistic value, that completely baffle us when we try to denote by one word the mood they are supposed to convey. This alone suffices to make the conception of music as a sentimental art, or an art of expressing sentiments, quite untenable." [57] And A. Gehring, pointing out that one cannot prove every musical phrase or figure to mean some nameable feeling, memory, or idea, declares, "Until this is done, we must deny that symbolization accounts for the essential charm of the art." [58]

But this is a fallacy, based on the assumptions that the rubrics established by language are absolute, so that any other semantic must make the same distinctions as discursive thought, and individualize the same "things," "aspects," "events," and "emotions." What is here criticized as a weakness, is really the strength of musical expressiveness: that *music articulates forms which language cannot set forth.* The classifications which language makes automatically preclude many relations, and many of those resting-points of thought which we call "terms." It is just because music has *not* the same terminology and pattern, that it lends itself to the revelation of non-scientific concepts. To render "the most ordinary feelings, such as love, loyalty or anger, unambiguously and distinctly," would be merely to duplicate what verbal appellations do well enough.

I cannot agree, therefore, with Professor Urban's statement: "It is true that there are other symbols than those of language, namely, the symbols of art and mathematics, by means of which meanings may be communicated. But these symbols themselves require interpretation, and interpretation is only possible in terms of language." [59] His very combination of art and mathematics seems to me to bespeak a misunderstanding; for mathematics is discursive and literal,

---

[56] Paul Moos, *Die Philosophie der Musik* (1922), p. 297.

[57] F. Heinrich, "Die Tonkunst in ihrem Verhältnis zum Ausdruck und zum Symbol," *Zeitschrift für Musikwissenschaft*, VIII (1925–26), 66–92. See p. 75.   [58] *The Basis of Musical Pleasure*, p. 90.

[59] W. M. Urban, *Language and Reality*, p. 55.

a specialized and abbreviated language. It appeals essentially to the eye, and is therefore most easily "done on paper," but all its symbols have names; a complex like $\dfrac{\sqrt{a+b}}{c^{m+n}}$ may always be verbally expressed as "the square root of a-plus-b, over c to the m-plus-nth power." This is not a non-linguistic symbolism; it is merely a highly technical jargon, and the teaching of mathematics is its interpretation to the uninitiate. But in art such interpretation is vicious, because art — certainly music, and probably all art — is formally and essentially untranslatable; and I cannot agree that "interpretation of poetry is the determination of what poetry says. . . . One of the essential functions of the teaching of literature is its interpretation. . . . Now a character of such interpretation is that it is always carried out in non-poetic terms or in *less* poetic terms than the thing interpreted." [60] Evidently Professor Urban would extend this sort of explanation even to music, for he says elsewhere: "Even in such non-linguistic arts as music or pure design, where the element of assertion is apparently absent, it is, I should hold, only apparently so." [61]

In that case, of course, Moos and Heinrich and Gehring are justified in denying "emotive" meanings to music on the ground that no propositions about feelings can be assigned, with any confidence, as the contents of its forms. But it seems to me that truth rests rather with another statement of Urban's, which is hard to reconcile with his prevailing, explicit views about the primacy and supremacy of language: "The poet . . . does well to speak in figure, to keep to his own symbolic form. For precisely in that symbolic form an aspect of reality is given which cannot be adequately expressed otherwise. It is not true that whatever can be expressed symbolically can be better expressed literally. For there *is* no literal expression, but only another kind of symbol." [62]

For the musician, this other kind of symbol is not con-

[60] *Ibid.*, pp. 487–488.   [61] *Ibid.*, p. 478.
[62] *Ibid.*, p. 500. Oddly enough, this same passage concludes with the words:

stantly obscured by something that is said; wherefore musicians have grasped its character and importance more clearly than literary critics. If music is a symbolism, it is essentially of this untranslatable form. That is the gist of Wagner's description of the "orchestral language." Since this "language" has no conventional words, it can never appeal to discursive reason. But it expresses "just what is unspeakable in verbal language, and what, viewed from our rationalistic (Verstandesmenschlichen) standpoint, may therefore be called simply *the Unspeakable*." [63]

Because the forms of human feeling are much more congruent with musical forms than with the forms of language, music can *reveal* the nature of feelings with a detail and truth that language cannot approach. This peculiar articulateness of music as a semantic of vital and emotional facts was discovered nearly two centuries ago by one of the contributors to Marpurg's famous *Beyträge zur Musik*. This writer (the same Hüller who objected to ducks and sneezing fleas in "modern music") says:

"There are feelings . . . which are so constantly suppressed by the tumult of our passions, that they can reveal themselves but timidly, and are practically unknown to us. . . . Note, however, what response a certain kind of music evokes in our hearts: we are attentive, it is charming; it does not aim to arouse either sorrow or joy, pity or anger, and yet we are moved by it. We are so imperceptibly, so gently moved, that we do not know we are affected, *or rather, that we can give no name to the affect*. . . .

"Indeed, it is quite impossible to *name* everything fascinating in music, and bring it under definite headings. Therefore music has fulfilled its mission whenever our hearts are satisfied." [64]

"But when all is said and done, it remains true that poetry is covert metaphysics, and it is only when its implications, critically interpreted and adequately expressed, become part of philosophy that an adequate view of the world can be achieved." What *is* this critical and adequate expression, if not literal interpretation?

[63] *Oper und Drama*. See Gatz, *Musik-Aesthetik*, p. 192.

[64] Hüller, "Abhandlung von der Nachahmung der Natur in der Musik," pp. 515 and 523. Italics mine.

Since the day when this was written, many musicologists — notably Vischer, Riemann, and Kurth — have emphasized the impossibility of interpreting the "language of feeling," although they admit its function to be, somehow, a revelation of emotions, moods, or subtle nameless affects. Liszt warned specifically against the practice of expounding the emotive content of a symphonic poem, "because in such case the words tend to destroy the magic, to desecrate the feelings, and to break the most delicate fabrics of the soul, which had taken this form just because they were incapable of formulation in words, images or ideas." [65]

But there are musicians for whom it is not enough to recognize the ineffable character of musical significance; they must remove their art from the realm of meaning altogether. They cannot entertain the idea that music expresses anything in any way. The oddest thing about this perfectly legitimate problem of musical meaning is that it seems impossible for people to discuss it with anything like detachment or candor. It is almost like a religious issue; only that in matters of faith the proponents of a doctrine are usually the vehement believers, the passionate defenders, whereas in this musicological argument it is apt to be the non-believers, the scoffers and critics, who are most emotional about it. Those who deny that music is a language of feelings do not simply reject the symbolistic theory as unconvincing or indemonstrable; they are not content to say that they cannot find the alleged meaning in music, and therefore consider the hypothesis far-fetched; no, they reject with horror the very attempt to construe music as a semantic, they regard the imputation of any meaning — emotional or other — as an insult to the Muse, a degradation of the pure dynamic forms, an invidious heresy. They seem to feel that if musical structures should really be found to have significance, to relate to anything beyond themselves, those structures would forthwith cease to be musical. The dignity of music demands that it should be autonomous; its existence should have no explanation.

[65] Franz Liszt, "Berlioz und seine Harold-Synphonie," reprinted by Gatz from Liszt's *Gesammelte Schriften*. See Gatz, *op. cit.*, p. 127.

To add "meaning" to its sensuous virtues is worse than to deny it any virtue — it is, somehow, to destroy its life.[66]

Yet the most vehement critics of the emotive-content theory seem to have caught a germ from the doctrine they attacked: in denying the very possibility of any content of music, they have fallen into the way of thinking about it in terms of form and content. They are suddenly faced with the dichotomy: *significant or meaningless.* And while they fiercely repudiate the proposition that music is a semantic, they cannot assert that it is meaningless. It is the problem, not the doctrine, that has infected them. Consequently they try to eat their cake and have it too, by a logical trick that is usually accepted only among mathematicians — by a statement which has the form of an answer to the question in hand, and really commits them to nothing. Musical form, they reply, is its own content; its means itself. This evasion was suggested by Hanslick when he said, "The theme of a musical composition is its essential content." He knew that this was an evasion; [67] but his successors have found it harder and harder to resist the *question* of content, and the silly fiction of self-significance has been raised to the dignity of a doctrine.[68] It is really just a talisman against any and every assignment of specific content to music; and as such it will presently appear justified.

Whenever people vehemently reject a proposition, they do so not because it simply does not recommend itself, but

[66] The importance of this conflict was recognized by Dr. Wierling, who says: "The great reaction which Hanslick evoked with his book shows by its harshness that here was no contest of opinions, but a conflict of forces like that of dogma against heresy. . . . The reaction against Hanslick was that of persons attacked in their holiest convictions." (*Das Tonkunstwerk als autonome Gestalt und als Ausdruck der Persönlichkeit,* pp. 24–25.) Exactly the same spirit was certainly evinced by Hanslick himself, who repulsed what he considered not a mere error, but a pernicious doctrine.

[67] See Hanslick, *op. cit.,* p. 133: "In the art of music there is no content opposed to form, because music has no form over and above its content." This is an effectual repudiation of the form-and-content dichotomy, a rejection of the problem, not of its answers.

[68] See, e.g., E. J. Dent, *Terpander: or, the Music of the Future* (1927), p. 12; Carroll C. Pratt, *The Meaning of Music* (1931), p. 237; and F. Heinrich, "Die Tonkunst in ihrem Verhältnis zum Ausdruck und zum Symbol," p. 67.

because it *does*, and yet its acceptance threatens to hamper their thinking in some important way. If they are unable to define the exact mischief it would do, they just call it "degrading," "materialistic," "pernicious," or any other bad name. Their judgment may be fuzzy, but the intuition they are trying to rationalize is right; to accept the opponent's proposition *as it stands*, would lead to unhappy consequences.

So it is with "significant form" in music: to tie any tonal structure to a specific and speakable meaning would limit musical imagination, and probably substitute a preoccupation with feelings for a whole-hearted attention to music. "An inward singing," says Hanslick, "and not an inward feeling, prompts a gifted person to compose a musical piece." [69] Therefore it does not matter what feelings are afterward attributed to it, or to him; his responsibility is only to articulate the "dynamic tonal form."

It is a peculiar fact that some musical forms seem to bear a sad and a happy interpretation equally well. At first sight that looks paradoxical; but it really has perfectly good reasons, which do not invalidate the notion of emotive significance, but do bear out the right-mindedness of thinkers who recoil from the admission of specific meanings. For *what music can actually reflect is only the morphology of feeling*; and it is quite plausible that some sad and some happy conditions may have a very similar morphology. This insight has led some philosophical musicologists to suppose that music conveys *general forms of feeling*, related to specific ones as algebraic expressions are related to arithmetic; a doctrine put forward by Moritz Hauptmann [70] and also by Moritz Carrière. [71] These two excellent thinkers saw in music what most aestheticians failed to see — its intellectual value, its close relation to concepts, not by reason of its difficult academic "laws," but in virtue of its *revelations*. If it reveals the rationale of feelings, the rhythm and pattern of their rise and decline and intertwining, to our minds, then it is a

[69] *Op. cit.*, p. 75.
[70] *Die Natur der Harmonik und Metrik* (1853).
[71] *Aesthetik*, 2 vols. (1859).

force in our mental life, our awareness and understanding, and not only our affective experience.

Even Hanslick granted this logical analogy between music and emotions; [72] but he did not realize how much he had granted. Because he considered nothing but conventional denotation as "meaning," he insisted that music could not mean anything. Every mathematician knows how hard it is to convince the naive beginner in algebra that its letters have any meaning, if they are not given specific denotations: "Let $a = 5$, let $b = 10$," etc. Presently the novice learns that it makes no difference to the validity of the equation how the meanings of terms have been assigned; then he understands the generality of the symbolism. It is only when he sees the balance of the equation as a form in itself, apart from all its possible arithmetical instances, that he grasps the *abstraction*, the real concept expressed through the formula.

Algebraic letters are pure symbols; we see numerical relationships not *in* them, but *through* them; they have the highest "transparency" that language can attain. In likening music to such a symbolism, Hauptmann and Carrière claimed for it that peculiar "significance" that belongs to abstractions — a general reference to the realm of reality from which the form is abstracted, a reflection of the laws of that realm, a "logical picture" into which all instances must fit, yet not a "picture" of any actual instance.

But this explanation of music as a high abstraction, and musical experience as a purely logical revelation, does not do justice to the unmistakably sensuous value of tone, the vital nature of its effect, the sense of personal import which we meet in a great composition every time it is repeated to us. Its message is not an immutable abstraction, a bare, unambiguous, fixed concept, as a lesson in the higher mathematics of feeling should be. It is always new, no matter how well or how long we have known it, or it loses its meaning; it is not transparent but iridescent. Its values crowd each other, its symbols are inexhaustible.

The fact is, I think, that Hanslick, who admitted only the

[72] *Op. cit.*, p. 26.

formal similarity of music and emotive experience but denied the legitimacy of any further interpretation, and those authors who realized that formality, but took it for the nature of musical *meanings* rather than of musical symbols, were very close to a correct analysis. For music has all the earmarks of a true symbolism, except one: the existence of an *assigned connotation*. It is a form that is capable of connotation, and the meanings to which it is amenable are articulations of emotive, vital, sentient experiences. But its import is never fixed. In music we work essentially with free forms, following inherent psychological laws of "rightness," and take interest in possible articulations suggested entirely by the musical material. We are elaborating a symbolism of such vitality that it harbors a principle of development in its own elementary forms, as a really good symbolism is apt to do — as language has "linguistic laws" whereby words naturally give rise to cognates, sentence-structures to subordinate forms, indirect discourse to subjunctive constructions "by attraction," noun-inflections to inflections of their modifiers "by agreement." No conscious intellectual intent determines vowel changes, inflections, or idioms; the force of what has been called "linguistic feeling" or a "sense of words" — "the Spirit of Language," as Vossler says — develops the forms of speech. To make up a language upon a preconception of what it is to express never leads to a real language, because language grows in meaning by a process of articulation, not in articulate forms by a process of preconceived expression.

What is true of language, is essential in music: music that is invented while the composer's mind is fixed on what is to be expressed is apt not to be music. It is a limited idiom, like an artificial language, only even less successful; *for music at its highest, though clearly a symbolic form, is an unconsummated symbol*. Articulation is its life, but not assertion; expressiveness, not expression. The actual function of meaning, which calls for permanent contents, is not fulfilled; for the *assignment* of one rather than another possible meaning to each form is never explicitly made. Therefore music is "Significant Form," in the peculiar sense of "significant" which Mr. Bell and Mr. Fry maintain they can grasp, or feel, but not define; such significance is implicit, but not conventionally fixed.

The fact that in music we have an unconsummated symbol, a significant form without conventional significance, casts some light on all the obscure conflicting judgments that the rise of program music has evoked. The expression of an idea in a symbolic mode may be successful or unsuccessful; easy and adequate, or halting, askew, inexact. Ordinarily we have no precise "logical picture" of affects at all; but we *refer to* them, chiefly by the indirect method of describing their causes or their effects. We say we feel "stunned," "left out," "moved," or "like swearing," "like running away." A mood can be described only by the situation that might give rise to it: there is the mood of 'sunset and evening star,' the mood of a village festival, or of a Vienna soirée. If, now, a composer's musical idiom is not so rich and definite that its tonal forms alone are perfectly coherent, significant, and satisfying, it is the most natural thing in the world that he should supplement them by the usual, non-musical ways of expressing ideas of feeling to ourselves and others; by envisaging situations, objects, or events that hold a mood or specify an emotion. He may use a mental picture merely as a scaffolding to organize his otherwise musical conception. Schumann tells of occasions when he or another composer had envisaged a scene or a being so that the vision directly inspired a coherent, well-wrought musical work.[73] Sometimes the mere suggestion of what Huber calls a "sphere," e.g. "a medieval realm," "a fairy world," "a heroic setting," effected by one title-word such as "Scheherazade" or "Oberon," serves to crystallize a shifting and drifting musical theme into artistic form. Sometimes a composer sets himself an elaborate program and follows it as he might a libretto or a choreographer's book. It is true, and natural enough,

[73] Robert Schumann on Berlioz' *Synphonie Fantastique*, reprinted by Gatz from *Gesammelte Schriften über Musik und Musiker*. See Gatz, *op. cit.*, pp. 299–303.

that this latter practice produces a less perfect musical expression than purely thematic thinking, for it is not single-minded; not everything relevant is contained in the music; and there is nothing *in the work* to force the composer's helpful fancies on the listener. Nothing can constrain us to think of Till Eulenspiegel's escapades while listening to music.

But similarly, nothing can prevent our falling back on mental pictures, fantasies, memories, or having a *Sphärenerlebnis* of some sort, when we cannot directly make subjective sense out of music in playing or hearing it. A program is simply a crutch. It is a resort to the crude but familiar method of holding feelings in the imagination by envisaging their attendant circumstances. It does not mean that the listener is unmusical, but merely that he is not musical enough to think in entirely musical terms. He is like a person who understands a foreign language, but thinks in his mother tongue the minute an intellectual difficulty confronts him.

To a person of limited musical sense, such ideation seems the most valuable response to music, the "subjective content" which the listener must supply. People of this persuasion often grant that there may also be an appreciation of pure beautiful sounds, which "gives us pleasure"; but we can *understand* the music better when it conveys a poetic content.[74] Goethe, for instance, who was not musical (despite his interest in the art as a cultural product), tells how, in listening

[74] Henri Prunières (the same "interpreter" who tells us so categorically how Beethoven felt when he invented his themes) writes of Strauss's programmatic works: "These works are endowed with a form sufficiently beautiful in itself to afford the auditor lively pleasure, even should he not perceive all the author's intentions. It must be remembered, however, that his pleasure is doubled when he is capable of grasping, of gradually discovering, the hidden symbols." ("Musical Symbolism," p. 20.)

D. M. Ferguson, in an essay entitled "How can Music Express Emotion?" claims that music, "being unable, as words and pictures can do, to present to our attention the causes or external circumstances of feeling *(from which we largely infer the nature of the feeling itself)*, begins *in medias res*, with the nervous disturbance itself and . . . instead of representing the conditions which arouse emotion and demanding that the observer observe therefrom the emotional meaning, music represents the emotional disturbance itself *and demands that for its fullest comprehension its hearers shall infer the cause.*"

to a new piano quartet, he could make no sense out of any part save an allegro, which he could interpret as the Witches' Sabbath on the *Blockberg*, "so that after all I found a conception which could underlie this peculiar music." [75]

Where such interpretation is spontaneous, it is a perfectly legitimate practice, common among musically limited persons, and helpful; but it becomes pernicious when teachers or critics or even composers initiate it, for then they make a virtue out of walking with a crutch. It is really a denial of the true nature of music, which is unconventionalized, unverbalized freedom of thought. That is why the opponents of program-music and of hermeneutic are so vehement in their protests; they feel the complete misconception of the *artistic* significance of tonal structures, and although they give doubtful reasons for their objection, their reaction is perfectly sound.

The real power of music lies in the fact that it can be "true" to the life of feeling in a way that language cannot; for its significant forms have that *ambivalence* of content which words cannot have. This is, I think, what Hans Mersmann meant, when he wrote: "The possibility of expressing opposites simultaneously gives the most intricate reaches of expressiveness to music as such, and carries it, in this respect, far beyond the limits of the other arts." [76] Music is revealing, where words are obscuring, because it can have not only a content, but a transient play of contents. It can articulate

---

(*Proceedings of the Music Teachers' National Association*, 1925, pp. 20–32. See pp. 26–27. Italics mine.)

Another purveyor of interpretations, F. Nicholls, says (after classifying "chords of fear" and "arpeggios of joy"): "It is now desired to illuminate a piece of pure music by reading into it — in accordance with our acquired knowledge of musical symbolism — some more *definite* and *particular* meaning. . . . The music is the higher or cosmic interpretation of definite things. . . . An interpretation, nevertheless, is often very helpful; and a 'parable,' so to speak, in words often, and quite justifiably, adds to the enjoyment of the music." (*The Language of Music, or, Musical Expression and Characterization*, 1924, pp. 77–78.) Hereupon he writes doggerel words to a Beethoven piano sonata.

[75] J. P. Eckermann, *Gespräche mit Goethe* (ed. of 1912), p. 158.

[76] "Versuch einer musikalischen Wertaesthetik," *Zeitschrift für Musikwissenschaft*, XVII (1935), 1: 33–47.

feelings without becoming wedded to them. The physical character of a tone, which we describe as "sweet," or "rich," or "strident," and so forth, may suggest a momentary interpretation, by a physical response. A key-change may convey a new *Weltgefühl*. The assignment of meanings is a shifting, kaleidoscopic play, probably below the threshold of consciousness, certainly outside the pale of discursive thinking. The imagination that responds to music is personal and associative and logical, tinged with affect, tinged with bodily rhythm, tinged with dream, but *concerned* with a wealth of formulations for its wealth of wordless knowledge, its whole knowledge of emotional and organic experience, of vital impulse, balance, conflict, the *ways* of living and dying and feeling. Because no assignment of meaning is conventional, none is permanent beyond the sound that passes; yet the brief association was a flash of understanding. The lasting effect is, like the first effect of speech on the development of the mind, to *make things conceivable* rather than to store up propositions. Not communication but insight is the gift of music; in very naive phrase, a knowledge of "how feelings go." This has nothing to do with "*Affektenlehre*"; it is much more subtle, complex, protean, and much more important; for its entire record is emotional satisfaction, intellectual confidence, and *musical* understanding. "Thus music has fulfilled its mission whenever our hearts are satisfied."

It also gives substance to a theory that sounds very odd outside some such context as this, a theory advanced by Riemann, and more recently developed by Professor Carroll Pratt, who (apparently quite independently) came to the conclusion that music neither causes nor "works off" real feelings, but produces some peculiar effects we mistake for them. Music has its special, purely auditory characters, that "intrinsically contain certain properties which, because of their close resemblance to certain characteristics in the subjective realm, are frequently confused with emotions proper." [77] But "these auditory characters are not emotions

<hr>

[77] Pratt, *The Meaning of Music*, p. 191.

at all. They merely *sound* the way moods *feel*. . . . More often than not these formal characters of music go unnamed: they are simply what the music is. . . ." [78]

The notion that certain effects of music are so much *like* feelings that we mistake them for the latter, though they are really entirely different, may seem queer, unless one looks at music as an "implicit" symbolism; then, however, the confusion appears as something to be expected. For until symbolic forms are consciously abstracted, they are regularly confused with the things they symbolize. This is the same principle that causes myths to be believed, and names denoting powers to be endowed with power, and sacraments to be taken for efficacious acts; the principle set forth by Cassirer, in a passage which I have quoted once before,[79] but cannot refrain from repeating here: "It is typical of the first naive, unreflective manifestations of linguistic thinking as well as the mythical consciousness, that its content is not sharply divided into symbol and object, but both tend to unite in a perfectly undifferentiated fusion." [80] This principle marks the line between the "mythical consciousness" and the "scientific consciousness," or between implicit and explicit conception of reality. Music is our myth of the inner life — a young, vital, and meaningful myth, of recent inspiration and still in its "vegetative" growth.

[78] *Ibid.*, p. 203. Compare Hugo Riemann, *Wie Hören Wir Musik?* (1888), pp. 22–23: "It is really not a question of *expressing* emotions at all, for . . . music only moves the soul in a way *analogous* to the way emotions move it, without pretending, however, in any way to arouse them (wherefore it does not signify anything that entirely heterogeneous affects have similar dynamic forms, and therefore may be 'expressed' by the same music, as has already been observed, quite rightly, by Hanslick). . . ."

[79] In *The Practice of Philosophy*, p. 178.

[80] This identification of symbol and object in music is given remarkable illustration by a passage from Gehring's *The Basis of Musical Pleasure*, which reads: "If the sequence of thoughts which fills our mind from minute to minute bears any close resemblance to melodic structure, it is so subtle that nobody has yet been able to detect it. However, is it necessary to trace an analogy? May not the mental phenomenon and the musical counterpart here melt together? May not the melody be substituted for the important train of thought which it is supposed to mirror? In the case of measure, force, and tempo, music duplicates or photographs the mind; in the case of melody, it coincides with it." (Page 98.)

CHAPTER IX

The Genesis of Artistic Import

THE roots of music go far back in history, but in its beginnings it probably was not art. There seems to have been a long pre-musical period, when organized sounds were used for rhythmatization of work and ritual, for nervous excitation, and perhaps for magical purposes. In this period the elementary *materials* of music became established, tonal forms which finally reached a stage of articulation that made them, quite spontaneously, instinct with meaning. That is why Bücher, in his famous book *Arbeit und Rhythmus*,[1] can actually trace so many motifs back to sailors' cries, the long breaths of corn-grinders, to threshers' flail-strokes and the measure of bounding hammers in the smithy. All those mechanical sounds and spontaneous utterances had to be long familiar before their tonal quality could become abstracted for the listening ear; they had to attain fixed forms before they could become elements for musical imagination. Probably *song* of some kind, as well as drummed dance-rhythm, is older than any *musical* interest. If indeed, as von Humboldt says, "Man is a singing creature," then music is not necessarily given as soon as there is song; then he may have sung his reveilles and musters, his incantations and his dances, long before he knew that vocal forms were beautiful and could be sung without signifying anything. Group speaking is necessarily chanting. The length of a sentence that can be spoken in one breath is a natural verse-limit, as the hold on the end of a choral verse indicates. Work rhythms, dance measures, choric utter-

[1] Karl Bücher, *Arbeit und Rhythmus* (4th ed. 1908; first published in 1896).

ance, these are some of the influences that formed music out
of the sounds that are natural to man, that he utters at work,
or in festal excitement, or in imitation of the world's sounds
— the cuckoo's cry, the owl's hoot, the beat of hooves, feet,
drums, or hammers.

All such noises are incipient "themes," musical models
which artistic imagination may seize upon to form tonal
ideas. But they do not themselves enter into music, as a
rule; they are transformed into characteristic motifs; intervals, rhythms, melodies, all the actual ingredients of song
are not *supplied* but merely *inspired* by sounds heard in
nature. The auditory experiences which impress us are
those which have musical possibilities, which allow themselves to be varied and developed, expanded, altered, which
can change their emotional value through harmonic modifications. Ernst Kurth, in his excellent *Musikpsychologie*,
has made a searching study of these proto-musical elements,
which he calls *Ursymbole*; his words are the best statement
I can find of the way familiar sounds are transformed into
music, so I quote them here:

"In investigating the *thematic* roots of folksong, one soon
comes upon *psychological* roots as well; among all races
there appear certain recurrent, simple idioms that are really
nothing but ultimate symbols of their vital consciousness:
calls, chimes, cradle-rhythms, work-rhythms; dance-forms,
often intimately related to certain bodily movements and
steps; shouts, hunting-calls and military signals, highland
themes (*Alphornweisen*) and tallyhos (symbols of popular
humor persisting even in high artistic composition); also
plenty of borrowings from the national liturgy; in short, all
sorts of motifs in which an undercurrent of popular imagination reveals itself.

"Especially impressions from the first phases of childhood
leave their imprint here; hence the fondness for (hidden)
cradle-rhythms in folktunes, for certain beckoning calls,
furthermore for religious motifs and the many clear or merely
suggested bell sounds. . . .

"All these themes are easily detected in folksongs, either

frankly or obscurely present, sometimes clearly interpretable, sometimes of indeterminate symbolic character. They are by no means simply expressive of the momentary literal meaning of the text, but rather may be said to emanate directly (and sometimes even in defiance of the text) from musical reflection and formulation in its own right. . . . They can hardly be discerned as separate motif-values in the general easy flow of the tune; neither musically nor ideationally can a folksong ever be schematically analyzed as a sheer synthesis of such ultimate symbols." [2]

All these sounds which meet our alert and retentive ear in the course of the day's work become fixed forms for our minds, because they are heard over and over again in nature, industry, or society; but they give rise to music because they are intrinsically expressive. They have not only associative value, but value as rhythms and intervals, exhibiting stress and release, progression, rise or fall, motion, limit, rest. It is in this musical capacity that they enter into art, not in their original capacity of signs, self-expressions, religious symbols, or parrot-like imitation of sounds.

There is a widespread and familiar fallacy, known as the "genetic fallacy," which arises from the historical method in philosophy and criticism: the error of confusing the *origin* of a thing with its *import*, of tracing the thing to its most primitive form and then calling it "merely" this archaic phenomenon. In a philosophy of symbolism this mistake is particularly fatal, since *all elementary symbolic forms have their origin in something else than symbolistic interest*. Significance is always an adventitious value. Words were probably ritualistic sounds before they were communicative devices; that does not mean that language is now not "really" a means of communication, but is "really" a mere residue of tribal excitement. Musical materials, likewise, presumably had other uses before they served music; that does not imply that music is "really" not an intellectual achievement, and expression of musical ideas, at all, but is in reality a mere invocation of rain or game, or a rhythmic aid to dancers, or what not.

[2] Kurth, *Musikpsychologie*, p. 291.

But just as it is a mistake to reduce music to its origins, so it is, I think, to elevate primitive emotional sounds, like bird-songs or the sing-song speech of sentimental persons, to the dignity of music. They are musical materials, but their unconscious use is not art. This is true even of certain tunes. "The Old Gray Mare" was made for marching, and is a real aid to rhythmic tramping, but its musical function is quite secondary. Certain spinning songs are musically just bad. They have been developed in order to carry the words of a ballad, and no one cares about the melody. The same is true of drummed dance-rhythms interspersed with shouts or verses. Tonal forms arise casually in answer to practical demands, just as architectural, ceramic, and pictorial forms do, and attain some degree of conventional development before anyone sees them as artistic forms at all.

The plastic arts find natural models everywhere. Nature is full of individual, beautiful, characteristic forms, and anyone molding clay or marking with his finger in the sand naturally recalls some object to give sense to the shapes that produce themselves under his hand. It is so easy to achieve organic unity in a design by making it *represent* something, that even when we would experiment with pure forms we are apt to find ourselves interpreting the results as human figures, faces, flowers, or familiar inanimate things. Geometric forms require purely intellectual and original organization to recommend themselves to the eye as sensible *Gestalten*, and must be relatively simple to be handled by their inventor or beholder as beautiful forms. But natural objects, by virtue of their practical significance, carry a certain guarantee of unity and permanence, which lets us apprehend their forms, though these forms would be much too difficult to grasp as mere visual patterns without extraneous meaning. An artistically sensitive mind sees significant form where such form presents itself. The profusion of natural models undoubtedly is responsible for the early development of plastic art.

But there is a danger in that asset, too; for the purely visual arts very easily become *model-bound*. Instead of merely providing artistic ideas, a model may dictate to the artist; its practical functions, which served to organize the conception of it as a form, may claim his attention to the detriment of his abstractive vision. Its interest as an object may conflict with its pictorial interest and confuse the purpose of his work.

For the average beholder judging an artistic work, this confusion is inevitable. The first naive comment is always apt to be that the picture is, or is not, *quite accurate*; next, that the subject is or is not worthy of being represented; and then, probably, that the work is "pleasant" or "unpleasant." All three of these comments are based on standards which have nothing to do with art; all three place a premium on qualities which usually detract from "significant form." The first demands that the artist should be primarily interested in the object — as a storekeeper might be, who was to judge it for his stock. The second concerns the object, not in relation to the picture — not its visual virtues or failings — but in relation to everything else in the world *but* the picture. Its practical, moral, or historical significance is the criterion of value here. The third treats the picture in what is really an "aesthetic" capacity, its power to excite or soothe our senses, to effect either annoyance or repose, as the colors of a living-room do; or, if the "pleasure" derives from the theme of the picture (a pastoral landscape being "pleasant," a St. Sebastian full of arrows "unpleasant" art), it is expected to stimulate the imagination in agreeable ways.

But all these virtues may belong to mediocre pictures; they are, in fact, usually exemplified in the landscapes, marines, and *genre* paintings that serve as covers for magazines whenever the pretty-girl-portrait is not appropriate. A painter of no insight, judgment, or imagination worth mentioning might follow Goethe's suggestions for a picture, find a graceful and perfect model to impersonate a noble character, and depict it with skillful accuracy — "*getreue Nachahmung der Natur*," as his mentor called it — in colors chosen with faultless taste; [3] and produce a picture that might hang in every parlor, but mean exactly nothing to the sensibilities

---

[3] See "Zu malende Gegenstände" and "Maximen und Reflexionen über Kunst." In *Werke* (Cotta ed.), vol. XXXV.

of any real artist. All these factors may, indeed, be *materials* for artistic conception; but they are not the conception itself, they offer no criterion of excellence. A subject which has emotional meaning for the artist may thereby rivet his attention and cause him to see its form with a discerning, active eye, and to keep that form present in his excited imagination until its highest reaches of significance are evident to him; then he will have, and will paint, a deep and original conception of it. That is why men long in love or in religious fervor are inspired to produce great, convincing works of art. Not the importance of the theme, nor the accuracy of its depiction, nor the fantasies stirred in the beholder, make a work of art significant, but the articulation of visual forms which Hoeslin would call its "melody."

If the origin of art had to wait on somebody's conception of this inner meaning, and on his intention to express it, then our poor addle-brained race would probably never have produced the first artistic creation. We see significance *in* things long before we know what we are seeing, and it takes some other interest, practical or emotional or superstitious, to make us produce an object which turns out to have expressive virtue as well. We cannot conceive significant form *ex nihilo*; we can only *find* it, and create something in its image; but because a man has seen the "significant form" of the thing he copies, he will copy it with that emphasis, not by measure, but by the selective, interpretative power of his intelligent eye. A savage may have this insight; in fact, Bushmen and Indians, Polynesians and Indonesians, seem to be prone to it, sensitive to forms as the early Egyptians and the nameless cave-dwellers of paleolithic ages were. Apparently primitive mankind has a "vegetative" period of artistic activity, as he has of linguistic and mythological and ritual growth. A crude pre-Athenian peasant makes a Herm for the protection of his home, and produces a statue of archaic beauty; an Indian carves a totem-pole, and achieves a composition; he fashions a canoe or molds a water-jar, and creates a lovely form. His model is the human body, the treetrunk, the curled dry leaf floating, the shell or skull or cocoanut from which he drinks. But as he imitates such models for practical ends he sees more than the utilitarian import of their shapes; he literally *sees* the reflection of human feeling, the "dynamic" laws of life, power, and rhythm, in forms on which his attention is focussed; he sees things he cannot name, magical imports, rightness of line and mass, his hands unwittingly express and even overdraw what he sees, and the product amazes and delights him and looks "beautiful." But he does not "know," in discursive terms, what he is expressing, or why he deviates from the model to make the form more "significant." When he emerges from his savage state and takes discursive reason seriously he tries to copy more accurately; and the ambition for naturalistic, literal representation, for rational standards of art, moral interpretations, and so forth, confuse his intuition and endanger his visual apprehensions.

It has often been remarked that music as we know it, i.e. as an artistic medium, is of very recent date. William Wallace was so impressed with the lateness of its evolution that he attributed this sudden growth to the emergence of a new faculty of hearing, a neurological development which man was supposed to have just attained. In *The Threshold of Music*, he asserted that the Greeks, and even our ancestors of five or six hundred years ago, could not hear what we can; they could not distinguish consonance from dissonance. He points out some interesting facts in support of this theory, notably that to the Greeks, as to the Chinese before them, music was essentially an intellectual exercise. Instrumental music was practiced only as a craft supplying one of the physical pleasures of life, like catering or massage, and had none of the prestige of the true arts; wherefore musical instruments were few and crude, and the ingenious Greeks who could cast all sorts of delicate sculptured forms in bronze did not use that same skill to make even the most obvious improvements in the flute and the lyre. So he concludes that ancient musicians simply had not the "inner ear" that is normal, now-a-days, not only for gifted persons, but for the average man, who quite naturally hears melodies in the context of some harmonic structure. "While the Greeks had reached the highest attainments in eye-training and mind-training," he concludes, "as shown by their works of art, by their dialectics and their poetry, the existing records of their music go to prove that their sense of hearing lacked the faculty of discerning the finer shades and subtleties of sound." [4] Since the professional Greek rhapsodists prided themselves on singing quarter-tones accurately on pitch, this statement is certainly open to doubt. Yet it is indeed remarkable that, although the organ existed throughout the Middle Ages, no one discovered the possibilities of *simultaneous* tonal combinations; and also that the great classical period of music is centuries later than that of the other arts — drama, sculpture, or painting. If we reject Wallace's hypothesis, that "musical sense" evolved only with a recent neurological development, we assume the burden of a better explanation.

This lies, I think, in the fact that *music has very few natural models.* Bird songs, cries, whistles, traditional cattle-calls, and metallic clangs are scant materials; even the intonations of the human voice, whether purely emotional (as with us), or semantic (like the Chinese speech-tones), are indefinite, elusive, hard to hold in memory as precise forms. There are hardly any given musical configurations in nature to suggest organized tonal structures, and reveal themselves as significant forms to a naive, sensitive, savage ear.

The molds and scaffoldings in which music had to take shape were all of extraneous character. Pictures have visual models, drama has a direct prototype in action, poetry in story; all may claim to be "copies," in the Platonic sense or in the simple Aristotelian sense of "imitations." But music, having no adequate models, had to rest on the indirect support of two non-musical aids — *rhythm*, and *words.*

Rhythms are more fixed and stable, more definite than intonations. That is probably why the rhythmic structure is the first aspect of music to become formalized and precise. Rhythm can be simultaneously expressed in many ways — in

[4] William Wallace, *The Threshold of Music* (1908), esp. pp. 35–42.

shouts, steps, drum-beats, by voice, bodily motion, and instrumental noises. Words and acts and cries, whistles, rattles,
and tom-toms, may all be synchronized in one single rhythm;
no wonder the rhythmic figure is easily abstracted, when it is
rendered in such multiple modes! It is obviously one and
the same metric pattern, a general dynamic form, that may be
sung, danced, clapped, or drummed; this is the element that
can always be repeated, and therefore traditionally preserved.
Naturally it offers us the first logical frame, the skeletal structure of the embryonic art of music.[5]

The most obvious tonal material is, of course, the human
voice; and the spontaneous function of the voice is natural
utterance — cry or speech. In adults, speech has become such
a dominant habit that even our purely emotional exclamations tend to verbal forms like: "Alas!" "*Ach!*" "*Tiens!*" And
Bücher has shown how meaningless vocables carrying out
rhythms are gradually replaced by assonant words, without
any particular regard to meaning. Tennyson's farmer heard
his horse's hooves say: "Property, property, property," which
made sense enough to his mind; but the fisherman who hears
the sails say: "Jerry and Josh, Jerry and Josh," or the child
who listens to the train's wheels repeating: "Jerusalem, Jerusalem, Jerusalem," is simply yielding to the force of linguistic
habit. This sort of mental formulation seems to underlie
the construction of occupational songs, and probably of many
festal songs. The adjustment of speech-impulses to the demands of rhythmic tonal figure is the natural source of all
chanting, the beginning of vocal music.[6]

Since singing aloud requires some resonant, sustained
vowel sounds, one cannot help singing syllables, and their
suggestion of words makes the opportunity for poetic expression too obvious to be missed. But as soon as the silly
random verbiage first dictated by rhythmic figures and tonal
demands is imbued with poetic sense, a new source of artistry
has been created: for the *poetic line* becomes the *choral*

[5] Cf. R. Wallaschek, "On the Origin of Music," *Mind*, XVI (1891), 63:
375–386.
[6] Bücher, *Arbeit und Rhythmus*, p. 380.

verse, which determines the elementary melodic form, the musical phrase. Patterns of pitch follow patterns of word-emphasis, and melodic lines begin and end with propositional lines. This is the second extraneous "model" for musical form.

For a long age music was dependent on these two parents, dance and song, and was not found without them. As ritual dancing disappeared, and religion became more and more bound to verbal expression, to prayer and liturgy, occupational and secular festive music became wedded to dance forms, sacred music to the chant; [7] so that Goethe, reviewing the history of the art, and mistaking its guide-lines for its intrinsic characteristics, was led to say: "The holiness of sacred music, the jocund humor of folk-tunes, are the pivots round which all true music revolves. . . . Worship or dance." [8]

But the folksong is by no means restricted to jocose sentiments nor always based on dance-rhythms; it derives from sacred sources as well as from secular excitements, and very soon abstracts from both the first independent *musical* product — the "air." Old airs, like our modern hymn tunes, are neither sad nor gay; any words in the proper metrical pattern may be sung to them. Such melodies belong to no special occasion, no special subject-matter, but are merely *used* for the purpose of singing a variety of poems. Thus airs themselves often acquire names, after places, composers, saints, as well as after their original words. Airs are national possessions; they may convey ballads, or find their way into semi-religious settings, solemn graduations, patriotic exercises and

[7] Cf. the observation of Kathi Meyer: "In antiquity, ritual was a cult act, a genuine sacrifice which was really carried out. Prayers and songs were mere accompaniments and remained secondary matter, hence the low development of these parts of the rite. Now, in the Christian service, the actual sacrifice is no longer really performed, it is symbolized, transcendentalized, spiritualized. The service is a parable. So prayers and chants became the realities which had to be emphasized more and more; they too served ultimately the process of spiritualization. If, in the past, a symbol was needed for the cult, one could replace the act or even the god by an image, in painting or sculpture. Now, with the conceptualizing of religion, one can spiritualize only the psychic processes, the 'anima.' That is effected by the word, or better yet in music." *Bedeutung und Wesen der Musik* (1932), p. 47.

[8] Goethe, "Maximen und Reflexionen über Kunst."

the like, creep into revivalist meetings, and end up in the most dignified hymnology.[9] If their rhythmic accent is light and definite they are more apt to have a career on the village green, the barn floor, the dance hall, sung to endless silly words and played on fiddles or bagpipes without any words at all. The dance seems to be their excuse for being; but presently they are played or whistled on the street where no one requires their rhythmic measure for any but musical purposes. At this point music stands without its poetic or terpsichorean scaffolding, a tonal dynamic form, an expressive medium with a law and a life of its own.

Because its models are non-musical, they are not as vital to its mature artistic products as the models of pictures, statues, plays, or poems are apt to be. Of course a certain dance has left its stamp on all Mozart's minuets, and another on Chopin's waltzes; yet the musical works called minuets and waltzes do not *represent* those respective dances as pictures represent objects. They are abstracted forms reincarnated in music, and we can take the music and forget the dance far more easily than we can take a painting and forget what it portrays. The dance was only a framework; the air has other contents, musical characteristics, and interests us directly, not by its connotation of a "step" which we may not even know.

The same is true of words that have served to frame a tune. The melody, heard by someone who does not hear or understand the words, recommends itself as a tonal pattern on its own merit, and makes perfectly good sense when it is played instead of sung. Music dispenses easily with its models, because it could never really do them justice as a representative; they are merely its foster-parents, and it was never their true image anyway. This orphan estate belated its growth as an art, and kept it long in a merely auxiliary, even a utilitarian position; but it has the compensating virtue of making music more independent of its natural models than any other art when it does attain its selfhood. We perceive it as "significant form," unhampered by any fixed, literal meaning, by any-

[9] Cf. Bücher, *Arbeit und Rhythmus*, p. 401.

thing it represents. It is easier to grasp the *artistic* import of music than of the older and more model-bound arts.

This artistic import is what painters, sculptors, and poets express *through* their depiction of objects or events. Its semantic is the play of lines, masses, colors, textures in plastic arts, or the play of images, the tension and release of ideas, the speed and arrest, ring and rhyme of words in poetry — what Hoeslin calls *"Formenmelodie"* and *"Gedankenmelodie."* Artistic expression is what these media will convey; and I strongly suspect, though I am not ready to assert it dogmatically, that the import of artistic expression is broadly the same in all arts as it is in music — the verbally ineffable, yet not inexpressible law of vital experience, the pattern of affective and sentient being. This is the "content" of what we perceive as "beautiful form"; and this formal element is the artist's "idea" which is conveyed by every great work. It is this which so-called "abstract art" seeks to abstract by defying the model or dispensing with it altogether; and which music above all arts can reveal, unobscured by adventitious literal meanings. That is presumably what Walter Pater meant by his much-debated dictum, "All art aspires to the condition of music." [10]

This does not mean, however, that music achieves the aim of artistic expression more fully than other arts. An ideal condition is its asset, not a supreme attainment, and it is this *condition* for which the other arts must strive, whereas music finds it fulfilled from the first stage in which it may be called an art at all. Its artistic mission is more visible because it is not obscured by meanings belonging to the represented object rather than to the form that is made in its image. But the artistic *import* of a musical composition is not therefore greater or more perfectly formulated than that of a picture, a poem, or any other work that approaches perfection as closely after its kind.

Whether the field of musical meanings, over which its unassigned symbols play — the realm of sentient and emotional

[10] Walter Pater, *The Renaissance. Studies in Art and Poetry* (1908; 1st ed. 1873), p. 140.

experience — is ultimately the subject-matter of all art, is a moot question. In a general way it probably is so; but within this very great and uncharted domain there may well be many special regions, to one or another of which the medium of one art is more suited than that of another for its articulate expression. It may well be, for instance, that our physical orientation in the world — our intuitive awareness of mass and motion, restraint and autonomy, and all characteristic feeling that goes with it — is the preëminent subject-matter of the dance, or of sculpture, rather than (say) of poetry; or that erotic emotions are most readily formulated in musical terms. I do not know; but the possibility makes me hesitate to say categorically, as many philosophers and critics have said,[11] that the import of all the arts is the same, and only the medium depends on the peculiar psychological or sensory make-up of the artist, so that one man may fashion in clay what another renders in harmonies or in colors, etc. The medium in which we naturally conceive our ideas may restrict them not only to certain forms but to certain fields, howbeit they all lie within the verbally inaccessible field of vital experience and qualitative thought.

The basic unity of all the arts is sometimes argued from the apparent beginning of all artistic ideas in the so-called "aesthetic emotion" which is supposed to be their source and therefore (by a slightly slipshod inference) their import.[12] Anyone who has worked in more than one medium probably can testify to the sameness of the "aesthetic emotion" accompanying creation in the various arts. But I suspect that this

[11] Cf. S. T. Coleridge's essay, "On the Principles of Genial Criticism Concerning the Fine Arts, More Especially those of Statuary and Painting," appended to *Biographia Literaria*, in the ed. of 1907; also D'Udine, *L'art et le geste*, p. 70.

[12] Cf. Clive Bell: "The starting-point for all systems of aesthetics must be the personal experience of a peculiar emotion. . . . This emotion is called the aesthetic emotion; and if we can discover some quality common to all and absent from none of the objects that provoke it, we shall have solved what I take to be the central problem of aesthetics." (*Art*, p. 6.) Mr. Bell forgets the logical rule that such a discovery would prove nothing, unless the quality in question were also *peculiar to* aesthetic objects; any quality common to all objects whatever would fulfil the condition he states.

characteristic excitement, so closely wedded to original conception and inner vision, is not the source, but the effect, of artistic labor, the personal emotive experience of revelation, insight, mental power, which an adventure in "implicit understanding" inspires. It has often been stated that it is the same emotion which overtakes a mathematician as he constructs a convincing and elegant proof; and this is the beatitude which Spinoza, who knew it well, called "the intellectual love of God." Something like it is begotten in appreciation of art, too, though not nearly in the same measure as in producing; but the fact that the difference is one of degree makes it plausible that the emotion springs from the one activity which the artist and the beholder share in unequal parts — the comprehension of an unspoken idea. In the artist this activity must be sustained, complete, and intense; his intellectual excitement is often at fever pitch. The idea is his own, and if he loses his command of it, confused by the material or distracted by pressing irrelevancies, there is no symbol to hold it for him. His mind is apt to be furiously active while an artistic conception takes shape. To the beholder the work is offered as a constant source of an insight he attains gradually, more or less clearly, perhaps never in logical completeness; and although his mental experience also wakens the characteristic emotion, variously called "feeling of beauty," "aesthetic emotion," and "aesthetic pleasure," he knows nothing like the exhilaration and tense excitement of an artist before his pristine marble or clay, his unmarked canvas or paper, as the new work dawns in his brain.

Perhaps it is inevitable that this emotion which one really *has* in producing or contemplating an artistic composition should become confused with the content of the work, since that content is itself emotive. If there is feeling in the work, and both artist and spectator experience a feeling, and moreover the artist has *more* of a feeling than the spectator, would it not take a very careful thinker to refrain from jumping to the conclusion that the emotion embodied in the form is felt by the artist before he begins his work, is "expressed" in the process of creating as it might be in shouting or weeping, and is sympathetically felt by the audience? Yet I believe the "aesthetic emotion" and the emotional content of a work of art are two very different things; the "aesthetic emotion" springs from an intellectual triumph, from overcoming barriers of word-bound thought and achieving insight into literally "unspeakable" realities; but the emotive content of the work is apt to be something much deeper than any intellectual experience, more essential, pre-rational, and vital, something of the life-rhythms we share with all growing, hungering, moving and fearing creatures: the ultimate realities themselves, the central facts of our brief, sentient existence.

"Aesthetic pleasure," then, is akin to (though not identical with) the satisfaction of discovering truth. It is the characteristic reaction to a well-known, but usually ill-defined, phenomenon called "artistic truth" — well-known to all artists, creative or appreciative, but so ill-defined by most epistemologists that it has become their favorite aversion. Yet truth is so intimately related to symbolism that if we recognize two radically different types of symbolic expression we should logically look for two distinct meanings of truth; and if both symbolic modes are rational enough, both senses of truth should be definable.

Here it must be noted that the distinction between discursive and presentational symbols does not correspond to the difference between literal and artistic meanings. Many presentational symbols are merely proxy for discourse; geometric relations may be rendered in algebraic terms — clumsy terms perhaps, but quite equivalent — and graphs are mere abbreviated descriptions. They express facts for discursive thinking, and their content *can be verbalized*, subjected to the laws of vocabulary and syntax. Artistic symbols, on the other hand, are untranslatable; their sense is bound to the particular form which it has taken. It is always *implicit*, and cannot be explicated by any interpretation. This is true even of poetry, for though the *material* of poetry is verbal, its import is not the literal assertion made in the words, but *the way the assertion is made*, and this involves the sound, the tempo, the aura of associations of the words, the long or short sequences of ideas, the wealth or poverty of transient imagery that contains them, the sudden arrest of fantasy by pure fact, or of familiar fact by sudden fantasy, the suspense of literal meaning by a sustained ambiguity resolved in a long-awaited key-word, and the unifying, all-embracing artifice of rhythm. (The tension which music achieves through dissonance, and the reorientation in each new resolution to harmony, find their equivalents in the suspensions and periodic decisions of propositional sense in poetry. Literal sense, not euphony, is the "harmonic structure" of poetry; word-melody in literature is more akin to tone-color in music.)

The poem as a whole is the bearer of artistic import, as a painting or a drama is. We may isolate significant lines, as we may isolate beauties in any work, but if their meaning is not determined and supported by their context, the entire work, then that work is a failure despite the germ of excellence it contains. That is why Professor Urban's restatement of T. S. Eliot's cryptic lines:

"And I see the damp souls of the housemaids
    Sprouting disconsolately at area gates,"

namely: "That housemaids' souls are damp and sprout," and his demand for a *more adequate rendering* of this assertion by way of philosophical interpretation, seems to me a fundamental misconception of poetic import.[13] A "more adequate rendering" would be more, not less, poetic; it would be a better poem. "Artistic truth" does *not* belong to statements in the poem or their obvious figurative meanings, but to its figures and meanings *as they are used*, its statements *as they are made*, its framework of word-sound and sequence, rhythm and recurrence and rhyme, color and image and the speed of their passage — in short, to the poem as "significant form." The material of poetry is discursive, but the product — the artistic phenomenon — is not; its significance is purely im-

---

[13] Urban, *Language and Reality*, see passage quoted p. 234, above. To anyone who cannot grasp the poet's meaning and vision here, Professor Urban's "interpretation" certainly would make matters worse rather than better.

plicit in the poem as a totality, as a form compounded of sound and suggestion, statement and reticence, and no translation can reincarnate that. Poetry may be approximated in other languages and give rise to surprisingly beautiful new versions revealing new possibilities of its skeletal literal ideas and rhetorical devices; but the product *is* new, like an orchestral scoring of an organ-fugue, a piano version of a string quartet, or a photograph of a painting.

An artistic symbol — which may be a product of human craftsmanship, or (on a purely personal level) something in nature seen as "significant form" — has more than discursive or presentational meaning: its form as such, as a sensory phenomenon, has what I have called "implicit" meaning, like rite and myth, but of a more catholic sort. It has what L. A. Reid called "tertiary subject-matter," beyond the reach of "primary imagination" (as Coleridge would say) and even the "secondary imagination" that sees metaphorically. "Tertiary subject-matter is subject-matter imaginatively experienced *in* the work of art . . . , something which cannot be apprehended apart from the work, though theoretically distinguishable from its expressiveness." [14]

"Artistic truth," so called, is the truth of a symbol to the forms of feeling — nameless forms, but recognizable when they appear in sensuous replica. Such truth, being bound to certain logical forms of expression, has logical peculiarities that distinguish it from propositional truth: since presentational symbols have no negatives, there is no operation whereby their truth-value is reversed, no *contradiction*. Hence "the possibility of expressing opposites simultaneously," on which Mersmann commented. Falsity here is a complicated failing, not a function of negation. For this reason Professor Reid calls it not falsity but *inexpressiveness*; and Urban, in a moment undisturbed by epistemology, abandons not only the term "falsity," but also "truth," and suggests that artistic forms should rather be designated as *adequate* or *inadequate* to the ideas they embody.[15] Perhaps

[14] "Beauty and Significance," p. 132.
[15] Urban, *op. cit.* See pp. 439–442.

he did not see that this shift of terminology belies his doctrine that all art makes assertions which must ultimately be paraphrased in language; for assertions are true or false, and their adequacy has to be taken for granted before we can judge them as assertions at all. They are always debatable and may be tested for their truth-values by the nature of their explicable consequences. Art, on the other hand, has no consequences; it gives form to something that is simply there, as the intuitive organizing functions of sense give form to objects and spaces, color and sound. It gives what Bertrand Russell calls "knowledge by acquaintance" of affective experience, below the level of belief, on the deeper level of insight and attitude. And to this mission it is either adequate or inadequate, as images, the primitive symbols of "things," are adequate or inadequate to give us a conception of what things are "like." [16]

To understand the "idea" in a work of art is therefore more like *having a new experience* than like entertaining a new proposition; and to negotiate this knowledge by acquaintance the work may be adequate *in some degree.* There are no degrees of literal truth, but artistic truth, which is all significance, expressiveness, articulateness, has degrees; therefore works of art may be good or bad, and each must be judged on our experience of its revelations. Standards of art are set by the expectations of people whom long conversance with a certain mode — music, painting, architecture, or what not — has made both sensitive and exacting; there is no immutable law of artistic adequacy, because significance is always *for* a mind as well as *of* a form. But a form, a harmony, even a *timbre*, that is entirely unfamiliar is "meaningless," naturally enough; for we must grasp a *Gestalt* quite definitely before we can perceive an implicit meaning, or even the promise of such a meaning, in it; and such definite grasp requires a certain familiarity. Therefore the most original

[16] Lord Russell fails to appreciate, I think, the logical, formulative mission of sense, or else he evades it because it has kept company with idealism. But *to see in certain forms* is not to create their contents, though it is a source of that relativistic character of "data" which makes them less final and absolute than his empiricism lets him admit.

contemporary music in any period always troubles people's ears. The more pronounced its new idiom, the less they can make of it, unless the impulse which drove the composer to this creation is something of a common experience, of a yet inarticulate *Zeitgeist,* which others, too, have felt. Then they, like him, may be ready to experiment with new expressions, and meet with an open mind what even the best of them cannot really judge. Perhaps some very wonderful music is lost because it is too extraordinary. It may even be lost to its composer because he cannot really handle his forms, and abandons them as unsuccessful. But intimate acquaintance with all sorts of music does give some versatile minds a power of grasping new sounds; people so inclined and trained will have a "hunch," at least, that they are dealing with true "significant form" though they still hear a good deal of it as noise, and will contemplate it until they comprehend it, for better or worse. It is an old story that Bach, Beethoven, and Wagner were "hard to hear" in their own time. Many people today, who can follow Rimsky-Korsakoff or Debussy as easily as Schumann, cannot hear music in Hindemith or Bartok; yet the more experienced probably know, by certain signs, that it is there.

On the other hand, artistic forms are exhaustible, too. Music that has fulfilled its mission may be outgrown, so that its style, its quality, its whole conception, palls on a generation that is ardently expressing or seeking to express something else.[17] Only very catholic minds can see beauty in many styles even without the aid of historical fancy, of a conscious "self-projection" into other settings or ages. It is probably easiest in music, where typical forms are not further bound down by literal references to things that have a transient and dated character.

The worst enemy of artistic judgment is literal judgment, which is so much more obvious, practical, and prompt that it is apt to pass its verdict before the curious eye has even taken in the entire form that meets it. Not blindness to "significant form," but *blindedness,* due to the glaring evi-

[17] Cf. Hanslick, *Vom Musikalisch-Schönen,* p. 57.

dence of familiar things, makes us miss artistic, mythical, or sacred import. This is probably the source of the very old and widespread doctrine that the so-called "material world" is a curtain between humanity and a higher, purer, more satisfying Truth — a "Veil of Maya," or Bergson's false, "spatialized" Reality.

Is it conceivable that mysticism is a mark of inadequate art? That might account for the fact that all very great artistic conceptions leave something of mysticism with the beholder; and mysticism as a metaphysic would then be the despair of implicit knowledge, as skepticism is the despair of discursive reason.

To us whose intelligence is bound up with language, whose achievements are physical comforts, machines, medicines, great cities, and the means of their destruction, theory of knowledge means theory of communication, generalization, proof, in short: critique of science. But the limits of language are not the last limits of experience, and things inaccessible to language may have their own forms of conception, that is to say, their own symbolic devices. Such nondiscursive forms, charged with logical possibilities of meaning, underlie the significance of music; and their recognition broadens our epistemology to the point of including not only the semantics of science, but a serious philosophy of art.

CHAPTER X

The Fabric of Meaning

ALL thinking begins with *seeing*; not necessarily through the eye, but with some basic formulations of sense perception, in the peculiar idiom of sight, hearing, or touch, normally of all the senses together. For all thinking is conceptual, and conception begins with the comprehension of *Gestalt*.

The first product of intellectual seeing is literal knowledge, the abstracted conception of things, to which those things themselves stand in the relation of instances. So-called "common sense" does not carry this literal formulation of its ideas of things, acts, persons, etc., very far in the way of elaboration. Common-sense knowledge is prompt, categorical, and inexact. A mind that is very sensitive to forms as such and is aware of them beyond the common-sense requirements for recognition, memory, and classification of things, is apt to use its images metaphorically, to exploit their possible significance for the conception of remote or intangible ideas; that is to say, if our interest in *Gestalten* goes beyond their common-sense meanings it is apt to run us into their dynamic, mythical, or artistic meanings. To some people this happens very easily; in savage society, at least in certain stages of development, it seems to be actually the rule, so that secondary imports of forms — plastic, verbal, or behavioral forms — often eclipse what Coleridge called the "primary imagination" of them. Sense-data and experiences, in other words, are essentially *meaningful structures*, and their primary, secondary, or even more recondite meanings may become crossed in our impression of them, to the detriment of one value or another.[1] But our first awareness of presented forms usually

[1] Roger Fry has said in this connection: "Biologically speaking, art is a

serves to label them according to their *kinds,* and add them
to the general stock of our "knowledge by acquaintance."

It is fortunate that our first understanding of forms is
normally a literal comprehension of them as *typical things*
or *such-and-such events;* for this interpretation is the basis
of intelligent behavior, of daily, hourly, and momentary
adjustment to our nearest surroundings. It is non-discursive,
spontaneous abstraction from the stream of sense-experience,
elementary sense-knowledge, which may be called *practical
vision.* This is the meeting-point of thought, which is symbolic, with animal behavior, which rests on sign-perception;
for the edifice which we build out of literal conceptions, the
products of practical vision, is our systematic spatio-temporal
world. The same items that are *signs* to our animal reflexes
are contents for certain *symbols* of this conceptual system.
If we have a literal conception of a house, we cannot merely
think of a house, but *know one when we see it;* for a sensory
sign stimulating practical action also answers to the image
with which we think.

This dual operation of a datum as sign and symbol together is the key to realistic thinking: the envisagement of
fact. Here, in practical vision, which makes symbols for
thought out of signs for behavior, we have the roots of
practical intelligence. It is more than specialized reaction
and more than free imagination; it is conception anchored
in reality.

"Fact" is not a simple notion. It is that which we conceive
to be the source and context of signs to which we react
successfully; this is a somewhat vague definition, but when
all is said, "fact" is a somewhat vague term. When logicians
try to define it, it becomes a hypostatized proposition; [2] there

---

blasphemy. We were given our eyes to see things, not to look at them."
(*Vision and Design,* p. 47.)

[2] As it certainly is, in the writings of Moore, Stebbing, Ramsey, Wisdom,
and other British philosophers. Cf. L. S. Stebbing, "Substances, Events, and
Facts," *The Journal of Philosophy,* XXIX (1932), 12: 309–322; F. P. Ramsey
and G. E. Moore, "Symposium: Facts and Propositions," *Proceedings of the
Aristotelian Society,* suppl. vol. VII (1927), 153–206; John Wisdom, "Time,
Fact, and Substance," *ibid.,* N.S. XXIX (1928–29), 67–94.

are positive and negative, specific and general, universal and particular facts; [3] Professor Lewis even speaks of actual and unreal facts. [4] On the other hand, when psychologists or their philosophical cousins, the pragmatists, offer a definition, fact becomes hardly distinguishable from the animalian sign-response. The best attempt I have seen at a definition of "fact," in relation to what might be called "stark reality" on the one hand, and language, or literal formulation, on the other, is made by Karl Britton in his recent book, *Communication.*

"A fact," says Britton, "is essentially abstract but *there.* It is what is an object of attention, of discriminating awareness, in present events. . . . A fact is that in events to which we make a learned and discriminating response determined in part *by the understanding of statements.* . . .

"A fact is that which determines assent or dissent, without inference and in accordance with the rules. . . .

"The formal rules of language determine the structure of propositions and show in a general way the sort of thing that a proposition is. . . . But the fact which shows the proposition to be *true,* is that in events to which I make *a response that has the same structure* as the proposition p. Can I then learn about the general structural character of *facts* from the formal laws of language? Yes, but not about the general structural character of *events.* . . .

"To the same events an infinite variety of responses is possible: he who understands 'p' makes only certain responses and not others. It is this that *introduces* limitation, structure; *events as such have no structure.* . . .

"It follows that it is only for thinking minds that there is structure in nature. . . . A world without minds is a world without structure, without relations and qualities, *without facts.*" [5]

    [3] Cf. Hugh Miller, "The Dimensions of Particular Fact," *The Journal of Philosophy,* XXXVI (1939), 7: 181–188.
    [4] C. I. Lewis, "Facts, Systems, and the Unity of the World," *The Journal of Philosophy,* XX (1923), 6: 141–151. See p. 142.
    Karl Britton, *Communication: A Philosophical Study of Language* (1939), pp. 204–206.

This excerpted passage shows at once the logician's conviction that the *form* of fact is the form of proposition, and the behaviorist's desire to dispense with concepts and speak only in terms of "response." So the form of a fact becomes the form of a specific human response to a specific event. This response, I take it, is his conceiving of the event (though I should regard his conceiving as only a component of the "response," which probably has other aspects not determining the fact at all). At any rate, allowing for special wordings required by operationalism, behaviorism, etc., we probably agree on the main tenet that *a fact is an intellectually formulated event*, whether the formulation be performed by a process of sheer vision, verbal interpretation, or practical response. A fact is an event as we see it, or would see it if it occurred for us. It is something to which a proposition is applicable; and a proposition that is not applicable to any event or events is *false*. We can construct propositions that apply to *all* events; these are necessary propositions, or, in Wittgenstein's phrase, "tautologies." Some propositions apply directly, some indirectly, to events; hence our specific and general, universal and particular, positive and negative facts. Only "unreal facts" seem to me to be pure hypostatizations of propositional content, and defy the purpose of the concept "fact," which is to recognize the link between symbolic process and signific response, between imagination and sensory experience.

In a naive stage of thought, facts are taken for granted; matters of fact are met in practical fashion as they become obvious. If it requires further facts to explain a given state of affairs, such further facts are simply assumed. Imagination supplies them, philosophical interest sanctions them, and the popular mind accepts them on quite other grounds than empirical evidence. This pre-scientific type of thought, systematic enough in its logical demonstrations, but unconcerned about any detailed agreement with sense-experience, has been described and commented on as often as the history of philosophy has been written: how Plato ascribed circular orbits to the planets because of the excellence of circular motion, but

Kepler plotted those orbits from observation and found them to be elliptical; how the schoolmen argued about the speed of falling bodies until Galileo, that *enfant terrible* of learning, dropped his weights from the leaning tower, and so forth. And everybody knows how these and other demonstrations undermined and finally demolished scholasticism, and gave birth to science; for, as Francis Bacon said, all it required was "that men should put their notions by, and attend solely to facts."

Now if men had *really* "put their notions by," and merely paid attention to facts, they would have returned to the condition of Hobie Baker the cat, whose mentality Mr. Stuart Chase covets so wistfully. Religion, superstition, fantastic Biblical world-history, were not demolished by "discoveries"; they were *outgrown* by the European mind. Again the individual life shows in microcosm the pattern of human evolution: the tendency of intellectual growth, in persons as in races, from dreamlike fantasy to realistic thinking. Many of the facts that contradicted theology had been known for ages; many discoveries required no telescope, no test-tube, no expedition round the world, and would have been just as possible physically hundreds of years before. But so long as the great Christian vision filled men's eyes, and systems of ethical symbols or great artistic ventures absorbed their minds, such facts as that wood floats on water and stones sink, living bodies have a uniform temperature and others vary with the weather, were just meaningless. Surely sailors had always known that ships showed their topsails over the horizon before they hove into full view. Surely the number of known animal species, had any hunter or farmer bothered to count them up, would always have made it obvious that the measurements of the ark could not have accommodated them by two and two, with food-supplies for eight or nine months. But nobody had chosen to take stock of these numbers while reading the measurements. For mythological purposes, the ark was "very big," the animals "very many," and their *Lebensraum* was God's problem.

Not in better information, but in *a natural tendency of*

maturing thought toward realism, lay the doom of the dogmatic age. When logical acumen reaches a certain height, and the imaginative power has been disciplined into real skill and ingenuity, then the normal growth of men's interest in facts reveals a new challenge to philosophical thinking — the intellectual challenge of "contingent" things. The most insistent facts have always been respected in practice, or we would not be here. But a society that has its mind fixed on religious symbols deals with facts in a purely practical spirit and disposes of them as fast as they arise. To take philosophical interest in their concomitant variations, their sequences, their uniformities, demands a change of outlook.[6] It sets up a new aim for constructive thought: not only to form a system out of traditional premises, but to construct a logically coherent cosmology such that its premises shall imply certain propositions exemplified by observable facts. When this challenge is felt (it need not be consciously recognized), its immediate effect is a new interest in facts, not as distracting interruptions to pure thought, but as its very sources and terminals, the fixed points on which theories and inventions must hinge.

The power that comes with scientific knowledge could become apparent only after science had attained a considerable growth. Practical gain, dominion over nature, were therefore not its early motives; its motives were intellectual, they lay in the restless desire of an ever-imaginative mind to exploit the possibilities of the factual world as a field for constructive thought.[7] Just as a person addicted to cross-

[6] The importance of this change has been pointed out and discussed by A. N. Whitehead, in *Science and the Modern World* (1926), chap. i.

[7] In this opinion, too, I find myself supported by the judgment of Professor Whitehead, who said in one of his published lectures: "Science has been developed under the impulse of speculative Reason, the desire for explanatory knowledge. Its reaction on technology did not commence until after the invention of the improved steam engine in the year 1769. Even then, the nineteenth century was well advanced before this reaction became one of the dominating facts. . . . There was nothing systematic and dominating in the interplay between science and technical procedure. The one great exception was the foundation of the Greenwich Observatory for the improvement of navigation." (*The Function of Reason,* 1929, pp. 38–39.)

word puzzles becomes a maniac for new words, so the pioneers of science were avid for facts that could conceivably be used in their business. Looking, measuring, analyzing things, became something like sports in their own right. But great scientists were never distracted by the fact-finding rage; they knew from the first what they were doing. Their task was always *to relate facts to each other,* either as different cases of the same general fact, or as successive transformations of an initial fact according to some systematic principle, or (at an elementary stage of conception) as more and more exemplifications of "contingent laws," or generally observed uniformities.

The interest in facts led to their progressive discovery, to the invention of aids and implements of discovery, and so to an unprecedented acquaintance with the world. But it was far less the information men acquired that undid their religious beliefs than the change of heart which prompted such research. The desire to construct a world-picture out of facts superseded the older ambition to weave a fabric of "values," in which things and events were interpreted as manifestations of good and evil, related to powers, wills, minds, but not essentially to each other; their own laws having been given short shrift as mere "contingencies," which might even be expected to yield, upon occasion, to higher principles, with the result known as "miracle." No matter how much the old order thundered against new facts, declaring them not so, unknowable, uncertain, dangerous half-truths, or what-not, the new facts were not its real destroyers, but *the new eyes that saw them.*

We have inherited the realistic outlook and its intellectual ideal, science. We have inherited a naive faith in the substantiality and ultimacy of facts, and are convinced that human life, to have any value, must be not only casually and opportunely adapted to their exigencies (as even the most other-worldly lives have been), but must be intellectually filled with an appreciation of "things as they are." Facts are our very measure of value. They are the framework of our lives; thinking that leads to the discovery of observable fact takes us "down to reality"; Wittgenstein has really caught and recorded the modern man's intellectual attitude, in his metaphysical aphorisms: [8]

"The world is everything that is the case." (1)

"The totality of atomic facts is the world." (2.04)

"The world divides into facts." (1.2)

Our world "divides into facts" because we so divide it. Facts are our guarantees of *truth*. Every generation hankers for "truth," and whatever will guarantee the truth of propositions to its satisfaction, is its zero-point of theory where thought comes to rest in "knowledge." To us it seems utterly unimaginable that anyone could *really* resist a *demonstratio ad occulos* and hold his deepest convictions — those which command his actions — on any other basis. Yet people have acted with lordly disregard of "appearances," and do so yet. Christian Scientists flatly deny the reality of visible facts that are unpleasant, and act on their disbelief. Not only idealists, but even their great antagonist William James held it possible that, from the intellectual vantage-point of "higher beings" than men, our evils might prove to be illusions.[9] The ancient Greeks had such a respect for pure reason that they could seriously accept, on its logical merits, a doctrine of reality which was *never* exemplified in fact at all, but flatly contradicted by experience; Parmenides could declare all events to be illusory because change was not possible under the premises of his systematic thought. Such heroic independence from sense-evidence is not often found, and of course the most hard-bitten Eleatic could not act on this faith until he was ready to die in it (which, *ex hypothesi*, could not happen). But all these doctrines show how in different stages of thought people demand different kinds of security for their convictions.

We find sense-evidence a very gratifying conclusion to the process of thought. Our standards of rationality are the same as Euclid's or Aristotle's — generality, consistency, co-

[8] *Tractatus Logico-Philosophicus.*

[9] See "Is Life Worth Living?" in *The Will to Believe, and Other Essays in Popular Philosophy* (1905), p. 58.

herence, systematic inclusion of all possible cases, economy and elegance in demonstration — but our ideal of science makes one further demand: the demand of what has been called "maximal interpretability." This means that as many propositions as possible shall be applicable to *observable fact*. The systems of thought that seem to us to represent "knowledge" are those which were *designed as hypotheses*, i.e. designed with reference to experience and intended to meet certain tests: at definite points their implications must yield propositions which express discoverable facts. If and only if these crucial propositions do correspond to facts, a hypothesis is ranked as "truth," its premises as "natural laws."

I will not enlarge on the assumptions, methods, standards, and aims of science, because that has been done a dozen times over, since Henri Poincaré's *La Science et l'hypothèse*; [10] even the part played by symbolism in science has been exhaustively and, I think, well treated by mathematicians and philosophers from Charles Peirce to the Vienna Circle. The upshot of it all is that the so-called "empirical spirit" has taken possession of our scholarship and speculation as well as of our common sense, so that in pure theory as well as in business and politics the last appeal is always to that peculiar hybrid of concept and percept, the "given fact." [11]

The realistic turn of mind which marks our civilization, and is probably a sign of our coming-of-age as a race, is further manifested in our rigorous standards of *historical fact*. This is not at all the same thing as scientific fact; nor is historical truth judged by the same criteria as the truth of scientific propositions. For to science, as Lord Russell once remarked in an academic seminar,[12] "A miracle would not be important if it happened only once, or even very rarely"; but in history the point is to find out what did happen just once, what were the specific facts about a specific occasion. Science never cares about historic instances as such: its "given facts" are

[10] Published in 1903.

[11] Karl Schmidt has discussed the scientific versus the naive conception of fact, in his article, "The Existential Status of Facts and Laws in Physics," *The Monist*, XLIII (1933), 2: 161–172.

[12] Held at Harvard University in the autumn of 1940.

always noted as *illustrations*, and occurrences which do not illustrate anything are not "scientific." If miracles occurred — events which could not be explained, but also could not be repeated or expected to repeat themselves — we could discount them as "inexactnesses" in our general picture of nature. But to a historian a miracle, though there were but one in the world, would be of great importance if it had consequences which ultimately involved many people. If there were any indubitable record of it which clearly established it as a miracle, history would simply accept it; but science would either exclude the fact, or would have to be entirely rewritten. Now if this miracle were really unique, or so rare as to be *practically* unique, the disadvantages of rewriting science would make it advisable to put a "scientific fiction," such as for instance an unfounded denial of the alleged "fact," in place of its record.

Science is an intellectual scheme for handling facts, a vast and relatively stable *context* in which whole classes of facts may be understood. But it is not the most decisive expression of realistic thinking: that is the new "historical sense." Not our better knowledge of what *are* the facts of history — there is no judging that — but the passion for running down evidence, all the evidence, the unbiassed, objective evidence for specifically dated and located events, without distortion, hypothesis, or interpretation — the faith in the attainability and value of *pure fact* is that surest symptom; the ideal of truth which made the whole past generation of historians believe that in archives as such there was salvation.

Now this ideal may be as extravagant as Carl Becker esteemed it, when he wrote: "Hoping to find something without looking for it, expecting to obtain final answers to life's riddle by resolutely refusing to ask questions — it was surely the most romantic species of realism yet invented, the oddest attempt ever made to get something for nothing!" [13] But it does sum up the attitude of that mighty and rather terrible person, the Modern Man, toward the world: the complete

[13] "Everyman His Own Historian," *American Historical Review*, XXXVII (1932), 2: 221–236. See p. 233.

submission to what he conceives as "hard, cold fact." To exchange fictions, faiths, and "constructed systems" for facts is his supreme value; hence his periodic outbursts of "debunking" traditions, religious or legendary; his satisfaction with stark realism in literature, his suspicion and impatience of poetry; and perhaps, on the naive uncritical level of the average mentality, the passion for *news* — news of any sort, if only it purports to *be so*; which, paradoxically enough, makes us peculiarly easy victims to propaganda. Where a former age would have judged persuasive oratory largely on its origins in God or Devil, i.e. in the right or the wrong camp, we profess to judge it on the merit of alleged *facts*, and fall to the party that can muster the most spectacular "cases."

The better minds of our age hold a heroic pride in being unafraid of truth, in wanting to face it and being able to "take it." William James, whose feeling was really rooted deeply in the old order of traditional "values," and bound to religious myths of Providence, progress, and the pilgrim soul, nevertheless had to cast his lot for the new ideal. His famous distinction between "tender-minded" and "tough-minded" philosophers and his praise of the latter, the truer breed, mark his confession of the new faith, despite his occasional nostalgic pleas for a "will to believe," for "life's ideals." The same sense of heroism, not to say heroics, rings in almost every paragraph of Bertrand Russell's early essay, *A Free Man's Worship*; [14] save that this thrilling disillusionment, this nobler worship of "hard fact," is never spoiled by any flirtation with the old gods. James' generation (at least its best souls, of whom he was one) could take the new standard of truth; Russell's generation can take it and like it. As for the children of the present age, they know no other measure, for fact-finding has become their common sense. Their unconscious orientation is empirical, circumstantial, and historical.

It is the historical mind, rather than the scientific (in the physicist's sense), that destroyed the mythical orientation of European culture; the historian, not the mathematician, introduced the "higher criticism," the standard of *actual fact*.

[14] In *Mysticism and Logic* (1918).

It is he who is the real apostle of the realistic age. Science builds its structure of hypothetical "elements" and laws of their behavior, touching on reality at crucial points, and if all those propositions which ought to correspond to observable events can be "cashed in" for the proper sense-experiences, the hypotheses that frame them stand acknowledged. But the historian does not locate known facts in a hypothetical, general pattern of processes; his aim is to link *fact to fact*, one unique knowable event to another individual one that begot it. Not space and time, but a geographical place and a date, B.C. or A.D., anchor his propositions to reality. Science has become deeply tinged with empiricism, and yet its ideal is one of universality, formalism, permanence — the very ideal that presided over its long life since the days of Euclid and Archimedes. The fact that it has shared the intellectual growth of the modern world is rather a mark of the continuity of human thought, the power of rationality to cope gradually with phase after phase of experience, than a novel departure. Science is almost as old as European culture; but history (not contemporaneous chronicle and genealogy, but epochal, long-range history) is only a few hundred years old; it is peculiarly a product of the realistic phase, the adult stage of judgment.

In a recent book entitled *History and Science*, Dr. Hugh Miller proposes to carry the ideal of *complete factual knowledge* even into the camp of the mathematical sciences. He regards the factual standard of knowledge in the light of a new generative idea; physical science, if perfected, should describe a system of reality in which each event would be uniquely determined, and the pattern of the physical world would appear as an *evolution*, fitting exactly the actual course of natural history. "The doctrine of evolution," he says, "is sometimes called a 'theory of evolution,' as if it were just one more theoretical hypothesis, and not a reorientation of all theoretical knowledge toward historical fact." [15] Here is the realistic ideal with a vengeance!

Underlying these great intellectual structures — science,

[15] Hugh Miller, *History and Science* (1939), p. 30.

history, and the hybrid we call "natural history" — is the dominant principle that rules our individual minds, the implicit belief in *causation.* On this belief we base our personal hopes and fears, our plans and techniques of action. It really *rules* our minds, for it inspires what I have called our "practical vision" — the carving out of general concepts in such a way that *temporal events* shall answer to a certain number of our images, which therefore function both as symbols of thought and as signs for behavior. The tendency to demand ever more signs to replace symbols at certain terminals of thought, more symbols to direct one to expect new signs, makes our lives more and more factual, intellectually strenuous, wedded to the march of mundane events, and beset by disconcerting surprises. Our increasing command of causal laws makes for more and more complicated activities; we have put many stages of artifice and device, of manufacture and alteration, between ourselves and the rest of nature. The ordinary city-dweller knows nothing of the earth's productivity; he does not know the sunrise and rarely notices when the sun sets; ask him in what phase the moon is, or when the tide in the harbor is high, or even how high the average tide runs, and likely as not he cannot answer you. Seed-time and harvest are nothing to him. If he has never witnessed an earthquake, a great flood, or a hurricane, he probably does not feel the power of nature as a reality surrounding his life at all. His realities are the motors that run elevators, subway trains, and cars, the steady feed of water and gas through the mains and of electricity over the wires, the crates of food-stuff that arrive by night and are spread for his inspection before his day begins, the concrete and brick, bright steel and dingy woodwork that take the place of earth and waterside and sheltering roof for him. His "house" is an apartment in the great man-made city; so far as he is concerned, it has only an interior, no exterior of its own. It could not collapse, let in rain, or blow away. If it leaks the fault is with a pipe or with the people upstairs, not with heaven.

Nature, as man has always known it, he knows no more.

Since he has learned to esteem signs above symbols, to suppress his emotional reactions in favor of practical ones and *make use of nature* instead of holding so much of it sacred, he has altered the face, if not the heart, of reality. His parks are "landscaped," and fitted into his world of pavements and walls; his pleasure resorts are "developments" in which a wild field looks unformed, unreal; even his animals (dogs and cats are all he knows as creatures, horses are parts of milk-wagons) are fantastic "breeds" made by his tampering. No wonder, then, that he thinks of human power as the highest power, and of nature as so much "raw material"! But human power is knowledge, he knows that; the knowledge of natural *facts* and the scientific laws of their transformation.

With his new outlook on the world, of course the old symbolism of human values has collapsed. The sun is too interesting as an object, a source of transformable energies, to be interpreted as a god, a hero, or a symbol of passion; since we know that it is *really* the ultimate source of what we call "power," transformable energy measurable by units, we take a realistic, not a mystical, attitude toward it; its image is no longer "distanced" in a perspective of non-discursive thought; our literal concepts have caught up with it. As for the moon, it is too rarely seen to be a real presence to us, and fits too well into the cosmological scheme governed by science to arouse wonder. We read about its beauties, more often than we actually see them unchallenged by neon-lights or blinking bulbs. The earth, laid bare in building-lots or parks, does not put forth unplanted life, as it always did for the savage; only our farmers — a small portion of mankind — know "Mother Earth" any longer; only our sailors — a still smaller portion — know the might of a raging sea. To most people, the ancient, obvious symbols of nature have become literary figures, and to many these very figures look silly. Their significance has been dissolved by a more mature, literal-minded conception of reality, the "practical vision" that sees sun and moon and earth, land and sea, growth and destruction, in terms of *natural law and historical fact.*

The modern mind is an incredible complex of impressions and transformations; and its product is a fabric of meanings that would make the most elaborate dream of the most ambitious tapestry-weaver look like a mat. The warp of that fabric consists of what we call "data," the *signs* to which experience has conditioned us to attend, and upon which we act often without any conscious ideation. The woof is symbolism. Out of signs and symbols we weave our tissue of "reality."

Signs themselves may be very complicated and form intricate chains; many signs are nameless, and linked into continuous *situations*, to which we react not with a single deed, but with a steady, intelligent behavior. Driving an automobile is an example of such a chain of reactions to signs. It is not a habitual act, though every individual response in it is a reaction to a certain sort of sign, facilitated by practice. The only single habit involved in the whole process is the habit of constantly obeying signs. A moment of yielding to habitual motions, as in distraction or stupor, is likely to wreck the car. We can drive *without thinking*, but never *without watching*.

Our response to a sign becomes, in its turn, a sign of a new situation; the meaning of the first sign, having been "cashed in," has become a context for the next sign. This gives us that continuity of actual experience which makes it the sturdy warp of reality, through which we draw the connecting and transforming woof-threads of conception.

As in an elaborate tapestry one often cannot tell how the fibers are involved with each other, so any namable item of reality may stem from a signific experience and enter into the role of a symbol, or a symbolic element, e.g. a word, uttered on an occasion, may act momentarily as a sign. Language is symbolical, but in communication it does more than express conceptions; it describes, but it also *points*. Whenever we talk in the present tense, saying: "Here is —," "Over there is —," "Look out," "I thank you," etc., we signify the realities to which our propositions apply. This signific function of language has become incorporated in its very structure; for in every proposition there is at least one word — the verb — which has the double function of *combining* the elements named into one propositional form, and *asserting* the proposition, i.e. referring the form to something in reality. It is because of this implicit function of assertion, involved in the very meaning of a true verb, that *every proposition is true or false*. A symbol that merely expresses a concept, e.g. an image or a name, is neither true nor false, though it is significant.

Sign and symbol are knotted together in the production of those fixed realities that we call "facts," as I think this whole study of semantic has shown. But *between the facts* run the threads of unrecorded reality, momentarily recognized, wherever they come to the surface, in our tacit adaptation to signs; and the bright, twisted threads of symbolic envisagement, imagination, thought — memory and reconstructed memory, belief beyond experience, dream, make-believe, hypothesis, philosophy — the whole creative process of ideation, metaphor, and abstraction that makes human life an adventure in understanding.

It is the woof-thread that creates the pattern of a fabric, howbeit the warp may be used here and there to vary it, too. The meanings which are capable of indefinite growth are symbolic meanings: connotations, not significations. There are two fundamental types of symbolism, discursive and presentational; but the types of meaning are far more numerous, and do not necessarily correspond to one or the other symbolic type, though in a general way literal meaning belongs to words and artistic meaning to images invoked by words and to presentational symbols. But such a rule is a crude, simplified, and very inexact statement. Maps, photographs, and diagrams are presentational symbols with purely literal significance; a poem has essentially artistic significance, though a great factor in its complex, global form is discursive statement. The sense of a word may hover between literal and figurative meaning, as expressions that were originally frank metaphors "fade" to a general and ultimately literal meaning. For instance, our newspapers overwork such figurative expressions as: "Candidate *Raps* Opponent," "Mayor *Flays* Council," "*Scores* New Dealers at Meeting." These words were originally strong metaphors; but we have learned to read them as mere synonyms for "scolds." [16] We still know them as figurative expressions, but they are rapidly acquiring a dual meaning, e.g. "To flay: (1) to remove the skin; (2) to criticize harshly."

Every word has a history, and has probably passed through stages where its most important significance lay in associations it no longer has, uses now obsolete, *doubles entendres* we would not understand. Even the English of Shakespeare has changed its color since it was written, and is lucid only to the historian who knows its setting. Sometimes a word of general import becomes a "technical term" and is practically lost to its former place in the language; sometimes a pre-eminent denotation narrows it again to a proper name (as for instance "Olympos," literally a high mountain, became the name of a *certain* mountain; and "Adam," first "man," then by abstraction, "Man," is to us the name of a *certain* man). And through all the metamorphoses of its meaning, such a word carries a certain trace of every meaning it has ever had, like an overtone, and every association it has acquired, like an aura, so that in living language practically no word is a purely conventional counter, but always a symbol with a "metaphysical pathos," as Professor Lovejoy has called it. Its meaning depends partly on social convention, and partly on its history, its past company, even on the "natural symbolism" or suggestiveness of its sound.

The intellect which understands, reshapes, and employs linguistic symbols, and at the same time tempers its activities to the exigencies of ever-passing, signific experience, really

[16] American English is full of such transient figures, passing swiftly from one literal meaning to another, by the twin bridges of literary device and popular slang. Perhaps the new country, the new race springing from a medley of nationalities, the new culture in its rapid growth, cause this instability of language, the tendency to extravagant metaphorical expression and the willingness of people to interpret and accept quite extreme figures of speech. Certainly no European language — not even the highly idiomatic French — is as rich in slang, in fashions, in informal expressive jargon, as our American dialect.

works with a minimum of actual perception or formal judgment. As Roger Fry has put it, "The needs of our actual life are so imperative, that the sense of vision becomes highly specialized in their service. With an admirable economy we see only so much as is needful for our purposes; but this is in fact very little, just enough to recognize and identify each object or person; that done, they go into our mental catalogue and are no more really seen. In actual life the normal person really only reads the labels as it were on the objects around him and troubles no further. Almost all the things which are useful in any way put on more or less this cap of invisibility." [17] Signs and discursive symbols are the stock-in-trade of conscious intelligent adjustment, and they are telescoped into such small cues of perception and denotation that we are tempted to believe our thought moves without images or words. The tiniest black spot of a certain shiny quality tells us that the cat is under the sofa with just its tail-tip showing. The word "cat," or a momentary, fragmentary image may be all that comes into our mind in recognition. Yet if someone asks us later: "Where's the cat?" we do not hesitate to answer: "I saw him under the sofa." By such signals we steer our course through the world of sense, and by one-word contacts we throw whole systems of judgment, belief, memory, and expectation into action.

Yet all these familiar signs and abbreviated symbols have to be supported by a vast intellectual structure in order to function so smoothly that we are almost unware of them; and this structure is composed of their full articulate forms and all their implicit relationships, which may be exhumed from the stock of our buried knowledge at any time. Because they do fit so neatly into the frame of our ultimate world-picture, we can think *with* them and do not have to think *about* them; but our full apprehension of them is really only suppressed. They wear a "cap of invisibility" when, like good servants, they perform their tasks for our convenience without being evident in themselves. Yet all our signs and symbols were gathered from sensuous and emotional experience and bear

[17] Fry, *Vision and Design*, pp. 24–25.

the marks of their origin — perhaps a remote historical origin. Though we ordinarily see things only with the economy of practical vision, we *can* look *at* them instead of *through* them, and then their suppressed forms and their unusual meanings emerge for us. It is just because there is a fund of possible meanings in every familiar form, that the picture of reality holds together for us, that we believe in the ultimate causal connection of all physical nature and the ultimate coherence of moral demands. A form that is both sign and symbol ties action and insight together for us; it plays a part in a momentary situation and also in the "science" we constantly, if tacitly, assume. A fine sunset demonstrates the earth's rotation with relation to the sun, marks a "time of day," signifies that dinner is ready or should be so, suggests continued fair weather, and also is sublime, peaceful, and beautiful. The chances are that most observers will take all its significations for granted and attend to its aesthetic significance only. Yet its reality in "nature" is a factor of that significance; were the display a product of screen and camera, it would lack its vague, traditional, religious meaning, and affect one very differently. It might be beautiful but not sublime. The interplay of beauty and reality, of spectacular color in empty air, lends it that cosmic importance which permeates our very vision of it.

Many symbols — not only words, but other forms — may be said to be "charged" with meanings. They have many symbolic and significs functions, and these functions have been integrated into a complex so that they are all apt to be sympathetically invoked with any chosen one. The cross is such a "charged" symbol: the actual instrument of Christ's death, hence a symbol of suffering; first laid on his shoulders, an actual burden, as well as an actual product of human handiwork, and on both grounds a symbol of his accepted moral burden; also an ancient symbol of the four zodiac points, with a cosmic connotation; a "natural" symbol of cross-roads (we still use it on our highways as a warning before an intersection), and therefore of decision, crisis, choice; also of *being crossed*, i.e. of frustration, adversity, fate; and finally, to the artistic eye a cross is the figure of a man. All these and many other meanings lie dormant in that simple, familiar, significant shape. No wonder that it is a magical form! It is charged with meanings, all human and emotional and vaguely cosmic, so that they have become integrated into a connotation of the whole religious drama — sin, suffering, and redemption. Yet undoubtedly the cross owes much of its value to the fact that *it has the physical attributes of a good symbol*: it is easily made — drawn on paper, set up in wood or stone, fashioned of precious substance as an amulet, even traced recognizably with a finger, in a ritual gesture. It is so obvious a symbolic device that despite its holy connotations we do not refrain from using it in purely mundane, discursive capacities, as the sign of "plus," or in tilted position as "times," or as a marker on ballot sheets and many other kinds of record.

There are many "charged" symbols in our thought, though few that play as many popular roles as the cross. A ship is another example — the image of precarious security in all-surrounding danger, of progress toward a goal, of adventure between two points of rest, with the near, if dormant, connotation of safe imprisonment in the hold, as in the womb. Not improbably the similar form of a primitive boat and of the moon in its last quarter has served in past ages to reinforce such mythological values.

The fact that very few of our words are purely technical, and few of our images purely utilitarian, gives our lives a background of closely woven multiple meanings against which all conscious experiences and interpretations are measured. Every object that emerges into the focus of attention has meaning beyond the "fact" in which it figures. It serves by turns, and sometimes even at once, for insight and theory and behavior, in non-discursive knowledge and discursive reason, in wishful fancy, or as a sign eliciting conditioned-reflex action. But that means that we respond to every new datum with a complex of mental functions. Our perception organizes it, giving it an individual definite *Gestalt*. Non-discursive intelligence, reading emotive import into the concrete form, meets it with purely sensitive appreciation; and even more promptly, the language-habit causes us to assimilate it to some literal concept and give it a place in discursive thought. Here is a crossing of two activities: for discursive symbolism is always general, and requires *application* to the concrete datum, whereas non-discursive symbolism is specific, is the "given" itself, and invites us to read the more general meaning out of the case. Hence the exciting back-and-forth of real mental life, of *living* by symbols. We play on words, explore their connotations, evoke or evade their associations; we identify signs with our symbols and construct the "intelligible world"; we dream our needs and fantasms and construct the "inner world" of unapplied symbols. We impress each other, too, and build a social structure, a world of right and wrong, of demands and sanctions.

Because our moral life is negotiated so largely by symbols, it is more oppressive than the morality of animals. Beasts have their moral relations, too; they control each other's actions jealously or permit them patiently, as a dog permits her puppies to bite and worry her, but growls at another dog that trespasses on her premises. But animals react only to the deed that is done or is actually imminent; they use force only to frustrate or avenge an act; whereas we control each other's merely incipient behavior with fantasies of force. We employ sanctions, threaten vague penalties, and try to forestall offenses by merely exhibiting the symbols of their consequences. That is why man is more cruel than any beast. We make our punishments effective as mere connotations, and to do so we have to make them disproportionately harsh. Misdemeanors that merit no more than a serious rebuke or a half-hour in jail have to carry a penalty of a month's imprisonment if the very thought of the punishment is to prevent them. Then, because symbols have to have reference to fact if they are to remain forceful at all, wherever the threat has not served as a deterrent it has to be fulfilled. And more than that; the power of symbols enables us not only to limit each other's actions, but to command them;

not only to *restrain* one another, but to *constrain*. That makes the weaker not merely the timid respecter of the strong, but his servant. It gives us duty, cónscription, and slavery. The story of man's martyrdom is a sequel to the story of his intelligence, his power of symbolical envisagement.

For good or evil, man has this power of envisagement, which puts on him a burden that purely alert, realistic creatures do not bear — the burden of understanding. He lives not only in a place, but in Space; not only at a time, but in History. So he must conceive a world and a law of the world, a pattern of life, and a way of meeting death. All these things he knows, and he has to make some adaptation to their reality.

Now, he can adapt himself somehow to anything his imagination can cope with; but he cannot deal with Chaos. Because his characteristic function and highest asset is conception, his greatest fright is to meet what he cannot construe — the "uncanny," as it is popularly called. It need not be a new object; we do meet new things, and "understand" them promptly, if tentatively, by the nearest analogy, when our minds are functioning freely; but under mental stress even perfectly familiar things may become suddenly disorganized, and give us the horrors. Therefore our most important assets are always the symbols of our general *orientation* in nature, on the earth, in society, and in what we are doing: the symbols of our *Weltanschauung* and *Lebensanschauung*. Consequently, in primitive society, a daily ritual is incorporated in common activities, in eating, washing, firemaking, etc., as well as in pure ceremonial; because the need of reasserting the tribal morale and recognizing its cosmic conditions is constantly felt. In Christian Europe the Church brought men daily (in some orders even hourly) to their knees, to enact if not to contemplate their assent to the ultimate concepts.

In modern society such exercises are all but lost. Every person finds his Holy of Holies where he may: in Scientific Truth, Evolution, the State, Democracy, *Kultur,* or some metaphysical word like "the All" or "the Spiritual." Human life in our age is so changed and diversified that people cannot share a few, historic, "charged" symbols that have about the same wealth of meaning for everybody. This loss of old universal symbols endangers our safe unconscious orientation. The new forms of our new order have not yet acquired that rich, confused, historic accretion of meanings that makes many familiar things "charged" symbols to which we seem to respond instinctively. For some future generation, an aeroplane may be a more powerful symbol than a ship; its poetic possibilities are perhaps even more obvious; but to us it is too new, it does not sum up our past in guarantee of the present. One can see this in the conscious symbol it presents to Marcel Proust, in *La Prisonnière*, as "one of these frankly material vehicles to explore the Infinite." Poetic simile, not spontaneous metaphor, is its status as yet; it is not a repository of experience, as nature-symbols and social symbols are. And virtually all the realities of our modern life are thus new, their material aspects are predominant, practical insight still has to cope with them instead of taking them for granted. Therefore our intelligence is keen but precarious; it lacks metaphysical myth, régime, and ritual expression.

There are relatively few people today who are born to an environment which gives them spiritual support. Only persons of some imagination and effective intelligence can picture such an environment and deliberately seek it. They are the few who feel drawn to some realm of reality that contains their ultimate life-symbols and dictates activities which may acquire ritual value. Men who follow the sea have often a deep love for that hard life, which no catalogue of its practical virtues can account for. But in their dangerous calling they feel secure; in their comfortless quarters they are at ease. Waters and ships, heaven and storm and harbor, somehow contain the symbols through which they see meaning and sense in the world, a "justification," as we call it, of trouble, a unified conception of life whereby it can be rationally lived. Any man who loves his calling loves it for more than its use; he loves it because it seems to have "meaning." A scholar who will defy the world in order to write or speak what he knows as "scientific truth," the Greek philosopher who chose to die rather than protest against Athens, the feminists to whom woman-suffrage was a "cause" for which they accepted ridicule as well as punishment, show how entirely realistic performances may point beyond themselves, and acquire the value of super-personal acts, like rites. They are the forms of devotion that have replaced genuflexions, sacrifices, and solemn dances.

A mind that is oriented, no matter by what conscious or unconscious symbols, in material and social realities, can function freely and confidently even under great pressure of circumstance and in the face of hard problems. Its life is a smooth and skillful shuttling to and fro between sign-functions and symbolic functions, a steady interweaving of sensory interpretations, linguistic responses, inferences, memories, imaginative prevision, factual knowledge, and tacit appreciations. Dreams can possess it at night and work off the heaviest load of self-expressive needs, and evaporate before the light of day; its further self-expressions being woven intelligently into the nexus of practical behavior. Ritual comes to it as a natural response to the "holiness" or importance of real occasions. In such a mind, doubts of the "meaning of life" are not apt to arise, for reality itself is intrinsically "meaningful": it incorporates the symbols of Life and Death, Sin and Salvation. For a balanced active intelligence, reality is historical fact and significant form, the all-inclusive realm of science, myth, art, and comfortable common sense.

Opportunity to carry on our natural, impulsive, intelligent life, to realize plans, express ideas in action or in symbolic formulation, see and hear and interpret all things that we encounter, without fear of confusion, adjust our interests and expressions to each other, is the "freedom" for which humanity strives. This, and not some specific right that society may grant or deny, is the "liberty" that goes necessarily with "life" and "pursuit of happiness." Professor Whitehead expressed this view precisely, when he said:

"The concept of freedom has been narrowed to the picture of contemplative people shocking their generation. . . . This is a thorough mistake. The massive habits of physical nature, its iron laws, determine the scene for the sufferings of men. Birth and death, cold and hunger, separation, disease, the general impracticability of purpose, all bring their quota to imprison the souls of women and men. Our experiences do not keep step with our hopes. . . . *The essence of freedom is the practicability of purpose. Mankind has chiefly suffered from the frustration of its prevalent purposes, even such as belong to the very definition of its species."* [18]

Any miscarriage of the symbolic process is an abrogation of our human freedom: the constraint imposed by a foreign language, or a lapse of one's own linguistic ability such as Sir Henry Head has described as loss of abstract concepts,[19] or pathological repression that causes all sorts of distorted personal symbols to encroach on literal thought and empirical judgment, or lack of logical power, knowledge, food for thought, or imagination to envisage our problems clearly and negotiably. All such obstacles may block the free functioning of mind. But the most disastrous hindrance is disorientation, the failure or destruction of life-symbols and loss or repression of votive acts. A life that does not incorporate some degree of ritual, of gesture and attitude, has no mental anchorage. It is prosaic to the point of total indifference, purely casual, devoid of that structure of intellect and feeling which we call "personality."

Therefore interference with acts that have ritual value (conscious or unconscious) is always felt as the most intolerable injury one man, or group of men, can do to another. Freedom of conscience is the basis of all personal freedom. To constrain a man against his principles — make a pacifist bear arms, a patriot insult his flag, a pagan receive baptism — is to endanger his attitude toward the world, his personal strength and single-mindedness. No matter how fantastic may be the dogmas he holds sacred, how much his living rites

[18] From A. N. Whitehead, *Adventures of Ideas* (1933), p. 84. (Italics mine.) By permission of The Macmillan Company, publishers.
[19] See "Disorders of Symbolic Thinking and Expression," *British Journal of Psychology,* XI (1920–21), part II, 179–193.

conflict with the will or convenience of society, it is never a light matter to demand their violation. Men fight passionately against being forced to do lip-service, because the enactment of a rite is always, in some measure, assent to its meaning; so that the very expression of an alien mythology, incompatible with one's own vision of "fact" or "truth," works to the corruption of that vision. It is a breach of personality. To be obliged to confess, teach, or acclaim falsehood is always felt as an insult exceeding even ridicule and abuse. Common insult is a blow at one's ego; but constraint of conscience strikes at one's ego and super-ego, one's whole world, humanity, and purpose. It takes a strong mind to keep its orientation without overt symbols, acts, assertions, and social corroborations; to maintain it in the face of the confounding pattern of enacted heresy is more than average mentality can do.

We have to adapt our peculiarly human mental functions — our symbolific functions — to given limitations, exactly as we must adapt all our biological activities. The mind, like all other organs, can draw its sustenance only from the surrounding world; our metaphysical symbols must spring from reality. Such adaptation always requires time, habit, tradition, and intimate knowledge of a way of life. If, now, the field of our unconscious symbolic orientation is suddenly plowed up by tremendous changes in the external world and in the social order, we lose our hold, our convictions, and therewith our effectual purposes. In modern civilization there are two great threats to mental security: the new mode of living, which has made the old nature-symbols alien to our minds, and the new mode of working, which makes personal activity meaningless, inacceptable to the hungry imagination. Most men never see the goods they produce, but stand by a traveling belt and turn a million identical passing screws or close a million identical passing wrappers in a succession of hours, days, years. This sort of activity is too poor, too empty, for even the most ingenious mind to invest it with symbolic content. Work is no longer a sphere of ritual; and so the nearest and surest source of mental satisfaction has dried up. At the same time, the displacement of the permanent homestead by the modern rented tenement — now here, now there — has cut another anchor-line of the human mind. Most people have no home that is a symbol of their childhood, not even a definite memory of one place to serve that purpose. Many no longer know the language that was once their mother-tongue. All old symbols are gone, and thousands of average lives offer no new materials to a creative imagination. This, rather than physical want, is the starvation that threatens the modern worker, the tyranny of the machine. The withdrawal of all natural means for expressing the unity of personal life is a major cause of the distraction, irreligion, and unrest that mark the proletariat of all countries. Technical progress is putting man's freedom of mind in jeopardy.

 In such a time people are excited about any general convictions or ideals they may have. Numberless hybrid religions spring up, mysteries, causes, ideologies, all passionately embraced and badly argued. A vague longing for the old tribal unity makes nationalism look like salvation, and arouses the most fantastic bursts of chauvinism and self-righteousness; the wildest anthropological and historical legends; the deprecation and distortion of learning; and in place of orthodox sermons, that systematic purveying of loose, half-baked ideas which our generation knows as "propaganda." There are committees and ministries of propaganda in our world, as there were evangelical missions and watch-and-ward societies in the world of our fathers. No wonder that philosophers looking at this pandemonium of self-assertion, self-justification, and social and political fantasy, view it as a reaction against the Age of Reason. After centuries of science and progress, they conclude, the pendulum swings the other way: the irrational forces of our animal nature must hold their Witches' Sabbath.

 A philosophy that knows only deductive or inductive logic as reason, and classes all other human functions as "emotive." irrational, and animalian, can see only regression to a prelogical state in the present passionate and unscientific ideologies. All it can show us as the approach to Parnassus is the way of factual data, hypothesis, trial, judgment, and generalization. All other things our minds do are dismissed as irrelevant to intellectual progress; they are residues, emotional disturbances, or throwbacks to animal estate.

But a theory of mind whose keynote is the symbolific function, whose problem is the morphology of significance, is not obliged to draw that bifurcating line between science and folly. It can see these ructions and upheavals of the modern mind not as lapses of rational interest, caused by animal impulse, but as the exact contrary — as a new phase of savagedom, indeed, but inspired by the rational need of envisagement and understanding. The springs of European thought have run dry — those deep springs of imagination that furnish the basic concepts for a whole intellectual order, the first discernments, the generative ideas of our *Weltanschauung*. New conceptual forms are crowding them out, but are themselves in the mythical phase, the "implicit" stage of symbolic formulation. We cannot analyze the contents of those vast symbols — Race, Unity, Manifest Destiny, Humanity — over which we fight so ruthlessly; if we could, it would mean that they were already furnishing discursive terms, clear issues, and we would all be busy philosophizing instead of waging holy wars. We would have the new world that humanity is dreaming of, and would be eagerly building the edifice of knowledge out of new insights. It is the sane, efficient, work-a-day business of free minds — discursive reasoning about well-conceived problems — that is disturbed or actually suspended in this apparent age of unreason; but the force which governs that age is still the force of *mind*, the impulse toward symbolic formulation, expression, and understanding of experience.

The continual pursuit of meanings — wider, clearer, more negotiable, more articulate meanings — is philosophy. It permeates all mental life: sometimes in the conscious form of metaphysical thought, sometimes in the free, confident manipulation of established ideas to derive their more precise, detailed implications, and sometimes — in the greatest creative periods — in the form of passionate mythical, ritual, and devotional expression. In primitive society such expression meets with little or no obstacle; for the first dawn of mentality has nothing to regret. Only as one culture supersedes another, every new insight is bought with the life of an older certainty. The confusion of form and content which characterizes our worship of life-symbols works to the frustration of well-ordered discursive reason, men act inappropriately, blindly, and viciously; but what they are thus wildly and mistakenly trying to do is human, intellectual, and necessary. Standards of science and ethics must condemn it, for its overt form is rife with error; traditional philosophy must despair of it because it cannot meet any epistemological criterion; but in a wider philosophy of symbolism it finds a measure of understanding. If there is any virtue in the theory of what I have called "symbolic transformation," then this theory should elucidate not only the achievements of that function, but also its miscarriages, its limitations, and its by-products of illusion and error. Freedom of thought cannot be reborn without throes; language, art, morality, and science have all given us pain as well as power. For, as Professor Whitehead has frankly and humbly declared: "Error is the price we pay for progress."

LIST OF BOOKS

LIST OF BOOKS

Acknowledgments

Passages from the following works have been quoted in this book: from *The Story of My Life*, by Helen Keller, by permission of Doubleday, Doran & Company; from *Tractatus Logico-Philosophicus*, by Ludwig Wittgenstein, *The Growth of Reason*, by Frank Lorimer, *The Mentality of Apes*, by Wolfgang Köhler, and *The Tyranny of Words*, by Stuart Chase, by permission of Harcourt, Brace and Company, publishers; from *The Ape and The Child*, by W. N. and L. A. Kellogg, by permission of McGraw-Hill Book Company, publishers; from "How Can Music Express Emotion?" by Donald N. Ferguson, reprinted by permission from the Music Teachers National Association *Volume of Proceedings* for 1925; from "Observations on the Mentality of Chimpanzees and Orang-Utans," by W. H. Furness, courtesy of the American Philosophical Society; from "Musical Symbolism," by Henri Prunières, by permission of *The Musical Quarterly*; from *Philosophy* and *Mysticism and Logic* by Bertrand Russell, courtesy of W. W. Norton and Company, publishers; from "Reason and Feeling," by J. E. Creighton, by permission of *The Philosophical Review*; from *Gestalt Psychology*, by Wolfgang Köhler, courtesy Liveright Publishing Corporation; from *Oceanic Mythology*, by Roland Dixon, by permission of the Marshall Jones Company; from *Primitive Culture*, by E. B. Tylor, courtesy of G. P. Putnam's Sons; from *Speech: its Function and Development*, by Grace De Laguna, by permission of the Yale University Press; from *Experience and Nature*, by John Dewey, Open Court Publishing Company; from *Five Stages of Greek Religion*, by Gilbert Murray, Columbia University Press, publisher.

My thanks are due to all these copyright holders.

I also wish to acknowledge my indebtedness to the following English publishers: to George Allen & Unwin, for passages from *Language and Reality*, by W. M. Urban, and *Language: its Nature, Development and Origin*, by Otto Jespersen; to Kegan Paul, Trench, Trubner & Company, for passages from *Philosophy and Logical Syntax*, by Rudolf Carnap, *Communication: a Philosophical Study of Language*, by Karl Britton, and *Art and the Unconscious*, by J. M. Thorburn; to Chatto and Windus, for some lines from *Vision and Design*, by Roger Fry; and to the editor of *Philosophy*, for quotations from "The Sense of the Horizon," by C. D. Burns.

LIST OF BOOKS

(Articles are not listed here, because the facts of their publication are fully given in footnotes.)

Aldrich, Richard, *Musical Discourse*. London: Milford, Oxford University Press, 1928.

Andersen, J. C., *Maori Life in Ao-tea*. Melbourne and London: no date.

Andrews, L., *Polynesian Comparative Dictionary*. Wellington, N. Z., 1891.

Avison, Charles, *An Essay on Musical Expression*. London, 1775.

Ayer, A. J., *Language, Truth, and Logic*. London: V. Gollancz, Ltd., 1936.

Bach, Carl Ph. Em., *Versuch über die wahre Art, das Klavier zu spielen*. Leipzig: C. F. Kahnt, 1925 (reprint from the second edition).

Beauquier, C., *Philosophie de la musique*. Paris, 1865.

Bell, Clive, *Art*. London, 1914.

Bergson, Henri, *La pensée et le mouvement*. Paris: Alcan, 1934.

Bethe, E., *Mythus — Sage — Märchen*. Leipzig, 1905 (reprinted from *Hessische Blätter für Volkskunde*, Vol. iv, nos. 2–3).

Boas, Franz, *The Mind of Primitive Man*. New York, 1911.

Brinton, D., *The Myths of the New World*. Philadelphia, 1896.

Britton, Karl, *Communication: A Philosophical Study of Language*. New York and London: K. Paul, Trench, Trubner & Co., 1939.

Bücher, Karl, *Arbeit und Rhythmus*. 4th ed. Leipzig, 1908 (first published as vol. xvii of *Abhandlungen der königlich-sächsischen Akademie der Wissenschaften*, 1896).

Bühler, Karl, *Sprachtheorie*. Jena: G. Fischer, 1934.

Burnett, J., Lord Monboddo, *Of the Origin and Progress of Language*. 6 vols., Edinburgh, 1773.

Burns, C. D., *The Horizon of Experience*. New York: W. W. Norton, 1934.

Cailliet, Émile, *Symbolisme et âmes primitives*. Paris: Boivin et cie, 1936.

Carnap, Rudolf. *The Logical Syntax of Language*. London: K. Paul, Trench, Trubner & Co., 1935 (German ed. Vienna: J. Springer, 1934).

Philosophy and Logical Syntax. London: K. Paul, Trench, Trubner & Co., 1935 (German ed. Vienna: J. Springer, 1934).

Carrière, Moritz, *Aesthetik*. 2 vols. Leipzig, 1859.

Caspari, Wilhelm, *Gegenstand und Wirkung der Tonkunst nach der Ansicht der Deutschen im 18. Jahrhundert*. Erlangen: 1903.

Cassirer, Ernst, *Die Philosophie der symbolischen Formen*. 3 vols., Berlin: Bruno Cassirer, 1923, 1924, 1929.

Clark, J. V., *History of Onondaga*. Syracuse, 1849.

Coleridge, S. T., *Biographia Literaria*. Oxford, 1907.

De Laguna, Grace, *Speech: its Function and Development*. New Haven: Yale University Press, 1927.

Dent, E. J., *Terpander: or the Music of the Future*. New York: E. P. Dutton & Co., 1927.

Dewey, John, *Experience and Nature*. Chicago & London: Open Court Publishing Co., 1925.

Dixon, Roland, *Oceanic Mythology*. Vol. ix of The Mythology of All Races, Boston, 1916.

D'Udine, Jean (A. Cozanet), *L'art et le geste*. Paris, 1910.

Durkheim, Émile, *Les formes élémentaire de la vie religieuse*. Paris, 1912.

Eaton, R. M., *Symbolism and Truth*. Cambridge, Mass.: Harvard University Press, 1925.

Eckermann, J. P., *Gespräche mit Goethe*. Houben's edition, Leipzig, 1912.

Ehrenreich, P., *Die allgemeine Mythologie und ihre ethnologischen Grundlagen*. Leipzig, 1910 (Mythologische Bibliothek vol. iv, 1).

Elster, A., *Musik und Erotik*. Bonn, 1925.

Frere, W. H., *The Principles of Religious Ceremonial*. London and New York: Longmans, Greene & Co., 1928.

Freud, Sigmund, *Totem and Taboo*. New York, 1918.
  Group Psychology and the Analysis of the Ego. London: International Psychoanalytic Press, 1922.
  Collected Papers. London: International Psychoanalytic Library (E. Jones editor), 1925.

Frobenius, Leo, *The Childhood of Man* ("*Aus den Flegeljahren der Menschheit*"). London, 1909.

Fry, Roger, *Vision and Design*. London: Chatto & Windus, 1925.

Garner, R. L., *The Speech of Monkeys*. New York, 1892.

Gätschenberger, R., *Zeichen, die Fundamente des Wissens*. Stuttgart: F. Fromanns, 1932.

Gatz, F. M., *Musik-Aesthetik*. Stuttgart: F. Encke, 1929.

Gehring, A., *The Basis of Musical Pleasure*. New York, 1910.

Graf, Max, *Die innere Werkstatt des Musikers*. Stuttgart, 1910.

Grudin, Louis, *A Primer of Aesthetics*. New York: Covici, Friede, 1930.

Hanslick, Eduard, *Vom Musikalisch-Schönen*. 5th ed. Leipzig, 1876 (1st ed. 1854).

Harrison, Jane, *Prolegomena to the Study of Greek Religion*. 2nd ed. Cambridge, 1908.

Hauptmann, Moritz, *Die Natur der Harmonik und Metrik*. Leipzig, 1853.

Helwig, Paul, *Seele als Äusserung*. Leipzig u. Berlin, B. G. Teubner, 1936.

Hitchcock, H. R., *English-Hawaiian Dictionary*. San Francisco, 1887.

Hoeslin, J. K. v., *Die Melodie als gestaltender Ausdruck seelischen*

Lebens. Leipzig, 1920 (reprinted from the *Archiv für gesammte Psychologie,* vol. xxxix).

Huber, Kurt, *Der Ausdruck musikalischer Elementarmotive. Eine experimentalpsychologische Untersuchung.* Leipzig: J. A. Barth, 1923.

Humboldt, Wilhelm v., *Die sprachphilosophischen Werke Wilhelm von Humboldts.* (Ed. Steinthal) Berlin, 1884.

Husserl, Edmund, *Logische Untersuchungen.* 2 vols. Halle a/S, 1913, 1921.

Itard, E. M., *The Savage of Aveyron.* Engl. transl. London, 1802.

James, D. G., *Skepticism and Poetry. An Essay on the Poetic Imagination.* London: Allen & Unwin, 1937.

James, William, *Principles of Psychology.* 2 vols. New York, 1899 (1st ed. 1890).

Jespersen, Otto, *Language: its Nature, Development, and Origin.* London: George Allen & Unwin, 1922.

Keller, Helen, *The Story of My Life.* Garden City: Doubleday, Doran & Co., 1936 (1st ed. 1902).

Kellogg, W. N. and L. A., *The Ape and the Child.* New York: McGraw-Hill Book Co., and London: Whittelsey House, 1933.

Kingsley, Mary, *Travels in West Africa.* London, 1897.

Koffka, Kurt, *Principles of Gestalt Psychology.* London: K. Paul, Trench, Trubner & Co., 1935.

Köhler, Wolfgang, *Gestalt Psychology.* New York: H. Liveright, 1929.
    The Mentality of Apes. London: K. Paul, Trench, Trubner & Co., and New York: Harcourt, Brace & Co., 1925.

Krappe, A. H., *La génèse des mythes.* Paris: Payot, 1938.

Kurth, Ernst, *Musikpsychologie.* Berlin: M. Hesse, 1931.

Lang, Andrew, *Myth, Ritual and Religion.* 2 vols. London, 1887.

Learned, B., *see* Yerkes.

Lessmann, H., *Aufgaben und Ziele der vergleichenden Mythenforschung.* Leipzig, 1907–1908 (Mythologische Bibliothek vol. i).

Lorimer, Frank, *The Growth of Reason.* London: K. Paul, Trench, Trubner & Co., and New York: Harcourt, Brace & Co., 1929.

Markey, J. F., *The Symbolic Process and its Integration in Children.* London: K. Paul, Trench, Trubner & Co., 1928.

Marpurg, F. W., *Historisch-kritische Beyträge zur Aufnahme der Musik.* 5 vols. Berlin, 1754–1760.

McAlpin, Colin, *Hermaia: A Study in Comparative Esthetics.* London and New York, 1915.

Meyer, Kathi, *Bedeutung und Wesen der Musik.* Strassburg: Heitz & Co., 1932.

Miller, Hugh, *History and Science.* Berkeley: University of California Press, 1939.

Moos, Paul, *Die Philosophie der Musik.* Stuttgart: deutsche Verlags-Anstalt, 1922.

Morris, Ch. W., *Foundations of the Theory of Signs*. Chicago: University of Chicago Press, 1938 (International Encyclopedia of Unified Science, vol. i, no. 5).

Murray, Gilbert, *Five Stages of Greek Religion*. Oxford: Clarendon Press, 1925.

Nadel, Siegfried, *Der duale Sinn der Musik*. Ratisbon: G. Bosse, 1931.

Nicholls, F., *The Language of Music, or, Musical Expression and Characterization*. London: K. Paul, Trench, Trubner & Co., 1924.

Noack, H., *Symbol und Existenz der Wissenschaft: Untersuchungen zur Grundlegung einer philosophischen Wissenschaftslehre*. Halle a/S: Niemeyer, 1936.

Nohl, Hermann, *Stil und Weltanschauung*. Jena, 1920.

Ogden, C. K., and I. A. Richards, *The Meaning of Meaning*. London: K. Paul, Trench, Trubner & Co., 1923 (International Library of Psychology, Philosophy, and Scientific Method).

Pater, Walter, *The Renaissance. Studies in Art and Poetry*. New York, 1908 (1st ed. 1873).

Peirce, Charles, *Collected Papers of Charles S. Peirce*. Vol. ii, "Elements of Logic." Cambridge, Mass: Harvard University Press, 1932.

Piaget, Jean, *Le langage et la pensée chez l'enfant*. Neuchatel and Paris: Delachaux & Niestlé, 1923.

Pirro, André, *L'ésthetique de Jean-Sebastien Bach*. Paris, 1907.

Poincaré, Henri, *La science et l'hypothèse*. Paris, 1903.

Pratt, Carroll C., *The Meaning of Music*. New York and London: McGraw-Hill Book Co., 1931.

Rank, Otto, *Psychoanalytische Beiträge zur Mythenforschung*. Leipzig, Wien u. Zürich: Internationaler psychoanalitischer Verlag, 1922.

Reid, L. A., *Knowledge and Truth*. London: Macmillan & Co., Ltd., 1923.

Richards, I. A., *see* Ogden.

Ribot, Th., *Essai sur l'imagination créatrice*. Paris, 1921 (1st ed. 1900).

Richet, Charles, *L'homme stupide*. Paris, 1919.

Riemann, Hugo, *Wie Hören wir Musik?* Leipzig, 1888.

Rignano, Eugenio, *The Psychology of Reasoning*. New York: Harcourt, Brace & Co., 1927.

Ritchie, A. D., *The Natural History of the Mind*. London: Longmans, Green & Co., 1936.

Russell, Bertrand, *A Critical Exposition of the Philosophy of Leibniz*. Cambridge, 1900.
   Mysticism and Logic. New York: W. W. Norton & Co., 1929 (first published in 1918).
   Philosophy. New York: W. W. Norton & Co., 1927.

Schenker, Heinrich, *Neue musikalische Theorien und Phantasien*. 3 vols. Stuttgart u. Berlin: J. G. Cotta, 1935.

Schoen, Max, *The Effects of Music*. London: K. Paul, Trench, Trubner & Co., and New York: Harcourt, Brace & Co., 1927.

Schoolcraft, H. R., *The Myth of Hiawatha*. Philadelphia and London, 1856.

Schweitzer, Albert, *J. S. Bach, le musicien-poète*. 2nd ed. Leipzig, 1905.

Seashore, Carl, *Psychology of Music*. New York and London: McGraw-Hill Book Co., 1938.

Shortland, E., *Maori Religion and Mythology*. London, 1882.

Sorantin, E., *The Problem of Musical Expression*. Nashville (Tenn.): Marshall & Bruce Co., 1932.

Spaier, A., *La pensée concrète: essai sur le symbolisme intellectuel*. Paris: F. Alcan, 1927.

Stekel, Wilhelm, *Die Träume der Dichter*. Wiesbaden, 1912.

Stern, Gustav, *Meaning and Change of Meaning*. Göteborg: Elanders boktryckeri aktiebolag, 1935.

Thimme, A., *Das Märchen*. Leipzig, 1909 (Handbücher zur Volkskunde, vol. ii).

Thorburn, J. M., *Art and the Unconscious*. London: K. Paul, Trench, Trubner & Co., 1925.

Tregear, E., *The Maori-Polynesian Comparative Dictionary*. Wellington, N. Z., 1891.

Urban, Wilbur M., *Language and Reality; the Philosophy of Language and the Principles of Symbolism*. London: G. Allen & Unwin, 1939.

Wallace, William, *The Threshold of Music*. London, 1908.

Wegener, Philip, *Untersuchungen über die Grundfragen des Sprachlebens*. Halle a/S, 1885.

Wertheimer, Max, *Drei Abhandlungen zur Gestalttheorie*. Erlangen: Philosophische Akademie, 1925.

Westervelt, W. D., *Legends of Maui, a Demigod of Polynesia, and of his Mother Hina*. Honolulu, 1910.

Whitehead, A. N., *Adventures of Ideas*. New York: The Macmillan Co., 1933.
  The Function of Reason. Princeton: Princeton University Press, 1925.
  Science and the Modern World. New York: The Macmillan Co., 1926.
  Symbolism: its Meaning and Effect. New York: The Macmillan Co., 1927.

Wierling, Gustav, *Das Tonkunstwerk als autonome Gestalt und als Ausdruck der Persönlichkeit*. Würzburg: K. Triltsch, 1931.

Wilson, Henry, *Wonderful Characters*. 2 vols. London, 1821.

Wittgenstein, Ludwig, *Tractatus Logico-Philosophicus*. London: K. Paul, Trench, Trubner & Co., 1922 (2nd ed. New York, Harcourt Brace & Co., 1933).

Yerkes, R. M. and A. W., *The Great Apes*. New Haven: Yale University Press, and London: Oxford University Press, 1929.

Yerkes, R. M., and B. Learned, *Chimpanzee Intelligence and its Vocal Expression*. Baltimore: Williams & Wilkins, 1925.

INDEX

INDEX

abstraction, 18, 19, 35, 72, 92, 127, 141, 145, 201, 239, 281
act, 152, 156
  audible —, 124
  expressive —, 127, 152, 159n
  religious —, 154, 155
  symbolic —, 114
AESOP, 174n
"aesthetic emotion," 258ff
aesthetics, 204, 207, 211, 218, 225
affect, *see* feeling
air, 255
ALDRICH, RICHARD, 220n; quoted, 221
analogy, 139, 145, 227, 232, 245n
ANAXIMENES, 7
animal activities, 29, 131, 286
  — fable, 174
  — intelligence, 59
  — mind, 31
  — semantic, 62, 104
  — worship, 163, 165, 166
  attributive —, 169
animals, 28, 29, 32, 35, 39, 40, 107, 113, 119, 150, 160, 162, 164, 199, 200, 279
apes, 32, 104, 105, 106, 110–119, *passim*, 126, 127, 128, 130, 135
application, 65, 66, 132, 202
ambivalence, 243
ANDERSEN, J. C., 184n, 185n
ANDREWS, L., 186n
appreciation, 97, 259, 286
architecture, 209
ARISTOTLE, 7, 9, 72, 153
art, 36, 102, 143, 174, 203, 209, 233, 243
  adequacy in —, 262, 263
  — and artifact, 204
  beginnings of —, Chapter IX *passim*
  function of —, 263
  logic of —, 218
  materials of —, 246, 249, 251, 253, 254, 260
  philosophy of —, 207
  plastic —, 205, 208, 249
  seriousness of —, 37, 38, 207

articulation, 92, 117, 153, 200, 205, 227, 240, 246, 251
assumption, 3, 4, 5, 25, 28, 87, 99
attitude, 153, 171, 202, 226, 290
AUGUSTINE, ST., 46
AVISON, CHARLES, quoted, 214
AYER, A. J., 21n

babble, 105, 116, 121, 123, 133
BACH, C. PH. E., quoted, 214, 215, 223
BACH, J. S., 209, 220, 231, 264
BACON, FRANCIS, 14, 15; quoted, 270
BADOUIN, CH., 206n
BARTOK, BELA, 264
BAUMANN, O., 104n
BEAUQUIER, C., 228n
beauty, 204, 208, 228n
BECKER, CARL, quoted, 275
BEETHOVEN, LUDWIG VAN, 209, 215, 224, 243n, 264
BELL, CLIVE, 241; quoted, 204, 211n, 258n
BERGSON, HENRI, 98, 265
BERLIOZ, HECTOR, 221, 236n, 241n
BETHE, E., quoted, 177n
BITTNER, JULIUS, 232n
BOAS, FRANZ, 49; quoted, 50, 133
BODKIN, A. M., 206n
BRIDGMAN, LAURA, 28
BRINTON, D., 182; quoted, 183
BRITTON, KARL, quoted, 268
BROWN, J. W., 206n
BRUNSCHWICG, LEON, 27
BÜCHER, KARL, 246n, 254n
BÜHLER, KARL, 73n, 136; quoted, 136n
BULLOUGH, EDWARD, 209n, 222; quoted, 223
BURNETT, J., LORD MONBODDO, 108n
BURNS, C. D., quoted, 5, 6, 7
BUSONI, FERRUCCIO, 216n; quoted, 223

CAILLET, ÉMILE, 149
CARNAP, RUDOLF, 21n, 22n, 27, 82; quoted, 83–84, 86, 215–216
CARRIÈRE, MORITZ, 238, 239

CASPARI, WILHELM, 215n
CASSIRER, ERNST, 21n, 27, 43, 87; quoted, 245
causation, 278
ceremonial, 150, 157, 287
chaos, 287
CHASE, STUART, 270; quoted, 34–35, 44
chatter, 32, 116, 122
CHIJS, A. VAN DER, 206n
childhood, *see* children
children, 28, 44, 106, 107, 109, 121, 122, 123, 126, 148, 150, 155, 156, 173, 178
"wild" —, 107, 108, 110, 119, 121
CLARCK, J. V., 182n
Christianity, 10, 11, 17
COHEN, FELIX, 4n
COLERIDGE, SAMUEL T., 89, 258n, 262
common sense, 3, 150, 171, 196, 266
communication, 120, 127, 129, 136, 138, 139, 243, 248, 280
composer, 215, 217, 221, 222, 240, 241, 242, 264
COMTE, AUGUSTE, 17
concept, 6, 7, 9, 13, 19, 23, 71, 77, 130, 202
non-scientific, 233
physical, 91
concepts and conceptions, 61n, 71, 72, 141
conception, 61, 62, 64, 71, 72, 110, 118, 133, 134, 147, 157, 245
power of, 151
CONDILLAC, ÉTIENNE B. DE, 121
connotation, 54, 64, 65, 67, 75ff, 138, 228, 232, 240, 256, 281
CONRADI, EDWARD, 122n
context, 136, 137, 139, 140, 145, 219
musical, 209, *228*
scientific, 275
CREIGHTON, J. E., quoted, 99
CROCE, BENEDETTO, 215

dance, 127, 130, 131, 152, 158, 174, 209, 226, 227, 246, 255, 256, 258
DAY, CLARENCE, quoted, 116
death, 150, 151, 153, 171, 176, 185, 188, 192
DEBUSSY, CLAUDE, 264
DELACROIX, HENRI, 27, 87

DE LAGUNA, GRACE, 27; quoted, 44, 47
denotation, 34, 62, 64, 65, 75ff, 78, 100, 114, 133, 138, 239
DENT, E. J., 237n
design, 208
DEWEY, JOHN, 27, 87; quoted, 156–157
diagram, *70*, 73
discourse, 66, 94, 97, 139
logic of, 67
DISSERENS, CH. M., 212n
dissonance, 205
DIXON, ROLAND, 171, 184n, 185n, 194n; quoted, 172, 187, 189
DONOVAN, J., 129, 133; quoted, 130, 131, 132
drama, 161n, 180, 185, 197, 209, 253
dream, 37, 38, 102, 127, 143, 149, 150, 171, 173, 176, 177, 178, 179, 181, 196, 199, 201, 207
D'UDINE, JEAN, 258n; quoted, 226, 227
DURKHEIM, ÉMILE, quoted, 164, 165

eating, 156, 159
ceremonial —, 47, 160, 164, 165
EATON, RALPH MONROE, 21n
ECKERMANN, J. P., 208, 243n
EGGAR, K., 206n
EHRENREICH, P., 175n
ELIOT, T. S., 206
ELLIS, HAVELOCK, 227
ELSTER, A., 206n
emendation, 136, 137
emotive theory, 211ff, 219, 223, 237
empiricism, 12, 14ff, 20, 21, 24
"empractic" speech, 136, 137, 138, 140
envisagement, 176, 202, 286
epistemology, 21, 51, 265
EUCKEN, RUDOLPH, 18
experience, 38, 98, 99, 100, 113, 124, 135, 148, 177, 202, 229
aesthetic, 110, 112, 207, *263*
animal, 89
— as a generative idea, 12, 18
continuity of, 280
formulation of, 6, 7, 88, 89
"horizons of —," 5, 6
transformation of, 45, 49, 51, 126
exposition, 137, 138, 140
expression, 85, 97, 123, 141
artistic, 257

logical, 150, 218, 223
— of feelings, 83, 84
— of ideas, 43, 49, 201, 203, 204, 248
self-, 152, 173, *214*, 215, 216, 217,
    221, 222, 223, 224, 289

fact, 14ff, 18, 20, 21, 33, 80f, 88, 202,
    267–279 passim, 97, 180
atomic, 79, 84, 273
historical, 274–277 *passim*, 289
significant, 134, 193
fairytale, 174, 175, 176f, 179, 181, 185,
    190
fantasy, 70, 100, 102, 124, 146, 147, 148,
    150, 171, 173, 174, 177, 178, 180,
    185, 193, 195, 196, 197, 198, 200,
    202, 206, 207
feeling, 92, 97, 100f, 123, 124, 152, 153,
    204, 223
    see also expression
    blind, 87
    — in music, 213, 214f, 216, 217, 218,
        221, 227, 238
    knowledge of, 221, 222, 234, 242
    morphology of, *238*
FERGUSON, D. M., quoted, 242n
fetish, 110, 113, 114, 150, 154, 162
fire, 181, 187, 190, 199
    origin of, 181
FLAUBERT, G., 205
form, 8, 70, 74, 89, 90, 91n, 93, 123,
    127, 141, 155, 164, 171, 172, 190,
    203, 209, 216, 225, 249
    — and content, 149, 208, 225, 226,
        234, 237, 257
    correct, 160
    discursive, 86
    expressive, 204, 206
    picture of, 70
    poetic, 197
    significant, 204, 205, 206, 211n, 219,
        238, 241, 249, 250, 251, 253, 256,
        261, 262, *264*, 289
forms, equivalence of, 82, 228
formulation, 248, 254
    logical, 97, 225
    — of conceptions, 118
    — of experience, 89, 98n, 149, *293*
    — of feelings, 222, *235*, 244
    — of problems, 4

freedom, 6, 289, *290*, 292, 294
FREGE, GOTTLOB, 82
FRERE, W. H., quoted, 161n–162n
FREUD, SIGMUND, 38, 50, 51, 177n
FROBENIUS, LEO, 46, 48; quoted, 47
FRY, ROGER, 204, 241; quoted, 266n–
    267n, 283
function, logical, *see* logical structure
    — of terms, 56, 57, 66
FURNESS, W. H., 117; quoted, 104, 105,
    117n–118n, 119n

GALILEI, GALILEO, 270
GARNER, R. L., 104n
GATEWOOD, ESTHER, 213n, 229
GÄTSCHENBERGER, R., 22n
GATZ, F. M., 210n, 215n, 224n, 235n,
    236n, 241n,
GEHRING, A., 234; quoted, 228n, 233,
    245n
generalization, 54, 67, 72, 96, 140, 210,
    239
    hasty, 209
generative idea, 8, 9, 11, 12, 13, 21,
    22, 23, 24, 25, 142, 277, 293
GESELL, ARNOLD, 108n
Gestalt, 74, 90, 97, 110, 123, 125, 226,
    231n, 249, 263, 266, 285
gesture, 51, 61, 74, 87n, 115, 117, 130,
    152, 153, 154, 155, 156, 160, 161,
    200, 218, 226f, 290
ghosts, 174, 178, 182, 185
god, gods, 47, 48, 49, 150, 154, 162–163,
    164, 165, 166, 167, 168, 169, 175,
    180, 181, 183, 185, 193, 194, 195,
    196, 202, 255n, 276
GOETHE, J. W. VON, 208n, 242, 250;
    quoted, 243, 255
GRAF, MAX, 206n
grammar, 67, 87, 88
    logical, 82
    musical, 228, 232
Great Hare, 183, 184
GREY, SIR GEORGE, quoted, 189
GRUDIN, LOUIS, 22
GUYAU, J.-M., 228n

HALE, HORATIO, 106, 108; quoted,
    107
HALL, G. S., 122n

HAUSEGGER, F. VON, 215
HANSLICK, EDUARD, 216n, 217, 224, 225, 226, 245n; quoted, 237, 238
HARRISON, JANE, 163, 167, 168, 174; quoted, 169–170, 196n–197n
HARTMANN, E. VON, 221
HAUPTMANN, MORITZ, 238, 239
HAYDN, JOSEPH, 220
HEAD, HENRY, 27, 290
HEINRICH, F., 234, 237n; quoted, 233
HELMHOLTZ, H. VON, 210
HELWIG, PAUL, 22n
HERDER, J. G. VON, 128, 210
hero, 175, 176, 178, 179, 180, 181, 182, 183, 185, 193, 196, 198, 202
  culture-, 181, 182, 184, 185, 193, 198
HERODOTUS, 169
HEVNER, KATE, 213n
Hiawatha, see Manabozho
Hina, 185, 190, 192
  stories of, 186–189 passim
HINDEMITH, PAUL, 264
HITCHCOCK, H. R., 185n
HOBBES, TH., 14
Hobie Baker (the cat), 34, 35, 44, 270
HOESLIN, J. K. VON, 227, 257
Holy One, 154, 162, 163
HOMER, 167, 169, 195, 197, 198
HUBER, KURT, 229ff, 232, 241; quoted, 230, 231n
HÜLLER, J. A., quoted, 220, 235
HUMBOLDT, WILHELM VON, quoted, 128
HUSSERL, EDMUND, 54

ideation, 42, 281
image, 144, 145, 149, 150, 163, 164, 177, 218, 263, 266
imagination, 36, 49, 89, 126, 130, 143, 155, 166, 174, 194, 197, 200, 238, 242, 246, 247, 250, 251, 269, 287
  frustrated, 291, 292
imitation, 131, 155, 156, 164, 232, 248, 253
insight, 92, 101, 157, 158, 164, 177, 200, 201, 209, 294
  artistic, 222, 223, 224, 259
  social, 179
instinct, 35, 98, 121, 123, 128
  myth-making –, 170, 174
  -theory of language, 107, 108, 109

interpretability, 274
interpretation, 10, 11, 18, 50, 73, 77, 78, 126, 180, 194, 233, 240
  – of music, 217, 220, 232, 243, 244
  – of poetry, 234, 261
  – of signs, 59, 60, 65
intuition, 92, 97, 122, 238, 252
ITARD, E. M., 108n, 119, 125; quoted 120, 121

JAMES, D. G., 89n; quoted, 26
JAMES, WILLIAM, 28n, 124, 273, 276, quoted, 210
JESPERSEN, OTTO, 104n, 128, 149n; quoted, 129, 133, 142

Kalevala, 198–200, passim
Kamala, 108, 121
KANT, IMMANUEL, 98n, 210
KELLER, HELEN, 28, 72, 119, 125; quoted, 62–63
KELLOGG, W. N., 122n
KELLOGG, W. N. & L. A., quoted, 105, 106, 111, 112, 113, 115
KEPLER, JOHANNES, 270
KIERKEGAARD, SØREN, 215
KINGSLEY, MARY, quoted, 103n–104n
KIPLING, RUDYARD, 116
KOFFKA, KURT, 27, 91, 227n
KÖHLER, WOLFGANG, 27, 111, 126, 127, 227; quoted, 90n, 91n, 112–113, 114, 115, 226
KRAPPE, A. H., 195; quoted, 197
KRETSCHMAR, HERMANN, 221
KURTH, ERNST, 212n, 236; quoted, 247–248

LA FONTAINE, J. DE, 174n
lalling, see babble
LANDQUIST, J., 206n
language, 8, 27, 36, 52, 73, 75, 76, 79–82, 87, 95, 97, 102, Chapter V passim, 144, 145, 147, 149, 201, 202, 216, 218, 234, 240, 243, 280
  – and thought, 63, 118n
  beginnings of, 33, 62, 106–109, 118, 127–135 passim, 142, 181, 232, 233
  characteristics of, 94, 96
  gesture –, 34, 103n, 104n

growth of, 33, *136–142 passim*, 200
limits of, 86f, 88, 100, 239, 265
logical, 89
— of feelings, 218, 221, 236
— of music, 94, 219, 220, 222, 224, 225, 228
— of religion, 49
— of sense, 94
LANG, ANDREW, quoted, 46, 192
LATIF, ISRAEL, 103; quoted, 122n
LEARNED, B., quoted, 112, 119n
legend, 177n, *181*, 186, 193, 196, 211
LESSMANN, H., quoted, 195
LEWIS, C. I., 268
life, 10, 17, 18, 28, 38, 52, 88, 98, 147, 148, 150, 151, 153, 157, 164, 171, 176, 188, *191.* 192, 201, 227, 289
eternal, 189
inner, 18, 222, 226, 228, 243, *245*
mental, 89, 101, 286
moral, 286
social, 47, 127, 200
LISZT, FRANZ, 215, 221; quoted, 236
LOCKE, JOHN, 14, 121
logic, 16, 17, 22, 23, 89, 101, 173
Aristotelian, 68
— of language, 84, 201
— of symbolism, 218
— of terms, 66
LONGFELLOW, H. W., 182n
LORIMER, FRANK, 27, 122n; quoted, 32–33
LOVEJOY, A. O., 282

magic, 36, 38, 46, 48, 49, 126, 154, *158f*, 187, 188, 197, 198, 199
Manabozho, 182f, 184
MARKEY, J. F., quoted, 131n
"material mode," 87, 91
mathematics, 18, 19, 25, 91, 102, 233, 239
MARPURG, F. W., 214, 215, 220n, 235
MATTHESON, J., 214
MATTHEWS, W., 154n
Maui, 184, 185, 193, 194
stories of, 186–189 *passim*
MCALPIN, COLIN, 220n
meaning, 35, 45, 52, 67, 85, 90, 94, 97, 110, 117, 123, 160, 229
artistic, 208, 209

complexity of, 281–286 *passim*
figurative, 139, 282
literal, 67, 83, 139, 140, 195, 224, 232, 248, 256, 257
logic of, 52, 55
musical, 217, 219, 223, 236, 238
— of signs, 59, 280f
— of symbols, 61, 280f
problem of, 21, 53, 102
psychological aspect of, 53, 55
— relation, 55, 64, 77
standard of, 83
types of, 54, 64, 266, 281
medium, 70, 209, *258*
melody, 227, 245n, 251, 257
MERSMANN, HANS, quoted, 243, 262
metaphor, 132, 136, 139, 140, 141, 142, 147, 148, 149, 165, 166, 173, 180, 191, 201, 281
dream-, 151
"faded," 140f, 281
MEYER, KATHI, quoted, 255n
MILL, J. S., 16, 17
MILLER, HUGH, 268n; quoted, 277
MILTON, JOHN, 195
mind, 10, 25, 26, 30, 32, 36, 42, 51, 90, 98, 99, 100, 110, 148, 180, 202
function of, 37, 38, 39, 41, 123, 127, 144, 291
growth of, 27, 31, 271
well-balanced, 289
mistake, 29, 31, 33, 36, 38, 46, 47, 59, 64, 65, 151, 158
model, 247, 250, 252, 255
natural, 249, 253, 256, 257
MOFFAT, ROBERT, 46
mood, 123, 212, 222, 241
moon, 180, 181, 182, 184, *190*, 191, 192, 193, 194, 196, 199, 279
MOORE, G. E., 267n
MOOS, PAUL, 234; quoted, 232–233
morale, 157, 287
MORE, K. C., 122n
MORRIS, CH. W., 22n
MOSONYI, D., 206n
MUDRAK, E., 175n
MÜLLER, MAX, 183n
MURRAY, GILBERT, quoted, 166, 167, 168
music, 101, 102, Chapter VIII *passim*

somatic effects of, 212, 229
program —, 220f, 241ff
myth, 5, 48, 102, 143, 157, 169, *Chapter VII passim*
  and fairytale, 174ff, 179, 245
  and legend, 193

NADEL, SIEGFRIED F., 232n
name, 60, 67, 73, 76f, 79, 80, 95, 105, 106, 119, 125, 135, 136, 139, 142, 180, 184, 190, 196, 226, 245
  call —, 62
  proper, 61, 62f, 65, *66*, 96, 162, 175, 186, 200
nature, 180, 185, 191, *278f*
  — myth, 181, 193, 194
  — symbol, 190, 197, 201
need, 28, 29, 36, *38ff*, 43, 45, 46, 49, 148, 149, 207
NEWELL, W. W., 154n
NICHOLLS, F., quoted, 243n
night, 180, 185, 194, 199
NOACK, H., 21n
novel predication, 136, 137, 138, 139, 140
novelty, *see* novel predication

OGDEN, C. K., 21n, 54n
OHMANN, 231n
orientation, 3, 12, 157, 158, 176, 258, 276, *287*, 291
OTTO, IRMGARD, 212n

PAGET, SIR RICHARD, 103n
painting, 71, 206, 209
PARMENIDES, 273
PATER, WALTER, quoted, 257
pattern, 55, 56, 64, 71, 77, 128, 130, 137, 153, 157, 191, 201, 225, 226, 227, 228, 229, 233, 254, 255, 256, 257, 281
PEIRCE, CHARLES S., 54, 77, 274
personification, 180, 190, 192, 193, 194, 197
Peter the Wild Boy, 108, 121, 125, 155
philosophy, 207, 219, 271, 293
  epochs of, 3, 4, 5, 9, 10, 11, 12, 13, 22
  Greek, 5, 6, 7, 211
  history of, 3, 5, 269
  of art, 265

of language, 82
PIAGET, JEAN, 27, 44
picture, 68, 70, 72ff, 94, 96, 144, 146, 206, 250, 253
  logical, 77, 79, 82, 222, 239, 241
  physiological, 227n
PIRRO, ANDRÉ, 221, 231, 232
pitch, 130, 253, 255
PITKIN, W. B., 34
PLATO, 7, 9, 48, 211, 269
play, 128, 155, 158
  festal, 130, 131
  — theory of art, 37
  — theory of sacrament, 157
  verbal, 44
pleasure, 205
  — theory of art, 211
PLOTINUS, 166
poetry, 142, 208, 209, 234, 235n, 253, *261*, 262
  epic, 196, *197–200 passim*, 201, 202, 203
POINCARÉ, HENRI, 274
PRATT, C. C., quoted, 244–245
prayer, 39, 48, 158, 255
predication, *see* novel predication
PREYER, W. H., 122n
primitive people, *see* savages
problems, *see* questions
projection, 79f, 81n, 82, 93, 144, 222, 226, 227
proposition, 66, 68, 79ff, 83f, 87, 268, 281
  — and fact, 268, 269, *274*
  expression of, 74
PRUNIÈRES, HENRI, quoted, 215, 242n
"psychical distance," 209n, 222, 223
psychoanalysis, 150, 173, 175, 206, 208
psychology, 16, 22, 24, 26, 86, 109, 180, 216
  Freudian, 23, 38, 207
  genetic, 27, 28, 32, 37, 39
purpose, 7, 9, 205, 209, 290, 291

questions, 3, 7, 8, 23, 84
  formulation of, 4, 6, 12
  importance of, 3, 4, 8
  new, 7, 9
  pseudo-, 9, 85
  rejection of, 3

RAMSEY, F. P., 267n
RANK, OTTO, 175n, 177n
realism, 271, 276f
reason, 4, 11, 25, 46, 99, 101, 142, 143, 201, 235, 252, 265
REID, LOUIS A., 92; quoted, 152n, 204, 262
relations, 73, 74, 81, 135, 165, 177, 211, 233
— among facts, 272, 277
artistic, 211n, 223
human, 178, 182
religion, 36, 47, 48, 150, 151, 154, 158, 159, 162, 163, 165, 167, 170, 171, 195, 202, 270, 292
repetition, 153, 156, *160*, 192
RESPIGHI, O., 220n
response, 24, 28, 34, 52, 90, 114, 121, 122, 136, 138, 153, 242, 244, 268, 269
emotional, 211, 227, 235
— to signs, *280*
rhythm, 130, 154, 162, 212, 227, 229, 231, 232, 246, *253f*, 261
RIBOT, TH., 27, 72n
RICHARDS, I. A., 21n, 54n
RICHET, CH., 34
RIEMANN, HUGO, 215, 218, 236, 244; quoted, 245n
RIGNANO, EUGENIO, 28n
RIMSKY-KORSAKOFF, N. A., 264
RITCHIE, A. D., quoted, 27, 41
ritual, 36, 38, 45, 46, 47, 48, 49, 102, 127, 128, 141, 143, *153*, 157, 158, 159, 163, 165, 169, 200
gods of, 168, 195
— in modern society, 287ff, 290, 291
mimetic, 154
ROUSSEAU, J.-J., 128, 214
RUSSELL, BERTRAND, 27, 68, 74, 76, 80, 82, 86, 263, 276; quoted, 75, 81, 84, 88, 274

SACHS, HANNS, 206n
sacra, 150, 151, 152, 153, 154, 174
sacrament, 159, 160, 165, 170, 171
SAPIR, EDWARD, quoted, 104n, 109-10, 126
savage, 28, 46f, 49, 103, 104n, 126f, 130f, 133, 138, 148, 151, 158, 159, 160, 162, 166, 174, 180, 190, 192, 193, 198, 251, 266
SCHENKER, HEINRICH, 231n
SCHMIDT, KARL, 274n
SCHOEN, MAX, 213n, 229
SCHOOLCRAFT, H. R., 182n
SCHOPENHAUER, ARTHUR, 210, 219
SCHUMANN, ROBERT, 215, 221, 241, 264
SCHWEITZER, ALBERT, 221, 231, 232
science, 7, 13, 14, 15, 16, 17, 21, 97, 102, 143, 203, 271n, 274f, 284
— and history, 277
— and metaphysics, 85, 265
— and religion, 202, 272
SEASHORE, CARL, quoted, 216n
self, the, 176, 179
self-expression, *see* expression
semantic, 35, 38, 54, 62, 75, 86, 87, 94, 97, 110, 147, 155, 200, 206, 233
— of art, 257
— of music, 101, 218, 219, 221, 225, 231, 232, 235, 236, 237
sense, 227
— data, 12, 14f, 20, 21, 26, 46, 72, 89f, 94, 124
— experience, *269*
— knowledge, 14f, *266*, *267*
— messages, 30, 42
musical, 253
sentence, 73, 74, 77, 138
one-word, 137, 138, 145
SHAW, GEORGE BERNARD, 67
SHORTLAND, E., 184n, 185n, 186n
sign, 27, *29ff*, 43, 74, 110, 120, 219, 248, *280*, 283
artificial, 58, 59
diacritical, 136
— language, 30
natural, 57, 59
signs and symbols, 31, 37, 42, 57, 60, 61, 62, 63, 66, 102, 200, 224, 266, 280
significance, 20, 50, 99, 101, 102, 110, 113, 114, 119, 132, 149, 164, 173, 178, 202, 206, 207, 218, 237, 248, 251, 293
lack of, 83, 116
musical, 203, Chapter VIII *passim*, 265

non-literal, 171
personal, 179
signification, 54, 57, 58, 64, 116, 281, 284
slang, 141, 282n
SOCRATES, 7, 8, 9
song, 101, 128, 129, 130, 131n, 199, 246, 247, 254, 255
SORANTIN, E., 232n
sound, 117, 118, 121, 122, 123, 124, 125, 128, 129, 131, 133, 134, 202, 246, 247, 248, 253
— painting, 220, 221
SPAIER, A., 22n
speech, 26, 45, 68, 75, 93, 101, 104, 105, 108, 110, 115, 116, 119, 121, 126, 129, 132, 142, 144, 244, 254
SPENCER, H., 17, 183n
SPINOZA, B. DE, 84, 259
SQUIRES, P. C., 122n
STEBBING, L. S., 267n
STEKEL, WILHELM, quoted, 207, 208n
STERN, GUSTAV, 22n, 122n
Story, 145, 146, 154, 169, 171ff, 176, 178, 180, 182, 190, 195
STOUT, G. F., 103
STRAUSS, RICHARD, 220n, 221, 242n
structure, logical, 52, 64, 68, 77, 102, 218, 219
    artistic, 208
    grammatical, 67, 137, 138
    musical, 209, 226, 227, 231, 236, 238, 243
    propositional, 68, 268
    sensory, 266
STUMPF, KARL, 211, 212n
sun, 180, 181, 182, 184, 187, 188, 190, 191, 192, 193, 194, 196, 199, 279
supernatural, the, 181
— being, 175, 176, 182, 186
superstition, 43, 110, 127, 162, 166, 178, 179, 197, 270
symbol, 18, 19, 20, 21, 22, 24, 26, 28, 29, 31, 68, 69ff, 98, 134, 149, 205, 225
— and object, 64, 74, 75, 94
"charged," 284f, 288
cosmic, 181, 190, 279
discursive, 67, 81f, 88, 95, 97, 98
dream —, 37, *147*, 148, 149

kinds of, 42, 45, 52, 94, 143, 219, 225, 260, *281*
logic of, 60, 70
misuse of, 34, 35
natural, 145, 150, 161, 191, 282, 284
non-discursive, 93, 94, 95, 201
presentational, 97, 98, 139, 145, 191, 218, 232, 260, 281
— situations, 54, 77
transparency of —, 75
symbolic mode, 203, 207
symbolic transformation, 43, 44, 45, 49, 99, 110, 115, 124, 127, 143, 227, 294
symbolism, mathematical, 18, 19, 234, 239
symbolization, 22, 24, 25, 27, 42
law of, 161
need of, *41*, 45, 46
symbols and signs, *see* signs
sympathy, 214, 222, 223
symptom, 31, 57, 83, 86, 105, 114, 126, 219, 222
synaesthesia, 123

taste, 211
telephone exchange, simile of, 31, 33, 34, 35, 36, 38, 41f, 60
terms, in meaning-relation, 55–58, 64, 233
THALES, 6, 7, 8, 166
THIMME, A., 177n
THORBURN, J. M., quoted, 208n
TOLSTOI, LEO, quoted, 69n
TOMB, J. W., 122
totem, 184, 200
— animal, 184
totemism, 164f, 166, 171
transformer, 42, 43
TREGEAR, E., 185n
truth, 9, 12, 15, 97, 259, 265, *273*, 274
and falsity, 60, 77, 263
artistic, 92, *262*, 263
literal, 202
TYLOR, E. B., quoted, 48, 192

understanding, 25, 89, 97, 99, 100, 143, 239, 268, 281, *287*, 293
"implicit," 259
musical, 101, 222, 226, 242, 244

URBAN, WILBUR M., 22n, 87n, 161n, 261, 262; quoted, 233, 234, 235n

value, 7, 8, 9, 75, 130, 133, 150, 151, 202
  artistic, 204, 205, 239, 248
  human, 276, 279
  practical, 272
verb, 67, 76, 77, 281
verse, 200, 246, 249
Victor, the Savage of Aveyron, 108, 119–121, 125, 155
VIERKANDT, ALFRED, quoted, 159n
VISCHER, THEODOR, 236
vocable, 75, 106, 110, 125, 137, 228

WAGNER, RICHARD, 224, 264; quoted, 221–222, 235
WALLACE, WILLIAM, 252; quoted, 253
WALLASCHEK, R., 254n
washing, 160, 161
WEGENER, PHILIP, 73n, 136–141
WERNAER, R. M., quoted, 205n–206n
WERTHEIMER, MAX, 91
WESTERVELT, W. D., 184n, 185n, 194n; quoted, 187, 188

WHITEHEAD, A. N., 12, 13, 22n, 27, 58n, 87, 149n; quoted, 4–5, 271n, 289–290, 294
WHITEHEAD, GEORGE, 206n
WIERLING, GUSTAV, 237n
WILSON, HENRY, 108n
WINCKELMANN, J. J., 210
WISDOM, JOHN, 267n
WITTGENSTEIN, LUDWIG, 22, 86, 269; quoted, 79, 82, 84, 273
woman, 185, 186, 190, 191, 193, 196
word, 34, 45, 61, 62, 75, 76, 82, 90, 96, 103, 105, 117, 118, 119, 121, 125, 133, 134, 136, 138, 139, 144, 228, 231, 232, 243, 248, 282
  — order, 73, 74, 77, 80, 81
  — tones, 129
words, and music, 253, 254, 255
  disconnected —, 67, 94, 104n, 283
  portraiture of —, 95
WUNDT, WILHELM, 211

YERKES, A. W., quoted, 105
YERKES, R. M., 111; quoted, 105, 112, 119n